Power, Media, Culture

Global Transformations in Media and Communication Research

This series contributes to exploring, in creative and transdisciplinary manners, the challenges posed by fast-evolving communication developments in an increasingly connected world. It provides a venue for collecting state-of-the-art, sound and innovative scholarly perspectives on specific aspects of communication transformations.

Due to ever-increasing global interactions among individuals, communities and communication devices, scholars face the challenge of rethinking the very categories – of space, time, boundaries and technology – through which communication and media studies have evolved, thus contributing to identifying and refining concepts, theories and methods to explore the diverse realities of communication in a changing world.

The International Association for Media and Communication Research (IAMCR) has a long tradition of being a truly international academic association, with members working in all corners of the globe. This unique feature makes it possible to include in the Palgrave/IAMCR series contributions from highly diverse geocultural and disciplinary traditions.

The series fosters and generates research that explores critical communication and media concerns from a variety of theoretical and methodological approaches. Outstanding contributions from non-Anglophone areas will also be made available to a global readership, after translation into English.

Titles include:

Claudia Padovani and Andrew Calabrese (*editors*)
COMMUNICATION RIGHTS AND SOCIAL JUSTICE
Historical Accounts of Transnational Mobilizations

Luis A. Albornoz (*editor*)
POWER, MEDIA, CULTURE
A Critical View from the Political Economy of Communication

Global Transformations in Media and Communication Research
Series Standing Order ISBN 978–1–137–43370–1 (hardback)
978–1–137–43371–8 (paperback)
(*outside North America only*)

Power, Media, Culture

A Critical View from the Political Economy of Communication

Edited by

Luis A. Albornoz
Carlos III University of Madrid, Spain

Translated by

Ian Barnett

palgrave
macmillan

First published in 2011 as *Poder, medios, cultura. Una mirada crítica desde la economía política de la comunicación*, published by Paidós.
978–950–12–2735–2
English edition published 2015 by
PALGRAVE MACMILLAN

Palgrave Macmillan in the UK is an imprint of Macmillan Publishers Limited, registered in England, company number 785998, of Houndmills, Basingstoke, Hampshire RG21 6XS.

Palgrave Macmillan in the US is a division of St Martin's Press LLC, 175 Fifth Avenue, New York, NY 10010.

Palgrave Macmillan is the global academic imprint of the above companies and has companies and representatives throughout the world.

Palgrave® and Macmillan® are registered trademarks in the United States, the United Kingdom, Europe and other countries.

ISBN 978–1–137–54007–2

This book is printed on paper suitable for recycling and made from fully managed and sustained forest sources. Logging, pulping and manufacturing processes are expected to conform to the environmental regulations of the country of origin.

A catalogue record for this book is available from the British Library.

A catalog record for this book is available from the Library of Congress.

This collective work is dedicated to all those researchers who, through their intellectual work and political commitment, contribute to the building of critical thinking

Contents

Figures and Tables

Figures

Tables

Foreword

Studying the political economy of communication (PEC) is no longer a marginal approach to media and communication studies in many parts of the world. Thus it is important for scholars within this perspective to share their work and discuss new and ongoing issues.

This volume was previously published by Ediciones Paidós in Spanish and includes mostly scholars from Spanish and Portuguese-speaking countries (Ibero-America). This English-language version is now part of the IAMCR's series with Palgrave Macmillan, *Global Transformations in Media and Communication Research*. The series aims to present key research and intellectual debates, to reflect the intellectual capital of the IAMCR, and to provide a forum for collective knowledge production and exchange through transdisciplinary contributions.

The series is an appropriate venue for the English-language edition of this collection, in that the Political Economy Section of the IAMCR has grown dramatically over the last decade or so, attracting numerous scholars from all over the world, including most of the authors in this volume (for a brief history of the Political Economy Section, see Wasko, 2014). The IAMCR has often met in Latin America and in Spanish- and Portuguese-speaking countries in Europe. There has also been active participation by Spanish- and Portuguese-speaking scholars in the IAMCR as a whole and the Political Economy Section in particular. We are often unable to share our thoughts and ideas, much less our research and writing, because of language barriers. A rich tradition in the study of political economy of the media/communication has developed in Latin America, Spain and Portugal, and those in the English-speaking world must become more aware and pay heed to these voices, as well as others around the world.

This volume addresses current theoretical issues related to the PEC in Ibero-American countries. The timing of the discussions is significant in light of contemporary developments in these countries. Not only have these regions been seriously affected by recent global financial crises but there have been important developments in media industries and media policies in many of these countries, especially (but not only) Brazil, Argentina, Venezuela, Mexico and Bolivia.

The volume presents overviews of the study of PEC in Ibero-America and elsewhere, followed by sections that focus on the creative industries and cultural consumption, and it concludes by paying attention to contemporary challenges.

The growth of the study of PEC

As more scholars direct their attention to applying the study of political economy to the study of media and communications, a range of issues and themes have emerged. Vincent Mosco's contribution to this volume (Chapter 2) highlights some of these areas, citing examples of work that explores globalization, history, resistance, new media and activism.

PEC has concentrated special attention on issues relating to international communication, transnationalization and (more recently) globalization. Some of the early work in the academic study of the PEC focused on these issues (e.g. work by Herbert Schiller and Thomas Guback). However, this has been an especially important theme for Ibero-American scholars as exemplified by work in the 1960s and 1970s related to cultural imperialism and the New World Information and Communication Order (NWICO), discussed by César Bolaño (Chapter 10). This focus has continued with ongoing analysis of the extension of media and communication markets and the consequences of such developments (see e.g. Becerra and Mastrini, 2011; Bolaño et al., 2012).

Meanwhile, Ramón Zallo (Chapter 1) explores the broad area of the political or critical economy of culture and communications, highlighting various theoretical trends and examples of research. His proposals for future priorities are especially intriguing and present a map of key areas for research, policies and action. Importantly, he notes that these emerge from important and urgent realities, and reminds us that 'It is not ideas that change the world, but rather changes in the world that force a change of ideas which, in turn, facilitate those changes or help to correct their less desirable dynamics or effects.'

Creative industries and other 'new' trends

One of the areas that has been challenged by many political economists has been 'creative industries'. As Philip Schlesinger explains (Chapter 3), the early development of the creative industry concept emerged in the UK. As Gaëtan Tremblay notes (Chapter 4), the creative industry concept and accompanying rhetoric of creativity has spread rapidly to government, policy-makers and academics around the world. Enrique Bustamante further outlines (Chapter 5) the activities in Ibero-American institutions that have embraced the creative industry trend.

Drawing on Antonio Gramsci, Schlesinger skewers the rhetoric of creativity. He argues that the distributive potential of social media and the Internet 'does not mean communicative equality barriers remain in respect of quality, extent of circulation, impact and profitability, among many others'.

While the creative industry fad is addressed and critiqued by these authors in this collection, a number of other 'new' approaches have emerged in media/cultural studies. These have taken various names, including convergence culture, production culture, production studies, cultural economy and media industry studies.[1] The explications of these 'new' approaches have often included a rejection of the study of political economy as a viable framework for studying the media. It is also rare to find truly critical analysis within this kind of work. Eileen Meehan and I have argued that

> It may be possible to argue that this current wave of ['new'] media industry approaches represent efforts to claim the study of media production/distribution in a more palatable form for cultural analysts, policy wonks, and the media industry itself. In other words, the aim might be seen as an approach that isn't necessarily heavily invested in (overtly) neoliberal economics (represented by media economics), nor one that has the taint of Marxism (represented by political economy).
>
> (Wasko and Meehan, 2013)

Cultural consumption and cultural studies

Another major theme addressed by many of the authors in this collection, including Armand Mattelart (Chapter 6), Micael Herschmann (Chapter 7), Francisco Sierra (Chapter 8) and Delia Crovi Druetta (Chapter 11), is the relationship between the PEC and cultural studies, or, more specifically, what has been referred to as cultural populism.

Mattelart directly confronts this matter in his discussion of various forms of culturalism that emphasize active reception and ignore ideology. He argues that this 'enthnographic turn' has had detrimental effects, especially on research new technologies, as well as the agendas of international institutions. He further notes that it has 'encouraged the articulation of the interests and object of so-called academic research with the demands of administrative research or that originating from the industry of marketing'.

Mattelart is also damning in his critique of the 'aberrant' use of the term 'citizen-consumer' and the 'quasi-religious views of the active status of audiences'. However, importantly, he points to the importance of reclaiming the role of citizens in building a 'counterhegemony', which is 'at the heart of the political economy of communication and culture project'. He also points to forms of intervention, including criticism of the media and democratization of communication.

While the tension between PEC and cultural studies is legendary, the integration of these approaches has also been increasingly accepted and implemented in a range of research. Such an integration of approaches is necessary, not only to fully examine the complexities of mediated communication but also to challenge other celebratory approaches in communication research. Many authors in this volume would agree with Graham Murdock's observation that 'We need to... work towards the construction of a more complete account of the central dynamics of contemporary culture and to mobilize those insights to defend the symbolic resources required to extend the rights and duties of citizenship in the service of revitalizing democracy' (Murdock, 1995: 94).

As Herschmann points out, borrowing from Stuart Hall's theory-methodological approach employing circuits of culture and encoding-decoding, 'The relationship between culture and economy is increasingly interconnected: it is a phenomenon that cannot be ignored given the growing move on the part of transnational corporations to monopolize the cultural space.' For Bustamante (Chapter 5), this means considering the study of contemporary culture within the framework of political economy 'since it easily overcomes the numerous errors and deviations – mediacentrism, eurocentrism – of the functionalist theory of communication'.

The tension between different critical approaches may be seen to be less of a problem these days, based on the increasing number of studies that actually succeed in integrating analysis of the cultural and the economic. Many scholars working in cultural studies, international communications, feminism, race-ethnic studies and other forms of social research have produced work that integrates these perspectives with PEC. In other words, they embrace a political economic perspective as only one of the lenses they use to understand media. This outpouring of research and its recognition of structuration and agency – whether individual, collective, corporate or institutional – have been ongoing for decades. For many contextual scholars, the conceptual or methodological divisions between or among political economy, cultural studies and social research have essentially collapsed, yielding scholarship that synthesizes these areas. In this volume, Crovi Druetta draws attention to the work that has been done along these lines, but also the necessity to continue to 'open up the richness of political economy' by combining it with other types of analysis.

While the authors in this collection mention examples of integrated studies by Ibero-American scholars, I'd like to add a few additional examples from English-language texts to illustrate the widespread acceptance of this principle.[2] A few studies have combined political economy with other approaches to examine a particular media phenomenon holistically. An excellent earlier example is Jostein Gripsrud's (1995) study of *Dynasty*, which traces the TV programme's production context, discusses its textual elements and examines its distribution and reception. In my own work on the Walt Disney Company, the history and political economy of the organization are presented, along with various readings of Disney's texts and people's reception of and resistance to Disney products (Wasko, 2001). Increasingly, scholars are successfully integrating political economy and cultural studies to achieve more complete and nuanced analyses. Other examples are Robert Babe (2010), Jyotsna Kapur (2005) and Richard Maxwell (2001), but there are many others.

The integration of feminism and political economy is well represented by Eileen Meehan and Ellen Riordan (2002), in which contributors examine media representations, consumer practices and commoditization. Carolyn Byerly and Karen Ross's (2006) collection considers how gender is implicated in media industries, among other issues. Meanwhile, Carol Stabile's (2006) study of gender, race and crime news combines historiography with textual, class and industrial analysis.

Collaborative research projects have also brought together researchers from different critical approaches and often from different national settings. For example, in the Global Disney Audiences Project, an international group of researchers using various critical approaches and multiple methodologies documented people's experiences of Disney's products and penetration into local economies (Wasko et al., 2001). Another example of work that addressed the commonalities and tensions between political economy and audience analysis was the Lord of the Rings Project, which examined the distribution of the film as well as fans' reactions (Barker and Mathijs, 2007). Meanwhile, Daniel Biltereyst and Philippe Meers (2011) have recently made important contributions to the integration of political economy and audience research.

Often these integrated approaches maintain the essence of political economy, in that the research examines the relationships of power that are involved in the production, distribution and consumption of media and communication resources within a wider social context. PEC still privileges issues relating to class power, not to the exclusion of other relationships, however, and emphasizes the complex and contradictory nature of such relationships. Most important, PEC challenges media and communication development that undermines equitable and democratic societies.

Dealing with the digital

Obviously the evolution of media technology must be taken into account in any assessment of media and culture. However, as Luis A. Albornoz points out (Chapter 9), caution must be taken not to reinforce technological determinism or symptomatic technology that is common in mainstream and celebratory approaches to the study of media and communication. He argues that analysis of the changes in digital communication technologies must be framed within important social, political and economic contexts that include attention to regulation, deregulation or reregulation; business concentration; production, distribution and consumption of cultural content; the internationalization of capital, agents and content; and trends in financialization. His chapter then outlines several current debates on digital communication technologies.

Albornoz's discussion fits well with the recent work that some political economists have been doing related to digital technologies. Digital labour has been analysed in a number of studies (e.g. Fuchs, 2014) and is the focus of a recent special issue of the journal *tripleC: Communication, Capitalism & Critique*, entitled 'Philosophers of the world unite! Theorising digital labour and virtual work – definitions, dimensions and forms'. Meanwhile, big data and cloud technology have been studied by Mosco (2014), while Patrick Burkart (2014) has recently analysed the policies and politics surrounding digitization. Important historical perspectives on the digitization process have been offered as well, with reminders that 'new' media technologies often present a good deal of continuity, especially in terms of corporate involvement, commercialization and commodification (for a historical overview of corporate intervention in new media development, see e.g. Tim Wu, 2010).

Theory and back to basics

Another interesting development within PEC generally is the return to classic theories and concepts to explain the evolution of media and communications. This is not new for Ibero-American scholars, who have consistently raised serious and important theoretical questions. Similar to Bolaño and others in this collection, many scholars are calling for a reinvigoration of Marxist analysis (see e.g. Terry Eagleton, 2011). As noted previously, most critical PEC scholarship draws on Marxist theory and practice, but a few media scholars and/or sociologists have emphasized the need to use Marxist theory more explicitly. Christian Fuchs (2008) has been especially active in these efforts, while John Bellamy Foster represents a sociologist who uses Marxist theory to study environmental and media issues (see McChesney et al., 1998).

Another concept that has been revived is the idea of the commons, which some media scholars have integrated into their analysis of the current media climate (see e.g. Graham Murdock, 2011; Benjamin Birkinbine, 2014; Dorothy Kidd, 2003). The concept of the commons has been integrated into a myriad of media-related projects, including media centres and websites. For instance, Wikimedia Commons is 'a media file repository making available public domain and freely-licensed educational media content (images, sound and video clips) to everyone, in their own language'.

Other debates also have ensued within the study of political economy of media and communication. For instance, Dwayne Winseck and Dal Yong Jin (2011) have argued that political economists studying the media need to pay more attention to empirical evidence and documentation, and have called for a broader definition of the approach that would include institutional and other types of analysis. Further distinctions and critiques are offered by Wasko et al. (2011) and Scott Fitzgerald (2012).

Role of intellectuals and challenges for the future

Along these lines, another theme that is addressed by several of the authors in this volume pertains to the role of intellectuals and academics in the changing world of media. For instance, Schlesinger addresses the complications of intellectuals' involvement in cultural politics and notes that, based on recent research, 'the legislative impulse remains strong in some intellectual quarters and disciplines'. It remains to be seen, however, what difference critical intellectuals and academics can make in policy arenas. Of course, such influence can vary greatly across diverse settings and different time periods.

The lure of the media world can be compelling, and certainly not all academics have resisted the (sometimes) lucrative appeal of working for dominant commercial media companies that others critique.

Bustamante comments on this trend, observing that 'part of the university and academic world, certainly already stripped of prominence and downgraded in its critical function, now accompanies this and many other similar fashions, indiscriminately accepting appointments with consultants, prophets and gurus, and acritically jumping on the bandwagon of market trends'.

The final chapter by Crovi Druetta speaks to this issue, as well as drawing attention to the privatizing trends in education. She argues that these tendencies are influencing research agendas in negative ways, including quality for quantity and preference for quick research that can contribute to the 'labyrinth of productivity'. Obviously, these trends have an influence on critical research such as PEC in a variety of ways, including (perhaps most importantly) a reduction in the range of funding sources.

Meanwhile, Mattelart calls on researchers and teachers, despite our 'precarious positions', to become key players in the future knowledge society and feels that we have not 'sufficiently questioned what it means to redefine our social contract with the citizenry as a whole'. The point, however, is to 'establish a knowledge economy and society that does not reproduce the power structure and power relations that have marked the development of industrial society'.

Conclusion

The notion of power is fundamental to this collection of articles and, therefore, it is not surprising that it is the first word in the title of this book. The question of power weaves its way through these discussions and is fundamental to the political economy approach. However, as noted by the authors, we must not accept a static approach to the study of the political economy of media, culture and communications. They likewise challenge us to respond to changes in media, changes in technology and changes in the world.

This collection of Ibero-American work is evidence of the growth and evolution of PEC. Again, this is not so surprising given the strong theoretical foundations and research that have been produced in this region over the years. Let's look forward to more translations in the future that can contribute to a better understanding of this important work.

Janet Wasko
University of Oregon, USA

Notes

1. Some examples include John Hartley, *Creative Industries* (Malden, MA: Blackwell, 2005); Henry Jenkins, *Convergence Culture: Where Old and New Media Collide* (New York: New York University Press, 2006); John Thornton Caldwell, *Production Culture: Industrial Reflexivity and Critical Practice in Film and Television* (Durham, NC: Duke University Press, 2008); Vicki Mayer, Miranda J. Banks and John Thornton Caldwell (eds) *Production Studies: Cultural Studies of Media Industries* (New York: Routledge, 2009); Paul du Gay and Michael Pryke (eds) *Cultural Economy* (London: Sage Publications, 2002). It also might be noted that some cultural studies scholars have recently discovered economics. See Lawrence Grossberg (2010) 'Standing on a Bridge: Rescuing Economies from Economists', *Journal of Communication Inquiry*, 34(4), 316–336.
2. This section draws on Meehan and Wasko (2013) and Wasko (2014).

References

Babe, Robert (2010) *Cultural Studies and Political Economy: Toward a New Integration*, Lanham, MD: Lexington.

Barker, Martin and Mathijs, Ernest (eds) (2007) *Watching Lord of the Rings*, New York: Peter Lang.

Becerra, Martin and Mastrini, Guillermo (2011) 'Communication economy paths: a Latin American approach', in Janet Wasko, Graham Murdock and Helena Sousa (eds) *The Handbook of Political Economy of Communications*, Malden, MA: Wiley Blackwell, 109–126.

Biltereyst, Daniel and Meers, Philippe (2011) 'The political economy of audiences', in Janet Wasko, Graham Murdock and Helena Sousa (eds) *The Handbook of Political Economy of Communications*, Malden, MA: Wiley Blackwell, 415–435.

Birkinbine, Benjamin (2014) 'Incorporating the commons: Towards a political economy of corporate involvement in free and open source software', paper presented at International Association for Media and Communication Research Conference, Hyderabad, India, July.

Bolaño, César, Mastrini, Guillermo and Sierra, Franscisco (eds) (2012) *Political Economy, Communication and Knowledge: A Latin American Perspective*, New York: Hampton Press.

Burkart, Patrick (2014) *Pirate Politics: The New Information Policy Contests*, Cambridge, MA: MIT Press.

Byerly, Carolyn M. and Ross, Karen (eds) (2006) *Women and Media: A Critical Introduction*, Malden, MA: Wiley Blackwell.

Eagleton, Terry (2011) *Why Marx Was Right*, London: Yale University Press.

Fitzgerald, Scott W. (2012) *Corporations and Cultural Industries: Time Warner, Bertelsmann, and News Corporation*, Lanham, MD: Lexington.

Fuchs, Christian (2008) *Internet and Society: Social Theory in the Information Age*, New York: Routledge.

Gripsrud, Jostein (1995) *The Dynasty Years: Hollywood Television and Critical Media Studies*, London: Routledge.

Kapur, Jyostna (2005) *Coining for Capital: Movies, Marketing, and the Transformation of Childhood*, New Brunswick, NJ: Rutgers University Press.

Kidd, Dorothy (2003) 'Indymedia.org: A new communications commons', in M. McCaughey and M. D. Ayers (eds) *Cyberactivism: Online Activism in Theory and Practice*, New York: Routledge, 47–69.
Maxwell, Richard (ed.) (2001) *Culture Works: The Political Economy of Culture*, Minneapolis, MN: University of Minnesota Press.
McChesney, Robert W., Wood, Ellen Meiksins and Foster, John Bellamy (eds) (1998) *Capitalism and the Information Age*, New York: Monthly Review.
Meehan, Eileen R. and Riordan, Ellen (eds) (2002) *Sex and Money: Feminism and Political Economy in the Media*, Minneapolis, MN: University of Minnesota Press.
Meehan, Eileen R. and Wasko, Janet (2013) 'In defence of a political economy of the media', *Javnost-Public*, 20(1), 39–54.
Mosco, Vincent (2014) *To the Cloud: Big Data in a Turbulent World*, New York: Paradigm Publishers.
Murdock, Graham (1995) 'Across the great divide: Cultural analysis and the condition of democracy', *Critical Studies in Mass Communication*, 12(1), 89–94.
—— (2011) 'Political economies as moral economies: Commodities, gifts and public goods', in Janet Wasko, Graham Murdock and Helena Sousa (eds) *The Handbook of Political Economy of Communications*, Malden, MA: Wiley Blackwell, 331–357.
Stabile, Carol (2006) *White Victims, Black Villains: Gender, Race, and Crime News in US Culture*, London: Routledge.
Wasko, Janet (2001) *Understanding Disney: The Manufacture of Fantasy*, Cambridge: Polity.
—— (2013) 'The IAMCR political economy section: A retrospective', *The Political Economy of Communication*, 1(1). Available at www.polecom.org/index.php/polecom/article/view/11/148.
Wasko, Janet, Murdock, Graham and Sousa, Helena (eds) (2011) *The Handbook of the Political Economy of Communications*, Malden, MA: Wiley-Blackwell/IAMCR.
Wasko, Janet, Phillips, Mark and Meehan, Eileen R. (2001) *Dazzled by Disney? The Global Disney Audiences Project*, Leicester: Leicester University Press.
Winseck, Dwayne and Jin, Dal Yong (eds) (2011) *The Political Economies of Media: The Transformation of the Global Media Industries*, London: Bloomsbury.
Wu, Timothy (2010) *The Master Switch: The Rise and Fall of Information Empires*, New York: Vintage.

Acknowledgements

As editor of this volume I should like to express my gratitude for the enthusiastic support of the following people: Rodrigo Gómez García (Metropolitan Autonomous University – Cuajimalpa Branch, Mexico), Janet Wasko (President of the International Association for Media and Communication Research), Belén Monclús (Autonomous University of Barcelona, Spain) and Ana I. Segovia (Complutense University of Madrid, Spain). I would also like to thank Manuel Palacio, María Trinidad García Leiva and Nacho Gallego, my colleagues in the Department of Journalism and Audiovisual Communication at Carlos III University of Madrid (UC3M). Finally, this volume could not have been completed without the dedicated work of Ian Barnett, translator of the chapters, and the helpful assistance of Claudia Padovani and Marjan de Bruin, editors of the Palgrave/IAMCR book series, and Felicity Plester and Sneha Kamat Bhavnani at Palgrave Macmillan.

Luis A. Albornoz

Notes

This volume is a partial update of the book *Poder, medios, cultura: Una mirada crítica desde la economía política de la comunicación* (Buenos Aires: Paidós, 2011), edited by Luis A. Albornoz. The translation of this text was supported by the scientific association Latin Union of Political Economy of Information, Communication and Culture (ULEPICC), the International Association of Mass Communication Research (IAMCR), the Audiovisual Communication and Advertising Department of the Basque Country University, and research funds from professors Gaëtan Tremblay (University of Quebec in Montreal) and Luis A. Albornoz (UC3M).

Contributors

Luis A. Albornoz is a founding partner and former president (2007–2013) of the scientific association ULEPICC. He is Associate Professor of Audiovisual System Structure in the Department of Journalism and Audiovisual Communication, UC3M, Spain. He is a member of UC3M's Television-Cinema: Memory, Representation and Industry Research Group and the author of *Al fin solos... La nueva televisión del Mercosur* (2000), *Periodismo digital. Los grandes diarios en la Red* (2007) and *La televisión digital terrestre. Experiencias nacionales y diversidad en Europa, América y Asia* (2012).

César Bolaño is a professor at the Federal University of Sergipe, Brazil, and founder and first president of ULEPICC. He was president of the Latin American Association of Communication Researchers (ALAIC) during 2009–2014, and Director of the journal *EPTIC OnLine*. His output includes *Mercado brasileiro de televisão* and *Indústria cultural, informação e capitalismo*. His most recent articles address issues such as the political economy of the Internet, the critique of the political economy of knowledge, and regulation and market forces in Brazilian TV.

Enrique Bustamante is Professor of Audiovisual Communication and Advertising at the Complutense University of Madrid, Spain. He is vice president of the Spanish Association of Communication Research and founder and general coordinator of *Telos – Revista Cuadernos de Pensamiento sobre Comunicación, Tecnología y Sociedad*. His publications include *Presente y futuro de la televisión digital*, *La televisión económica* and *Radio y televisión en España. Historia de una asignatura pendiente de la democracia*. His latest work as an editor is *La cooperación cultura-comunicación en Iberoamérica*.

Delia Crovi Druetta is a professor and researcher at the Faculty of Political and Social Sciences of the National Autonomous University of Mexico. She is the author of articles and books on topics relating to communication and new technologies. Her publications include *Bitácora de viaje. Investigación y formación de comunicólogos en América Latina*, *Periodismo digital en México*, *Educar en la era de las redes* and *Comunicación* *educativa y mediaciones tecnológicas*. She is a former scientific director of ULEPICC, and since 2014 she is president of ALAIC.

Micael Herschmann is a researcher with the National Council for Scientific and Technological Development, and deputy coordinator of research into media and sociocultural mediations of the postgraduate programme at the Federal University of Rio de Janeiro (UFRJ), Brazil, where he heads the research group Nucleus for Studies and Projects in Communication. He holds a PhD in communication from UFRJ. His publications include *Comunicação e história – interfaces e novas abordagens, Lapa, cidade da música, O funk e o hip-hop invadem a cena, Comunicação, cultura e consumo. A (des)construção do espetáculo contemporâneo* and *Mídia, memória e celebridades*.

Armand Mattelart is Professor Emeritus of Information and Communication Sciences at the University of Paris VIII, France. He is the author of numerous books on communication theories and the history of communication in their international dimensions. His publications include *Un mundo vigilado* and *Diversidad cultural y mundialización*.

Vincent Mosco holds the Canada Research Chair in Communication and Sociology and is Professor of Sociology at Queen's University, Canada. He holds a PhD in sociology from Harvard University, USA. His recent works include *The Political Economy of Communication, The Laboring of Communication: Will Knowledge Workers of the World Unite?* (with C. McKercher), *Knowledge Workers in the Information Society* (with C. McKercher) and *The Digital Sublime: Myth, Power, and Cyberspace*, which won the 2005 Olson Award for the most outstanding book in the field of rhetoric and cultural studies.

Philip Schlesinger is Professor of Cultural Policy at the University of Glasgow, UK, where he was also formerly Academic Director of the Centre for Cultural Policy Research. He is working on policies related to the creative industries, as well as a study on literary ethnography. He is an editor of the journal *Media, Culture & Society*. His most recent book (coedited with J.E. Fossum) is *The European Union and the Public Sphere: A Communicative Space in the Making?* He is also a member of the Royal Society of Arts and the Royal Society of Edinburgh, and a fellow of the Academy of Social Sciences.

Francisco Sierra is Associate Professor in Communication Theory at the University of Seville, Spain. He holds a PhD in information sciences from the Complutense University of Madrid. He is Director of the Centro Internacional de Estudios Superiores de Comunicación para América Latina (Ciespal) since 2014 and chief editor of the journal *Revista de Estudios para el Desarrollo Social de la Comunicación*. He is the author of *Políticas de comunicación y educación* and *Crítica y desarrollo de la sociedad del conocimiento*, which received the Award for Best Ibero-American Book on Communication 2008.

Gaëtan Tremblay is a professor at the University of Québec in Montréal, Canada, and Director of the Centre for Studies and Research on Brazil since 2004. He is a co-founder of the Interdisciplinary Research Group on Communication, Information and Society. He has headed the publication of various collective works, and has published many contributions to journals and books on communication, culture and media industries, distance learning and the information society. He belongs to the field of the PEC.

Janet Wasko is the Knight Chair in Communication Research at the University of Oregon in Eugene, Oregon, USA. She is the author, co-author or editor of 19 books, including *Understanding Disney: The Manufacture of Fantasy* and *How Hollywood Works*. Her research and teaching focus on the political economy of media, especially the political economy of film, as well as issues relating to democracy and media. She serves as the President of the IAMCR.

Ramón Zallo is Professor of Audiovisual Communication at the University of the Basque Country, Spain. He is president of the Spanish Section of ULEPICC. His latest book is *El Pueblo Vasco, hoy. Cultura, historia y sociedad en la era de la diversidad y del conocimiento*, and he is co-author of *Cultura y comunicación para el siglo XXI: Diagnóstico y políticas públicas*. A cultural advisor to the Basque Government on issues relating to communication, the audiovisual sector and culture (2002–2009), he was the chief framer of the Basque Plan for Culture (2004–2015) and contributed to the white paper for the Basque audiovisual sector.

Part I

The Political Economy of Communication

1
Current Challenges for the Critical Economy of Culture and Communication

Ramón Zallo

Our field, be it called the political economy of communication or the critical economy of culture and communication, is just one part (albeit a substantial one) of the critical viewpoint in that set of disciplines – economics, sociology or politics – that take a social analysis approach to culture and communication.[1] By this I mean that our field is not all-encompassing and that there is also a critical sociology of culture and communication (Raymond Williams, Pierre Bourdieu, etc.), or a critical political science (Antonio Gramsci, Ralph Miliband, Claus Offe, Norberto Bobbio, etc.), to which other fields will have to be added as they develop (a critical ecology, etc.).

Let us not forget that these disciplines and their critical versions emerged quite a few decades after work had begun on the construction of critical thinking, which in its early period gave a decisive, if not deterministic, role to the economic instance. The scientific advances in all currents of thought have enabled us to overcome that stage, and focus thematically and complement knowledge based on methodological respect, which in the case of critical thinking enjoys an added advantage: the close ties between the disciplines arising from shared epistemologies centring on the same social subject.

The founders on both sides of the Atlantic (including Dallas Smythe, Herbert Schiller, Armand Mattelart, Graham Murdock, Bernard Miège and Nicholas Garnham) were convinced of their project and had a dual mission to denounce the communication system and redefine paradigms, whether for the United Nations Educational, Scientific and Cultural Organization (UNESCO) or for application in states' national communication policies. We, on the other hand, since reality has changed on the other side of the neoliberal desert, are puzzled in a good many areas, such as the analysis of immaterial and global capitalism, either about the project to be defined (quite apart from the moral philosophy of change, which has never left us) or about what historical subject(s) will shape the future. Perhaps to our credit we have a more complex vision of society and its challenges.

Like the founders, we too have a vision that straddles critical contribution and denunciation. But it is for us already part of that three-sided dialectic of confrontation between the kindly Big Brother that is the communicative system of media groups and cultural merchandise; the massive, unfettered and stimulating social communication on the Web, which has led to a proliferation of communicators; and a few social majorities that haphazardly demand democratic communication. The subjects of reference represent, in the first case, cognitive capital; in the second, new demands and new forms of communication; and, in the third, a more mature society committed to qualitative progress.

This is not the place for a full stocktaking but a quick draft. Of little help to us right now when tackling these changes are two classic versions: that of Althusserian structuralism,[2] and that of the ideologized and monistic models that reduced the media to a propaganda system of power. For their part, two other more sophisticated models that incorporate key elements of a specific analysis of the media also fail to provide answers to all the questions. In one the central focus is owners and financiers,[3] who are certainly crucial but do not take into account certain internal variables. In the other the internal variables that influence information are taken into consideration but ownership and the system are not, meaning that a central aspect is missing: the economy itself.[4] The current social complexity is absent in the four types of models indicated. There, society is but a mirror, a passive subject and malleable mass at the mercy of the media. We need a fifth model that, in addition to picking up on the successes of previous models, is more refined and allows us to understand the complex relationship of the media with society and power at this time. The critical sociology of early cultural studies (Raymond Williams, Stuart Hall, E.P. Thompson, etc.) or of Pierre Bourdieu marked out an interesting path towards undoing that deficit.

There is therefore no single theory or tradition of political economy of communication, but many different traditions of critical economy of communication and culture. Part of the European tradition favoured models that ranged from cultural merchandise itself and the process of commercialization to the creation of structures (British, French (Grenoble), Spanish schools, etc.), and gradually pieced together a bottom-up interpretation, interspersed with the critical contributions of history, anthropology or political science.

Yet to be defined is a general and open model for interpreting the current media and social discourse management system in present-day capitalism. Today's capitalist system demonstrates a great capacity for self-transformation and continues to be based on goods, the exploitation of labour and the private accumulation of capital. And, at present, it establishes cognitive, technoinformational, intellectual, immaterial and digital capital – or whatever other name we give it – as the driving force of the whole system; with the emphasis on the appropriation and management of knowledge and all its derivatives: innovation, creation, education, learning or talent – forms of 'complex work', as Marx called them, that at present are expressed as intellectual work, which is already a direct production factor within the system.

However, in parallel to this, society has become *logos*, communication. The tension lies in who will be the keeper of the word, which goes beyond and overflows the more obvious confrontation between Internet users and system owners.

Economics in the strictest sense must focus on the economic function. That is its role. This does not detract from the fact that other disciplines can, and must, study culture and communication. On the contrary, the critical versions of anthropology, sociology, political science and so on are indispensable, as together, and along with the critical economy of communication and culture, they would make up a 'critique of culture and communication' of sorts or 'critical analyses of culture and communication' in which those versions of these various disciplines might come together in a complementary search for common know-how and paradigms. This would take us down an open road to knowledge rather than in the direction of the closed systems that believe they can explain everything.

Little progress will be made by practising economics that is not economics. We need explanatory legitimacy in the eyes of other more established and dominant versions. We will not explain complexity if we believe that economics is *science* or we do not cross it with other fields. Or to put it another way, critical economy, from the point of view of its own methodology, needs to be complemented by a social theory and by a theory of power, which invites flexibility and integration, or at least a grasp of various related fields.

Luckily, critical thinking does have a theory of history – albeit not a univocal one – linked to agents, particularly the working classes and their conflicts. Economic criticism cannot be divorced from society, its agents and effects; on the contrary, it incorporates them as a framework into its matrix. Economics would only appear to explain ownership, goods, work, relations between capital and labour force, production processes, specific output, sectors, boards of directors, concentration, corporate functioning, market behaviours, economic policy and son on. But not the rest. That requires the intersecting of its knowledge to produce social theory, of which economics is a part. Adding the word 'political' to 'economics', 'political economy', helps if it is understood as the 'critique of political economy', but it 'needs to be grounded in a realist, inclusive, constitutive and critical epistemology' (Mosco, 2006) to be added in to critical studies in general.

Social anchoring in the potential subjects of transformation is essential for progress towards a 'general theoretical model' without this needing to be done on the basis of purely laboratory-type thinking, or through a combination of various epistemologies, or from the viewpoint merely of ethics. Our 'economy of culture' must subordinate economic imperatives to strategies of cultural democratization and likewise subordinate the economic vision of culture – financing, sectors, regional policies and so on – to the cultural aspect of development.

Critical economy – unlike functionalism, behaviourism, positivism or postmodernism – will always place culture in the context of societies in conflict and, based on its own methodology, sets itself the function of revealing the structure and functioning of the system, and cannot, to analyse it, be detached from its relationship with collective welfare, domestic and international equality, or the rationality and fair distribution of resources and their uses, or with their opposites. This is to say, the defence of equality or respect for diversity are inherent in the very discourse of a critical economy that, due to its own definition and methodology, does not shrink from its role or its effects as a science for society.

With regard to culture, there is a difference between this and other perspectives, in which it is not economics that is instrumental but culture, which is regarded as a means for diversifying, reconstructing, maintaining, consolidating or developing cities and economies, including local cultural industries. Culture has been pervaded by other motivations. Indeed, in terms of cultural and communication policies on cultural products and equipment or networks, the liberal logic of the principle of subsidiarity has been gaining ground over classical logics in policies of intervention, promotion and stimulus. Similarly, in the deployment and management of equipment or programmes, uniqueness and 'spectacularity' have gained ground over social effectiveness.

In the absence of a metanarrative that is finalistic but grounded in the elements that define political economy, such as history, ethics, the concept of totality and *praxis*[5] – and one should, I think, add the continuous adaptation of methodologies – it is a matter of rebuilding a critical thinking of culture and communication[6] that will not be independent from a comprehensive system of thinking anchored in the potential subjects of change, such as workers' movements, alterglobalist and citizen-based social movements, be they alternative or reformist (see Waterman, 2006).

The advantage of the critical approach is that it offers a global vision and a number of tools. We will not easily fall into a formal conceptualist logic, or be swayed by fashions – for example, the 'creative industries' – nor will we disregard the social implications. But we also face certain risks, such as ideologism, a lack of rigour justified by a good cause, the hermeticism of models or subordination to political gains. In other words, we have no guarantee of getting it right, which is why we must be modest enough to study every version, because sometimes it is others that are entirely in the right, or partly so.

Having said that, we must confess that, in this age of social multiplication of the fragmented and socialized intellect, we are witnessing a monumental lapse of focus with regard to a possible project for change and an achievable utopia. In the case of culture and communication there is a proliferation of studies that – with the precision of an entomologist and like an intangible mosaic – detect the changes under way and the new subject matters. From that point on there are differences in the diagnoses, subjects, methodologies or centrality of knowledge. The result is considerable confusion within the main fields and topics of debate of our time and, consequently, in the alliances or the demands made on the administration in office with regard to public service or cultural and communication policies.

Recent research in the economy of culture and communication

The increasing importance of culture within the economy has, of course, led to a reappraisal not only of the economy of culture and communication, but also of critical perspectives on the economy.[7] Along with critical analyses by the now classic authors – Mattelart (2002, 2005), Miège (2004), Schlesinger (2007), Garnham (2005), Mosco and Schiller (2001) or Tremblay (1996) – there are also reflections associated with social movements[8] and a continuous output of academic papers.[9] But we are also seeing the emergence of new debates and original contributions by young or autonomous collectives.[10] In addition, now that the technological paradigm has completely changed, the debate about the type of regulation necessary for intellectual property offers interesting critical analyses that question the foundations of the creative market.[11]

But let us not be misled: what in general there are aplenty, on the one hand, are expert reports promoted by state administrations or suprastate regional organizations like the European Union (EU) or the Southern Common Market (Mercosur) – dealing with policies, agreements, harmonizations, observatories, the audiovisual sector and so on – or by cultural networks, be they of cities, regions, researchers or cultural managers, which in turn create the need for research of common interest on a variety of topics.[12] That is useful material for analysis.

On the other hand, there are significant theoretical works based on the conceptual apparatuses of neoclassical economics (Frey, 2000; Vogel, 2004; Towse, 2005; Lasuén Sancho et al., 2006), although the peculiarities of culture may not be of help in the useful or explanatory application of some of their vulnerable models.[13]

There are also macroeconomic and sectoral research efforts – with better results – provided by public or private institutional reports, and numerous statistics[14] accompanied by studies on the cultural gross domestic product (GDP), employment for the sector and the various cultural industries or by monitoring of public and private spending on culture (e.g. Jaén García, 2006). An increase has taken place in the 'observatory' function of governments, rights-management companies or foundations, for collecting and processing useful information. There are no longer any countries, either in Europe or in Latin America, that do not estimate the economic contribution of culture, albeit at the behest of suprastate institutions, with advances even being made in the detection of cultural indicators suitable for monitoring and assessing the state of culture and communication or of specific cultural policies.[15] On the microeconomic side a sizeable output of books describes communication enterprises (Población and García Alonso, 1997; Sánchez Tabernero, 2000; or Caro, 2007).

Given this thematic variety, there is often a certain syncretism at congresses, symposia and the like.[16]

In university research there is an explosion of studies on the important phenomenon of globalization (e.g. Tomlison, 1991; Beck, 1998; Quirós, 1998; Martín Barbero, 2000; García Canclini, 2001; Quirós and Sierra, 2001; Wolton, 2003; Mattelart, 2005; González Arencibia, 2006), as well as a proliferation of sectoral studies on culture and communication, or on communication alone,[17] the richness of which brings us back to reflecting on the world communication system, a subject that appeared to have been banished.

Abandoning the path of circumventing problems as if they did not exist, encouragement is being given at present – in a context in which democracies are being strengthened and a number of left-wing governments in Latin America are being consolidated – for the completion of studies on business concentration processes or on transnational power, and this at the same time that anti-concentration logics are being gradually dismantled in the world.[18]

In Europe, for example, the topic usually only bursts into the public arena when there is flagrant *ex post* abuse, with the resulting denouncement of the dominant market position and legal action from the competition's courts. But the liberal dismantling has not prevented a certain amount of university research along those lines. Indeed, the umbrella of globalization and that of diversity are encouraging a new renaissance in research and communication policy with regard to two problems that had been forgotten – the unbalanced flows between countries and processes of concentration – topics that until recently had only been addressed by scholars in Spain (e.g. Miguel de Bustos, 1993; Llorens, 2001; Bustamante, 2007a; García Santamaría, 2012).

Perhaps the novelty lies in the fact that there is no expectation of any geocultural solutions being provided externally or by international agencies, but rather through the efforts and understanding of the agents in each country. Regional agreements between countries can serve as coverage, as is the case of Mercosur. Concerns about the creation of the cultural sector are the order of the day, particularly in the publishing field and audiovisual sector, following the successes of several countries in the internationalized production of TV series.[19] Likewise, another traditional concern in Latin America – and in Spain too – is the relationships between information and power (see Jorge Alonso and García López, 2009; or the themes regularly addressed by Reig, 1998).

What is clear is that it is not enough to analyse the flows in themselves, be they transnational or international, and that what is needed instead is to provide the reference to origin (this shows us dominances) and to the territorial and cultural effects (this tells us about dependencies). Not to do so would be tantamount to not considering the problem of power in relation to culture and communication in the world and to the geoculture that it traces. This is not a problem of nationalisms but rather of mistreated social and cultural roots, and of uneven structural flows.

The preferred research approach to the communication system has in recent years made reference to information and communication technologies (ICTs), with applied studies such as those by Garitaonandia et al. (2003), Prado et al. (2006), Saperas (2007), Marzal Felici and Casero Ripollés (2007), Badillo and Ortega (2008) and Beceiro (2009). Indeed, there is a clear preference for research on the forms and effects of ICTs and the expectations this generates about the resulting communication system.

There is a variety of topics in the world of cyberculture, in which the right to knowledge and communication is being reformulated, the functionality of the system is even being questioned, and where reflection is taking place on democracy or education. It is a new social and cultural space, which must be subject to systematic monitoring from now on, and in which the dialogue between all cultures generates unimaginable flows. There are general prospective studies on the passage from analogue society to knowledge society;[20] or research studies on communication policies in the framework of technological and spatial convergence – the establishment of the information society in Spain, in the Spanish Autonomous Communities or in Argentina (Mastrini and Califano, 2006), reflections on the digital variants of traditional cultural industries (see Álvarez Monzoncillo et al., 2007) and the occasional withering critique of the next communicative model (Reig, 2001).

There have also been numerous studies on regulation relating to the Television Without Frontiers Directive, or the introduction of digital terrestrial TV in Spain or in the Autonomous Communities (García Leiva, 2006). Access is also available for the regular monitoring of the audiovisual sector in Europe (Crusafón, 2006).

It is evident from all these studies that the concerns about the various convergences are less and less focused on technological accumulation and more on their use for responding to specific needs, and that they appear to mark the leap from an information society of abstract items to knowledge societies with contents.

ICTs are proving instrumental not only in the emergence of a global information society – Castiñeira (2001) puts forward an integrative approach – but also in transforming industrial capitalism into digital, cognitive[21] or postindustrial capitalism. This centres on immaterial values, at the same time as a Web culture and a commercialized culture are spreading, with informational capital being located in the centre of the system and the human mind being a direct production force, as Castells (1999) stated, or a raw material. That capital should be understood not as the type of collective social capital described by Hamelink (1999), which would be a social quality – the degree of technical and economic capacity to access information, as well as the application of that information for specific ends – but first and foremost as sectoral or functional capital. This capital would have the function of a connector of the development of financial, energy-related, organizational, IT-related, cultural, ICT-related capital, for the appropriation of types of added value that are more substantial and drivers of the market, and that are now the dominant group of capital within the system.

Fortunately, thematic intersections also occur, such as those relating to sustainability (see Rodríguez and Vicario, 2005; Calderero et al., 2006; ASC, 2007; Esteban Galarza et al., 2008) or e-cultural policies (see Martínez Illa and Mendoza, 2004).

As far as strictly cultural management is concerned – micro- rather than macromanagement – there is a wealth of research, which is all very ground-level, functional and uncritical, on art consumers' preferences and their levels of satisfaction; or the determinants of the demand for cultural services (Colbert, 2003); or the functions of production and cost in firms; or the financing and pricing policy models in museums (Gombault and Petr, 2006), equipment, events and cultural centres; or the promotion models and support systems for the creation and management of cultural enterprises (Gómez de la Iglesia, 1999); or on the world of sponsorship and the conversion of sponsors into cultural promoters of their own projects; or on the most suitable relationships between public and private agents. This is a set of issues little known to economy of communication scholars. And it all straddles economics, the psychology of consumption or aesthetics, as topics featured in the historic *Journal of Cultural Economics* and other publications.[22]

Other repeated concerns, this time at the end of the value chain, are how to communicate events, brands, schedules or equipment, or how to achieve audiences and, as a related point, the more structural problem of creating new publics and building loyalty among them, or the secondary dilemma of making programmers the captives of loyal publics.

When it comes to the field of cultural management practices, the concerns are directed towards the training of cultural managers in general (Martinell Sempere, 2006a). The standardization of cultural public management sometimes makes it difficult to distinguish between right-wing and left-wing councils, which just goes to show that management is gaining the upper hand over political thinking. In terms of issues, priority is given, for example, to the use of business tools, creating networks and circuits, achieving synergies, economies of scale or network economies, new relations with private and social initiatives in the area of cooperation, the new generation of equipment designed for compactness, and the use of ICTs or administrative structural changes for improving cultural services.[23]

With regard to government intervention there is a significant output on cultural policy and audiovisual policy, and even more on communication policy or the redefinition of public services.[24] In Spain they revolve around the Spanish Radio and Television Corporation, the Autonomous Communities, and local radio and TV stations, and in France and the UK around the new missions of public services (CAC, 2001; Bustamante, 2006).

As can be observed, at present the concerns are being refocused and incorporate problems related to the cultural industries' own production – creating integrated complexes – or the media, as well as its social impacts, at the same time that interest has been aroused in taking advantage of ICTs *vis-à-vis* their technical and social organization for development purposes.

This is in part a reaction to the shift in concerns in the early 1990s from public to private spheres, in culture and communication also; as well as from homegrown production towards studies on demand, reception, uses and mediations – a variant of cultural studies (see García Canclini, 1990). The influence of transnational production was played down, perhaps excessively so, and concerns about developing a national culture industry with the support of national policies on culture and communication were put aside in almost every case. Perhaps this was the result of resignation in the face of the omnipresent market.

The current agenda deals with the setting up of observatories in many countries (Argentina, Mexico, Spain, Autonomous Communities, etc.) and the broadening of their content, as well as studies on culture and development (see García Canclini and Piedras, 2006; Miguel de Bustos, 2006). One particular variant – following in the wake of Florida (2002, 2005), Oakley or the consultants KEA European Affairs et al. (2006) – is the version applied to development from a proactive approach on the part of the so-called creative industries (see Piedras, 2004; Fonseca Reis, 2008; Fundación Este País, 2008; Guzmán Cárdenas, 2008).

In European research,[25] which seems to shift between institutional and economistic discourse, what is missing is an economic discourse of culture anchored more in the UNESCO tradition in terms of the values of diversity, access and equality,[26] which now have a certain continuity (UNESCO, 2001, 2005, 2009). There is also an evident contradiction between, on the one hand, the discourse of diversity led by the authorities in Canada, France, Brazil and Spain, among other countries, which generates a small amount of qualitative research, including concerns over international cooperation,[27] and, on the other hand, the economic discourse, dominant in fact in all countries, which generates far more utilitarian research on the profitable face of culture, without dealing with the problem of communicative and cultural power.

We are already installed in cultural economism. Also lacking is the cultural-political discourse and the resulting proposals that should encourage a contextualizing and instrumental type of economy of culture capable of correcting the errors that occur in policy options.

Recognizing the fact that most of the world is a collection of minorities means that diversity is a social reality to be managed in general and in particular. This has led to a clear conceptual expansion of what previously referred almost exclusively to ethnic minorities and is now a definition of the social state of health.[28] Currently it also refers to national minorities, groups participating in civil society, access, identities, the third sector and social movements, indigenous initiatives or virtual communities (on the 'associative undertakings' linked to social movements or the recovery of indigenous sounds, see Yúdice, 2006; on the third sector, see Martínez, 2005; Mayugo i Majó, 2005).

Now evident are integrative approaches centred on the concept of 'cultural development' or the cultural dimension of development in terms of proximity, citizenship, networks and interaction. This is a topic on which to keep a close watch.

Moreover, in spite of the compression of time and space in the Internet age, there is an increasing territorialization of research in parallel with the emergence as a cultural subject of substate, regional and city areas in terms of cultural strategic functions and partly in terms of interinstitutional international relations, both in Europe (see Congress of Local and Regional Authorities of Europe, 1999; Rausell Köster, 1999; Bonet, 2002; Palma Martos, 2003; Badillo, 2004; Guimerà i Orts, 2007; Casado, 2008; Gifreu i Pinsach and Corbella Cordomí, 2009) and in Latin America. This emergence is supported by discourses such as those produced by Agenda 21 for Culture,[29] the interlocal network or the noted presence of regions, stateless nations and social movements at the World Summit on the Information Society (WSIS). However, it must be said that while on some issues and in some places the perspective may be defensive, one of resistance, by certain movements – workers, women or communities – in other cases they can be alternative in nature, aimed at confronting models and projects, and making proposals with the opportunity and capacity to influence public policies (see Table 1.1).

Table 1.1 Holistic table for a critical economy of culture and communication

Areas	Topics	Objects of study 1	Objects of study 2	Objects of study 3	Objects of study 4	Objects of study 5	Objects of study 6
I. General and structural vision	**Desirable, reasonable and practicable cultural and contextual utopia (I)**	Values	Experiences	Discourses	Epistemological problems: **statute of the critical economy of communication and culture**; interdisciplinary fields		
	Characterization of present-day capitalism and trends	**Immaterial capitalism**	Globalization	**Crisis of civilization and cultural questioning: knowledge society?**	Accumulation and cultural and communicational power	**Concentration vs. accessible and multicentre communications**	Economic and cultural crisis
	Cultural and communication structures	*Structures of the current cultural and media system (II)*	Infrastructures, events, equipment, heritage: observatories and mappings	Spatial: global, international, states, substate, city International flows Cyberspace	Sectoral: branches, subsectors, segments	Intersectoral: chains, horizontal vertical and networks Innovation Education	GDP Employment
II. Micro- and mesoeconomy	Labour and valorization processes	Goods	*Cultural work*	Valorization	Value chains	Production	
	Mesocommunication	Accumulation processes	Groups: global, international, emerging, national champions, etc.	*Networks*			

	Cultural and communicative agents	Creators	Firms: management, strategies, financing, remuneration	Public agents	Social: third sector	Users	Agents and power
III. Markets	Markets and demands	Markets, GDP, indicators	Social expenditure on culture	Demand turnovers	Consumptions		
IV. Society	Society and cultural practices	Social changes	Practices and habits	Communities, genders, immigration, generations	Internet users	New publics	
V. Strategies and policies	Social and cultural strategies	**Paradigms (diversity, access, etc.) for the cultural and communication system**	Democratization of the media and the Web (III)	Cultural and communicative movements and communication by social movements	Alternative communications in response to the cultural divide	Demand	
	Cultural and communication policies	Cultural policies: visions, strategies, structures and instruments	Communication policies and regulations (Information Society (IS), Digital Terrestrial Television (DTT)) visions, strategies, structures, etc.	Public expenditure, public service	Governance	Intellectual property: mismatch between regulation and social culture	International and inter-regional cooperation

Note: Fields: I. Major trends (in bold); II. Driving realities (in italics); III. Responses (underlined).
Source: Author's own.

Traditionally, cultural policy was a mission of the state parallel to nation-building. However, it is becoming less so both for political reasons and due to questions of budgetary allocation. State administrations share cultural public expenditure with substate areas, provinces and cities, which are in charge of up to almost 70 per cent of public spending on culture. The emergence of new political subjects, decentralization, deconcentration, the shifting of cultural responsibility to more devolved power structures, in the form of 'subsidiarity, regionalism, local autonomy and federalism',[30] result in regional studies also being applied to the sphere of culture.

The other main area for cultural strategies and programming in the cultural life of culture-seeking citizens is municipal governments. The relationship between culture and city, in the context of diversity and as a reflection of the complexity and hybridization of the urban fabric, is being given significant momentum in all parts of the world, which is demonstrated, for example, in reports and books (for local or city-related issues, see López de Aguileta, 2000; Greffe, 2002; Lucchini, 2002; Bloomfield and Bianchini, 2004; Manito, 2006; Rausell Köster, 2007; and the applied study on music in Lapa, Rio de Janeiro, by Herschmann, 2007 and meetings (such as that of Eurocult 21)[31] or the specialization of cultural districts.

In the case of Spain there is a good deal of recent research on territorial cultural offerings and on structural cultural needs in regional areas and cities, which goes as far as producing diagnoses of the sector as well as of demand, habits and consumption. And it invites the possibility of general planning involving agents – with the democratic participatory development that this entails – which is unthinkable in macrospaces like states (as is the case with the Basque Government, 2004; Catalonia, Andalusia and Castilla La Mancha have also developed planning policies and Asturias, which has a white paper on cultural industries, and the Canary Islands is in the process of doing so). Certainly, with regard to territorial policies, none of the issues is univocal, and neither are each party's objectives and strategies. Within the institutional sphere, more information in this regard can be found in different lines of research such as the biennial series of the *Informe de la comunicació a Catalunya* report; the *Quaderns del CAC* of the Catalan Audiovisual Council (CAC); or the Audiovisual Foundation of Andalusia and the Institute of Regional Development, 2001. For works by university professors, see those of Zurbano (2005), Hernández i Martí (2006), Zallo (2007a) and López García (2008).

Challenges and priorities

Challenges and priorities do not derive from the scientific field itself but from the most significant and pressing realities to which research must respond. It is not ideas that change the world but rather changes in the world that force a change of ideas, which, in turn, facilitate those changes or help to correct their less desirable dynamics or effects.

Research in general – and ours in particular – follows very much in the wake of needs, be it relation to fields of knowledge or areas in which strategies, policies or actions are proposed.

Priority 1: Knowledge society and capitalism: The desirable and reasonable utopia and a critique of new capitalism

We may be in the midst of a crisis of civilization and of questioning what the place of culture in society is. Those in power point reassuringly towards the advent of a knowledge society.

Despite the fact that there are many existing descriptions of the profound changes[32] brought about by digitization and the Web, there are still many more questions than answers in the Internet era. We remain prisoners of the analogue imaginary in relation to immaterial capitalism, which, together with financial capital, and having become merged with it, has taken over the reins of leadership of the system, resulting in increasing concentration and inequality in the development of networks.

Defining this capitalism and its dual relationship with cultural and communication models, on the one hand, and with the centres of the economic system, on the other, is essential in order to explore alternative models and/or reforms of the cultural and communication systems.

Priority 2: Structural studies on cultural and communication systems in different spaces and sectors

The knowledge deficit surrounding cultural systems requires on-the-ground research, which will no doubt help to refine the methodologies and will test the explanatory capacity of the various schools of thought.

It is a matter of addressing the traditional topics, which have a long history, and ensuring their continuity. Special attention needs to be paid to territorial and international spheres, the monitoring of the Internet chain (rather than sector), and the impact of the economic and financial crisis on the communication system.

Priority 3: New sociabilities, networks and transformational subjects

Societies are undergoing accelerated change, and we are a long way from knowing what is taking place: what new sociabilities are emerging – with a particular impact on network systems – and how they relate to the pre-existing ones.

Economic, social and political agents, and new agents, are involved unequally in the process of shaping them. Are new subjects emerging that are the pioneers in the changes about to take place in the communication system?

Priority 4: Cultural work, social regulation in knowledge societies and intellectual property

Related to the above, the extent and centrality of knowledge and culture give cultural work a new role, at the same time as they make it more precarious and turn it into a source of added values that are systematically appropriated. The contrast between the possibility of comprehensively democratizing knowledge and its models of appropriation is a central contradiction which questions the models for regulating intellectual property.

The unanticipated mass uses of cyberspace throughout the world, the countertrends,[33] as well as the huge pockets of resistance to the private appropriation of technologies, applications, uses and content, individually, collectively or as a network, are tools for change or, at the very least, for limiting less welcome effects and promoting new values.

At the same time this begs questions about a viable social and economic statute for cultural creators.

Priority 5: Cultural and communication strategies and policies with an emphasis on diversity and equality, including the extension of public services and e-cultural policies

The new doctrinal approaches, paradigms or structuring criteria on a global scale, including new integrated development models, which seek to be efficient and respectful towards the citizenry, are a *governance* that participates in decision-making; a social demand for a cultural welfare state; sustainable development; access to knowledge; creativity and innovation in no matter what field; and the right to culture and cultural diversity.

These paradigms are allied with a strategy to change and democratize the cultural and communication system, with reference to the public space: public policies, pro-commons activities and so on. Since they have no ideological reference, they are generally accepted and – in addition to aiming in complementary directions – may provide solid foundations for beginning to address the most negative trends and for joining disparate forces.

They offer legitimization, discernment and balance when it comes to criticizing or implementing social strategies and public policies. We are living in a time of emphases or directions based on social objectives and, perhaps just as important as the issues and measures themselves is the method for dealing with them: through social participation and that of agents. After all, society is the bearer of culture and communication.

What are the appropriate communication policies? How are we to understand and preserve the function of public spaces as spaces of legitimization, management and democratic debate in the public arena? How is this to be achieved?

Cultural policies and regulations (heritage, arts, industries) and communicative ones (information society, digital terrestrial TV, etc.) become part of political centrality, and this requires clarification with regard to suitable visions, missions, strategies, structures and instruments for each society, and on an international scale. At any rate, when it comes to realizing this, the direct impact of ideologies and interests is assured.

Priority 6: Territories and transversality

As a functional and pragmatic derivative of the above, the usual spaces of intervention are territories, on one scale or another.

They require strategies that combine innovation, proximity, sociability, identification, democracy and development. The bonds of identity and knowledge between agents in a territory forged by history are fertile ground for multiplying the functionality of public strategies; as well as for the cooperation of interests via associations or clusters; and, without doubt, as places of confrontation between social actors and projects.

Culture as symbolic capital is also a tool for managing social change, a transversal component of innovative societies which provides recognized communities with identity, cohesion and visibility. The new progressive models should combine innovation, sustainability, equality, participation and knowledge to define cities, regions or countries, and make them smart, democratic, equalizing and connected.[34]

It is a challenge to ensure that culture should be present in these great transformations but maintaining its specificity rather than distorting it.

Priority 7: The critical economy of communication and culture

We can and must create a *political economy of culture* with the intention of encompassing at the same time those spheres most concerned (heritage, community and popular culture, arts, cultural industries – including creative advertising – the media and culture on the Web) and while carefully opening the way for cultural spheres of production in general – design and so forth. In order to so there are two requirements that must be met: a definable object of study and certain defining characteristics that are shared by all cultural expressions.

In culture and communication there is always an economic reality that needs to be explained, even if it is sometimes casuistry and dependent on the nature of the good or service, whether it be a public or private good.[35]

The question now is whether it is necessary to define a general statute for a critical and political economy of communication and culture as closely interrelated fields of study, and if this is the most suitable and promising approach, without precluding that there may be others – arts and culture; communications and telecommunications; creative economy; and the like – with which, in fact, it will compete as an explanatory model and approach.[36]

It should be possible to put together a general matrix for this purpose, based on productive and value-enhancing factors,[37] which includes in the exposition those elements relating to competing demands, social institutions and uses[38] – that is to say, an economy in interaction with the entire value chain and reproductive cycle of both culture and communication.

In my opinion and as an object of study of a social science such as economics, communicated cultural contents are born of acts of symbolic creation, owing to their very nature, they entail particular labour and valorization processes, they always involve some sort of aesthetic and communicative project regardless of its quality, they are expressed in cultural and communicative objects and services that are sought after as such, and they have a social efficiency in terms of social perception in the form of enjoyment, knowledge and social vertebration.[39]

Notes

1. Culture is a specific field of societies, but as an object of study it is shared by social sciences such as anthropology and sociology, which describe social phenomena and ways of life; economics, which considers it a sector; town planning, which understands it as a quality of the environment; and all

the possible intersections of different disciplines, as occurs in encounters between art, culture, science and technology.

2. The conceptualization of infrastructure-superstructure-ideological apparatuses, inherited from structuralism and Althusserianism, forgot about history and about agents in action.
3. The less refined and purely propagandistic models derived from the system of powers, as applied to the analysis of US information on revolutionary Nicaragua, would render the contribution of critical economy useless. If we examine the communication systems and models themselves, economics as a discipline has much to offer. For its part, the propaganda model developed by Chomsky and Herman (1988, 1995) with its five filters (owners/ownership, dependence on advertising, information sourcing from the power structure/establishment and elites, flak as a means of disciplining the media and reactionary ideology) does not give fundamental importance to the internal and professional variables that Shoemaker and Reese (1994) explain – characteristics of the informer, production routines, organizational work structure, various external forces and ideology – and which Martín Sabarís (2009) applies to the case of an election. For his part, Pedro (2008) adds a sixth filter (technology).
4. Shoemaker and Reese (1994) forget about none other than owners, profit and the power system.
5. See Mosco (2006), which was later taken up by Almiron (2008): 'In short, addressing the historical context, using moral philosophy as a guide, understanding the social as a whole and promoting scholars' commitment to reality. Four tasks that can bring together all political economists of communication, whatever their academic tradition.'
6. In the case of Latin America, Marques de Melo (2009) explores this thinking and assesses the research in the region over the past nearly 50 years. León Duarte (2008) also supports the current existence of a Latin American School of Communication, while Fuentes (1999) and other authors express a different idea. Whereas in the past it clearly applied when communicating dependency theories, that desirable common ground is now difficult to establish.
7. Summary and update of a part of the text presented, but not published, at the Tenth Ibercom Congress – Guadalajara, 2007 – which refers in particular to Spain and to a lesser extent to Europe and Latin America. May this humble and biased point serve as a tribute and homage to Daniel J. Jones, whose reports on the state of research we so sorely miss (see Jones, 1998).
8. For example, the Latin American Information Agency headed by Sally Burch with its continental campaign for communication rights, or the Civil Society Declaration in the first part of the WSIS, Geneva, 2003.
9. For example, those originating from the national and international congresses of the ULEPICC (Latin Union of Political Economy of Information, Communication and Culture), or Segovia's (2006).
10. This is the case with the European Institute for Progressive Cultural Policies or with YProductions (2007, 2009). Also the Traficantes de Sueños collective, publishing Moulier Boutang et al. (2004). The debates in My Creativity (Amsterdam, 16–18 November 2006) already pointed towards these new issues.

11. For example, the studies by the International Institute on Governance of Catalonia, the Ciberpunk and Cibersociedad websites, the reflections of Smiers (2006) or, from a radical liberal approach, Boldrin and Levine (2005).
12. See www.culturalpolicies.net, KEA European Affairs et al. (2006), International Network on Cultural Policy (INCP, 2006), European Commission (2001), Autissier (2005) and D'Angelo and Vesperini (2000). See also Cultural Information and Research Centres Liaison in Europe, which, for example, has studied the issue of European festivals with the prominent participation of Interarts and the systematic intervention of the European Audiovisual Observatory (2007).
13. Indeed, there are traits inherent to culture (e.g. the previous offer, the public good, the Baumol effect, certain rising costs, imperfect markets, exclusive rights, speculative logics, the subjectivity of the demand for experience, marketless demand, external economies, public interventions, the importance of regulations, social effects) which make culture a specific object of study. See some of these specificities described by Zallo (2007b).
14. See Ministerio de Cultura (2006, 2007, 2008), García Gracia et al. (2000, 2001), SGAE (2006), Departamento de Cultura del Gobierno Vasco (2008), EGEDA (2006), Cardona (2002), Wyman (2009), Seminario Internacional sobre Economía y Cultura: la tercera cara de la moneda (Bogotá, 2001), or Guzmán Cárdenas (2006).
15. See the Portal Iberoamericano de Gestión Cultural for articles about cultural indicators published in 2004 by authors including Romero, Bonet and Schuster.
16. At congresses and conferences a plurality of topics are often addressed. For example, at the 14th International Conference on the Cultural Economics (Vienna, 6–8 July 2006), the subjects dealt with were studies on demand (and art markets); subsidies and the value of culture; heritage, tourism, festivals and clusters; supply, innovation and cultural management firms; and the labour market for artists, international trade, diversity and globalization. At the symposia entitled Culture, Politics, Policy (University of Lille, 3 March 2007), the subjects dealt with were public policies; inequalities; attitudes; intellectual property, cultural practices, political uses of art; culture in the economy; decentralizations, committed art, market and regulation; cultural democratization, publics; and art and media.
17. In the case of Spain, for example, a good guide for examining both state-run and independent cultural industry sectors in the transition from 'analogue' to 'digital' culture are the books coordinated by Bustamante (2002, 2006). See also Díaz Nosty (2006), GECA (2006), Corominas et al. (2007), Moragas and Prado (2000), and Martí and Bonet (2006).
18. In the case of Latin America, let us remember that the crisis in the New World Information and Communication Order (NWICO), which emphasized the dependence between centre and periphery, and the international division of cultural and communicative labour, and advocated the need for national policies on communication and public service, was declared with the withdrawal of the USA and the UK from UNESCO in 1984. But it was the defeats suffered by the social and political change processes in the 1970s and 1980s with the advent of dictatorship that set the stage for it and gave way to less

bothersome concerns for the liberal models later instituted by those same dictatorships. Mastrini and Bolaño (1999) and Becerra and Mastrini (2006) classify and compare the process of concentration in each of the cultural industries, including telephony and the Internet, in Latin American countries. Also Fadul (1997) and Brittos and Bolaño (2005) analyse concentration in the Brazilian media. Equally valuable was the work of the late Stolovich et al. (2002). In Mexico there is the systematic research by Sánchez Ruiz (2006), Gómez García (2007), Crovi Druetta (2004) and Esteinou Madrid and Sánchez Rivera (2007).

19. The logics of sectoral promotion are now almost limited to the audiovisual sector for reasons of survival in the face of the US audiovisual invasion. Even the logic of governments has been to favour 'national groups' in order to confront transnational groups, with which they have sometimes ended up forming alliances.
20. See the pioneer Castells (1995, 1999, 2000, 2001, 2006). For his part, Echevarría published several books, the most ambitious being *Los señores del aire: telépolis y el tercer entorno* (1999), and Iriarte (2002) supports the International Institute of Governability. For a critical perspective, see Sierra (2001), Crovi Druetta (2004) and Bolaño (1999). Trejo Delarbre (1996, 2006) has made progress on these issues in Mexico, as has Tremblay (1996) in Quebec.
21. Some of its main theorists are Lazzarato (2007) – and his striking thesis on 'the worker as an entrepreneur of him/herself, being his/her own capital, being his/her own producer, being his/her own source of income' – and Rullani (2007).
22. Including *International Journal of Arts Management* (Montreal), *International Journal of Cultural Policy* (University of Warwick), without forgetting the new Portal Iberoamericano de Gestión Cultural, or the interesting *EC, cuadernos de economía de la cultura*, edited by the Observatorio Andaluz para la Economía de la Cultura y el Desarrollo (OIKOS).
23. For a review of these topics that applies to the case of the Basque Country, see López de Aguileta (2007).
24. For some general reflections on cultural policy, see Miller and Yúdice (2004). On cultural policy in Spain and the Autonomous Communities, see Marzo and Lozano (2005), Various Authors (2004), ICEX (2007) or Zallo (1995, 2002). In Latin America, Rubim and Bayardo (2008). The main authors on audiovisual policy are Bustamante (2007b) and Giordano and Zeller (1999), and in Mexico, Gómez García (2008). On communication policy in Europe, see Bustamante (2003). In the case of Spain, Fernández Alonso and Santana (2000), Díaz Nosty (2006) and Murciano (1992, 2006). In Latin America, see Mastrini (2006).
25. A general overview in the case of Europe can be found in the Council of Europe/ERICarts Institute (2007).
26. Monograph taken from the *Quaderns del CAC* on the 25th anniversary of the MacBride report (VV.AA., 2005).
27. This is how Martinell Sempere (2006b) sets out the foundations of the Spanish strategy on culture and development. See the OIS website, the Portal de Cultura de América Latina y Caribe, Olmos (2008), Bustamante (2007a), and the interesting reports by Mª Trinidad García Leiva (2009) and Luis A. Albornoz (2009) for the Fundación Alternativas, with support and funding

from the Agencia Española de Cooperación Internacional para el Desarrollo (AECID).

28. See Robins (2006). The 3rd International Meeting on Cultural Diversity (Buenos Aires, 2005) addressed the issues of heritage and development, local policies for culture and diversity, the media in the construction of identity and citizenship and its social influence, cooperation and so on.
29. Agenda 21 de la Cultura at www.barcelona2004.org; Rausell Köster (2007) summarizes its content as 'promoting diversity, increasing cultural goods and services, promoting creation and creative innovation and the democratization of access'.
30. As stated in point 18 of Council of Europe Recommendation 1811 (Council of Europe and ERICarts Institute, 2007) relating to the 'Regionalization of Europe' and designed to deal with issues involving national or cultural/linguistic minorities.
31. In United and Local Governments-Working-Group on Culture 'Local Policies for cultural diversity', see Robinson (2005), Laaksonen (2006) and Pascual (2006).
32. It is noted that some of the main items are the convergence of supports and the mix of expressive formats; the dematerialization of value with a certain symbolic overload; the disappearance of intermediaries in the production and distribution chain to the benefit of the ends of the chain (creation and user) and the emergence of new intermediaries (portals, search engines): the dilution of traditional models of profitability and the attempt to add income in successive windows and in different supports in search of different types of user; the drastic reduction in the cost of storage, now digital in nature, making it possible to meet specific mass demands; the combination of economies of scale with network and club economies, which lend value to the products themselves while benefiting from their presence.
33. Some of these are the trend towards communicational decentralization, 'proximity' communication, which seeks to manage the familiar, the experienced, and is present in national/regional or local communication; the search within communication for a drive towards coexistence and knowledge transfer; the doctrinal trends under way towards diversity on a global and national scale; the reopening of the debate on the public service sphere in the digital age; and the formulation of public policies for change.
34. One case in point is the conceptual model of 'smart territories' developed by TECNALIA (Espiga and Azkárate, 2007).
35. Its economic form is not uniform, since culture as a whole may be capital, a product or service, but it is possible to define common elements.
36. While some types of approach are no doubt useful for territorial or urban economic developments (*creative quarters* or *creative clusters*) or for synergies between sectors and activities, they are, on the other hand, questionable from the point of view of the statute of the object of study or of scientific taxonomies or statistics, which must always look at the economic logics of meaning or at their social linkage, objects as vast and cross-cutting as the information economy, communication hypersector, attention economy, *infonomics*, economy of creation or talent, knowledge economy and so forth. These approaches are useful for blending activities, for thinking about applicabilities, opportunities and combinations, but in a purely economic drift.

The economy of innovation or talent is too big and mixed a bag which fits in well with the continuous and irreversible process that the Frankfurt School noted in relation to desacralization, detranscendentalization of culture and the culturization of goods as a motivation to buy.

37. In the 1980s the focus was placed in particular on the microenvironment used as a basis for work processes and processes of valorization in an attempt to discover the use values and the commercial value of culture. In my opinion the most stimulating work in this field was that of Huet et al. (1978). The macroenvironment already had a more established tradition which some analysts like myself promoted in Spain (Torres, 1985; Bustamante and Zallo, 1988; Zallo, 1992; Bustamante, 2003).
38. This inclusion of the reproductive cycle is a still outstanding and complementary part in terms of the model of labour and value processes within culture and its sectors which we explored in the 1980s.
39. In Zallo (2007b), I described it rather than defined it as 'An economy of intangible or symbolic values generated by creative work, in the form of goods or services that are individually irreplaceable and whose contents and interpretations are being permanently renewed. It is an economy of multiple supply, a supply that creates demand and that has a functionality and social efficacy beyond its economic value. Its material and intellectual value tends to decrease historically but, on the other hand, there tends to be an increase in the cost of exclusivity, complexity and notoriety, meaning that the marginal cost in general tends to zero and there is a wide range of sunk costs, as well as uncertainty about the outcome of the act of valuing. It has extensive areas of public good, as well as imperfect markets and the inevitable presence of public administrations. All this makes it possible to regard culture economically as a sector with its branches, subsectors and ancillary activities.'

References

Albornoz, Luis A. (coord.) (2009) *Cultura y comunicación. Estado y prospectiva de la cooperación española con el resto de Iberoamérica, 1997–2007*, Madrid: Fundación Alternativas/AECID.

Almiron, Núria (2008) 'Economía política y comunicación: una aproximación epistemológica a los orígenes', 2nd Conference ULEPICC-Spain 'Nuevos retos para la perspectiva crítica en Comunicación y Cultura', Barcelona, 28 November (article published in *Revista Latina de Comunicación Social*, 64, 563–571).

Álvarez Monzoncillo, José María; Calvi, Juan; Gay, Celeste; Gómez-Escalonilla, Gloria and López, Javier (2007) *Alternativas de política cultural: las industrias culturales en las redes digitales*, Barcelona: Gedisa/Fundación Alternativas.

ASC (Academy for Sustainable Communities) (2007) *Mind the Skills Gap: The Skills We Need for Sustainable Communities*, Leeds: ASC.

Autissier, Anne-Marie (2005) *L'Europe de la culture. Histories et enjeux*, Arles: Actes Sud.

Badillo, Ángel (2004) *La desregulación de la televisión local en España: el caso de Castilla y León* (doctoral thesis), Barcelona: Autonomous University of Barcelona.

Badillo, Ángel and Ortega, Félix (2008) 'La nueva televisión local digital en España. Concentración, integración y desterritorialización del audiovisual de proximidad', Conference 'I+C Investigar la Comunicación', Spanish Association of Communication Research, Santiago de Compostela: University of Santiago de Compostela.
Beceiro, Sagrario (2009) *La televisión por satélite en España. Del servicio público a la televisión de pago*, Madrid: Fragua.
Becerra, Martín and Mastrini, Guillermo (2006) *Periodistas y magnates. Estructura y concentración de las industrias culturales en América Latina*, Buenos Aires: Prometeo.
Beck, Ulrich (1998) *¿Qué es la globalización? Falacias del globalismo, respuestas de la globalización*, Barcelona: Paidós.
Bloomfield, Jude and Bianchini, Franco (2004) *Planning for the Intercultural City*, Stroud-: Comedia.
Bolaño, César (1999) 'Sociedade da Informação: reestruturação capitalista e esfera pública global', Revista Latina de Comunicación Social, 15 – marzo de 1999, La Laguna.
Boldrin, Michele and Levine, David K. (2005) 'The Economics of Ideas and Intellectual Property', *Proceedings of the National Academy of Sciences of the United States of America*, 102(4), 1252–1256.
Bonet, Lluís (ed.) (2002) *El libro blanco de las industrias culturales de Cataluña*, Barcelona: Generalitat of Catalonia.
Brittos, Valério and Bolaño, César (eds) (2005) *Red Globo, 40 años de hegemonía*, Sao Paulo: Paulus.
Bustamante, Enrique (coord.) (2002) *Comunicación y cultura en la era digital. Industrias, mercados y diversidad en España*, Barcelona: Gedisa.
—— (coord.) (2003) *Hacia un nuevo sistema mundial de comunicación. Las industrias culturales en la era digital*, Barcelona: Gedisa.
—— (2006) *Radio y Televisión en España. Historia de una asignatura pendiente de la democracia*, Barcelona: Gedisa.
—— (ed.) (2007a) *La cooperación cultura-comunicación en Iberoamérica*, Madrid: AECI.
—— (coord.) (2007b) *Cultura y comunicación para el siglo XXI. Diagnóstico y políticas públicas*, Tenerife: Ideco/Cabildo de Tenerife.
Bustamante, Enrique and Zallo, Ramón (coord.) (1988) *Las industrias culturales en España*, Madrid: Akal.
CAC (Catalan Audiovisual Council) (2001) 'La definició del model de servei públic al sector de l'audiovisual', *Quaderns del CAC*, 10, 3–58.
Calderero, Alberto; Pérez, Juan and Ugalde Sánchez, Igone (2006) 'Territorios inteligentes: espacios de economía creativa', *Dyna*, 81(6), 40–44.
Cardona, Jeannine (2002) 'Les statistiques culturelles europeennes: bilan et perspectives', Proceedings of the International Symposium on Culture Statistics, 21–23 October, Montréal.
Caro, Francisco (2007) *Gestión de empresas informativas*, Madrid: McGraw-Hill.
Casado, Miguel Ángel (2008) *La promoción de la industria audiovisual en las comunidades autónomas españolas y en Escocia* (doctoral thesis), Leioa: University of the Basque Country.
Castells, Manuel (1995) *La ciudad informacional. Tecnologías de la Información, reestructuración económica y el proceso urbano-regional*, Madrid: Alianza.

—— (1999–2002) *La era de la información* (3 volumes), México: Siglo XXI.
—— (2001) *La galaxia internet*, Madrid: Areté/Plaza&Janés.
—— (2006) *La sociedad red*, Madrid: Alianza.
Castiñeira, Ángel (2001) 'Sociedad de la información, globalización y desarrollo humano', *Dhial Magazine*, doc. 84, Barcelona: Instituto Internacional de Gobernabilidad (IIG).
Chomsky, Noam and Herman, Edward S. (1988) *Manufacturing Consent. The Political Economy of the Mass Media*, Nueva York: Pantheon Books.
—— (1995) *Los guardianes de la libertad: propaganda, desinformación y consenso en los medios de comunicación de masas*, Madrid: Grijalbo.
Colbert, François (ed.) (2003) *Le marketing des arts et de la culture: une bibliographie analytique et sélective*, Montréal: HEC-Montréal.
Congress of Local and Regional Authorities of Europe (1999) 'La société de l'information locale et regionale', Sixth Session. Koivisto Rapport, 15–17 June, Strasbourg: Council of Europe.
Corominas, Maria; Bonet, Montse; Fernández Alonso, Isabel; Guimerà i Orts, Josep Àngel; Sanmartín, Julián and Blasco Gil, Joaquín (2007) 'La televisión digital terrestre local en España (TDT-L): los concesionarios privados', *Zer – Revista de estudios de comunicación*, 22, 69–95.
Council of Europe and ERICarts Institute (2007) *Compendium of Cultural Policies and Trends in Europe*, 8th edition, Brussels: Council of Europe/ERICarts Institute.
Crovi Druetta, Delia (coord.) (2004) *Sociedad de la información y el conocimiento: entre lo falaz y lo posible*, Buenos Aires: La Crujía.
Crusafón, Carmina (2006) 'Política audiovisual europea ante el reto de la digitalización', 1st Conference ULEPICC-Spain, 17 November 2006, Sevilla: University of Sevilla.
D'Angelo, Mario and Vesperini, Paul (2000) *Politiques culturelles en Europe: régions et décentralisation culturelle*, Strasbourg: Council of Europe.
Departamento de Cultura del Gobierno Vasco (2008) *Hábitos, prácticas y consumo en cultura, 2007–2008* (4 volumes), Vitoria-Gasteiz: Gobierno Vasco.
Díaz Nosty, B. (ed.) (2006) *Tendencias '06. Medios de Comunicación. El año de la televisión*, Madrid: Telefonica Foundation.
Echevarría, Javier (1999) *Los señores del aire: telépolis y el tercer entorno*, Barcelona: Destino.
EGEDA (Entidad de Gestión de Derechos de los Productores Audiovisuales) (2006) *Panorama Audiovisual 2005*, Madrid: EGEDA.
Espiga, Fernando and Azkárate Garai-Olaun, Gotzon (2007) *Hacia un futuro inteligente: 5 claves para diseñar las* smart cities, Donostia-San Sebastián: TECNALIA.
Esteban Galarza, María Soledad; Ugalde Sánchez, Miren Igone; Rodríguez Álvarez, Arantxa and Altuzarra Artola, Amaia (eds) (2008) *Territorios inteligentes: dimensiones y experiencias inter-nacionales*, A Coruña: Netbiblo.
Esteinou Madrid, Javier and Sánchez Rivera, Roberto (2007) 'Panorámica sobre el análisis de las políticas de comunicación en México', *Razón y Palabra*, 12(58), 1–31.
European Audiovisual Observatory (2007) *IRIS Special: The Public Service Broadcasting Culture*, Strasbourg: Council of Europe.
European Commission (2001) 'La cooperation culturelle en Europe', Cultural Cooperation in Europe Forum 2001, Brussels: Directorate-General for Education and Culture.

Fadul, Ana María (1997) 'La internacionalización de los grupos de medios en el Brasil de los años 90', *Diálogos de la Comunicación*, 50, 105–110.
Fernández Alonso Isabel and Santana, María Fernanda (2000) *Estado y medios de comunicación en la España democrática*, Madrid: Alianza Universidad.
Florida, Richard (2002) *The Rise of the Creative Class. And How It's Transforming Work, Leisure and Everyday Life*, New York: Basic Books.
—— (2005) *The Flight of the Creative Class. The New Global Competition for Talent*, New York: HarperCollins.
Fonseca Reis, Ana Carla (2008) *Economía creativa como estrategia de desarrollo: una visión de los países en desarrollo*, São Paulo: Itaú Cultural.
Frey, Bruno S. (2000) *La economía del arte*, Barcelona: La Caixa.
Fuentes, Raúl (1999) 'La investigación de la comunicación en América Latina: condiciones y perspectivas para el siglo XXI', *Diálogos de la Comunicación*, 56, 52–68.
Fundación Audiovisual de Andalucía-Instituto de Desarrollo Regional (2001) *Estudio de prospección del mercado de trabajo y detección de necesidades formativas en el sector audiovisual andaluz*, Sevilla: Consejería de Empleo y Desarrollo Tecnológico, Junta de Andalucía.
Fundación Este País (2008) *México ante el reto de la economía del conocimiento*, México City: Fundación Este País.
García Canclini, Néstor (1990) *Comunidades híbridas: estrategias para entrar y salir de la modernidad*, Buenos Aires: Grijalbo.
—— (2001) 'Por qué legislar sobre industrias culturales', *Nueva Sociedad*, 175, 60–69.
García Canclini, Néstor and Piedras, Ernesto (2006) *Las industrias culturales y el desarrollo de México*, México: Siglo XXI/FLACSO/Secretaría de Relaciones Exteriores.
García Gracia, Mª Isabel; Fernández Fernández, Yolanda and Zofío Prieto, José Luis (2000) *La industria de la cultura y el ocio en España: su aportación al PIB (1993–97)*, Madrid: Fundación Autor.
García Gracia, Mª Isabel; Zofío Prieto, José Luis and Fernández Fernández, Yolanda (2001) *La evolución de la industria de la cultura y el ocio por Comunidades Autónomas (1993–1997)*, Madrid: Fundación Autor.
García Leiva, María Trinidad (2006) 'La introducción de la TDT en España en el contexto de la política europea para la transición digital en televisión', *Revista EPTIC Online*, 8(1), 1–20.
—— (2009) 'Informe 1. España', in Albornoz, L.A. (coord.) *Cultura y comunicación. Estado y prospectiva de la cooperación española con el resto de Iberoamérica, 1997–2007*, Madrid: Fundación Alternativas/AECID, 25–49.
García Santamaría, José V. (2012) 'La concentración en los grupos españoles de comunicación: estrategias y tendencias', IV International Conference Latina de Comunicación Social, University of La Laguna, 4, 5 and 7 December, La Laguna.
Garitaonandia, Carmelo; Fernández Peña, Emilio; Oleaga, José and Ramajo, Natividad (2003) 'Del espectador pasivo al interactivo. La televisión digital interactiva en Estados Unidos, Europa y España', in Igartua, J.J. and Badillo, Á. (eds) *Audiencias y medios de comunicación*, Salamanca: University of Salamanca, 129–145.
Garnham, Nicholas (2005) *Emancipation, the Media, and the Modernity*, Oxford: Oxford University Press.

GECA (Gabinete de Estudios de la Comunicación Audiovisual) (2006) *El anuario de la televisión 2006*, Madrid: GECA.

Gifreu i Pinsach, Josep and Corbella Cordomí, Joan Maria (eds) (2009) *La Producció audiovisual a Catalunya 2005–2007*, Barcelona: Documenta Universitaria.

Giordano, Eduardo and Zeller, Carlos (1999) *Políticas de televisión*, Barcelona: Icaria.

Gombault, Anne and Petr, Christine (2006) *La gratuité des musées et des monuments côté publics*, Paris: Editions Documentation Française.

Gómez de la Iglesia, Roberto (dir.) (1999) *Valor, precio y coste de la cultura*, Vitoria-Gasteiz: Xabide S. Coop.

Gómez García, Rodrigo (2007) *El impacto del Tratado de Libre Comercio de América del Norte en la industria audiovisual mexicana (1994–2002)* (doctoral thesis), Bellaterra: Autonomous University of Barcelona.

—— (2008) 'Políticas e industrias audiovisuales en México. Apuntes y diagnóstico', *Comunicación y Sociedad*, 10, 191–223.

González Arencibia, Mario (2006) *Globalización cultural: sus interacciones socioeconómicas y políticas*, La Habana: Eumend.net.

Greffe, Xavier (2002) *Le développement local*, Paris: Editions de l'aube.

Guimerà i Orts, Josep Àngel (2007) *La televisió local a Catalunya: gestació, naixement i transformacions (1976–2006)*, Barcelona: Catalan Audiovisual Council (CAC).

Guzmán Cárdenas, Carlos E. (2006) 'La industria cinematográfica y su consumo en los países de Iberoamérica. Un análisis comparativo diacrónico', *Anuario ININCO*, 18(1), 349–363.

—— (2008) 'La economía creativa: TIC, industrias creativas y de los contenidos digitales. Una exploración conceptual', *Anuario ININCO*, 20(1), 209–262.

Hamelink, Cees J. (1999) 'Language and the Right to Communicate', *Media Development*, 46(4), 14–17.

Hernández i Martí, Gil-Manuel (2006) 'The Deterritorialization of Cultural Heritage in a Globalized Modernity', *Transfer: Journal of Contemporary Culture*, 1, 92–107.

Herschmann, Micael (2007) *Lapa, cidade da música. Desafios e perspectivas para o crecimiento do Rio de Janeiro e da industria da música independiente nacional*, Rio Janeiro: Mauad X.

Huet, Armel; Ion, Jacques; Lefebvre, Alain; Miège, Bernard and Peron, René (1978) *Capitalisme et industries culturelles*, Grenoble: PUG.

ICEX (Instituto Español de Comercio Exterior) (2007) *La internacionalización de las industrias culturales españolas*, Madrid: ICEX.

INCP (International Network on Cultural Policy) (2006) '¿Qué es la diversidad?', Working Group on Cultural Diversity and Globalization of the International Network on Cultural Policy, 5–6 February 2003, Paris.

Iriarte, Erick (2002) 'Creando una sociedad democrática en torno a Internet. Sobre el Comité Consultivo para la Administración de Nombres de Dominio', *Dhial Magazine*, 26.

Jaén García, Manuel (2006) 'Los efectos redistributivos de la política cultural en España', *EC. Cuadernos de Economía de la Cultura*, 6, 21–44.

Jones, Daniel E. (1998) 'Investigación sobre comunicación en España. Evolución y perspectivas', *Zer – Revista de estudios de comunicación*, 3(5), 13–51.

Jorge Alonso, Ana and García López, Marcial (eds) (2009) *Comunicación y poder. Reflexionando sobre el cambio social*, Málaga: Unicaja Foundation.

KEA European Affairs, Media Group and MKW GMBH (2006) *The Economy of Culture in Europe*, Brussels: Directorate-General for Education and Culture, European Commission.

Laaksonen, Annamari (2006) *Local Policies for Cultural Diversity. With Emphasis on Latin America and Europe* (report 1), Barcelona: UNESCO/Barcelona City Council/United Cities/Culture 21.

Lasuén Sancho, José Ramón; García Gracia, Mª Isabel and Zofio Prieto, José Luis (2006) *Cultura y economía*, Madrid: Fundación Autor.

Lazzarato, Maurizio (2007) 'The Misfortunes of the "Artistic Critique" and of Cultural Employment', *Transform.eipcp.net* – European Institute for Progressive Cultural Policies. Available at http://eipcp.net/transversal/0207/lazzarato/en, (consulted in September 2009).

León Duarte, Gustavo A. (2008) 'ELACOM. Referente histórico y conquista de la hegemonía en el pensamiento latinoamericano de la comunicación', *Razón y Palabra*, 13(61), 1–27.

Llorens, Carles (2001) *Concentración de empresas de comunicación y pluralismo: la acción de la UE* (doctoral thesis), Barcelona: Autonomous University of Barcelona.

López de Aguileta, Iñaki (2000) *Cultura y ciudad. Manual de política cultural municipal*, Gijón: Ediciones Trea.

—— (2007) 'Nuevas prácticas de gestión municipal', in VV.AA.: *I Conferencia Internacional sobre Políticas Culturales*, Vitoria-Gasteiz: Servicio Central de Publicaciones del Gobierno Vasco, 229–240.

López García, Xosé (ed) (2008) *A comunicación en Galicia 2007*, Santiago de Compostela: Consello da Cultura Galega.

Lucchini, Françoise (2002) *La culture au service des villes*, Paris: Anthropos.

Manito, Félix (2006) *Cultura y estrategia de ciudad. La centralidad del sector cultural en la agenda local*, Barcelona: Centro Iberoamericano de Desarrollo Estratégico Urbano.

Marques de Melo, José (2009) *Pensamiento comunicacional latinoamericano. Entre el saber y el poder*, Sevilla-Zamora: Comunicación Social Ediciones y Publicaciones.

Martí, Josep M. and Bonet, Montse (2006) 'Viejas tendencias, nuevos parámetros de análisis' (section Radio), in Díaz Nosty, B. (ed) *Tendencias '06. Medios de Comunicación. El año de la televisión*, Madrid: Telefonica Foundation, 185–196.

Martín Barbero, Jesús (2000) 'Globalización y multiculturalidad: notas para una agenda de investigación', in Moraña, M. (ed.) *Nuevas perspectivas desde / sobre América Latina. El desafío de los estudios culturales*, Santiago de Chile: Cuarto Propio/Instituto Internacional de Literatura Iberoamericana, 17–29.

Martín Sabarís, Rosa María (2009) '¿Información? ¿Política? It's the economy, again, stupid. ¿O no?', *Viento Sur*, 103, 68–76.

Martinell Sempere, Alfons (2006a) 'La formación en gestión cultural en Iberoamérica: reflexiones y situación', *Revista Digital de Cultura de la OEI, Pensar Iberoamérica*, 10, 72–90.

—— (2006b) 'Hacia una nueva política cultural exterior', Real Instituto Elcano, ARI no. 127/126, Madrid.

Martínez, Marcelo (ed.) (2005) *O Terceiro Sector e o audiovisual/El Tercer Sector y el audiovisual* (I Foro da Ciudadanía e da Comunicación), Santiago de Compostela: Unidixital.
Martínez Illa, Santi and Mendoza, Roser (2004) 'TIC y gestión de la cultura: ¿políticas e-culturales?', *Boletín GC*, 10, 1–23.
Marzal Felici, Javier and Casero Ripollés, Andreu (eds) (2007) *El desarrollo de la televisión digital en España*, A Coruña: Netbiblos.
Marzo, Jorge Luis (with Lozano, Amparo) (2005) 'Política cultural del Gobierno español en el exterior (2000–2004)', in VV.AA *Desacuerdos. Sobre arte, políticas y esfera pública en el Estado español. Cuaderno 2*, Barcelona: Arteleku-Diputación Foral de Gipuzkoa, Museu d'Art Contemporani de Barcelona-MACBA and Universidad Internacional de Andalucía-UNIA, 57–121.
Mastrini, Guillermo (ed) (2006) *Mucho ruido, pocas leyes. Economía y políticas de comunicación en Argentina (1920–2004)*, Buenos Aires: La Crujía.
Mastrini, Guillermo and Bolaño, César (eds) (1999) *Globalización y monopolios en la comunicación en América Latina. Hacia una economía política de la comunicación*, Buenos Aires: Biblos.
Mastrini, Guillermo and Califano, Bernadette (eds) (2006) *Sociedad de la información en la Argentina: políticas públicas y participación social*, Buenos Aires: Friedrich Ebert Foundation.
Mattelart, Armand (2002) *Historia de la sociedad de la información*, Barcelona: Paidós.
—— (2005) *Diversité culturelle et mondialisation*, París: La Découverte.
Mayugo i Majó, Carme (2005) 'El "Tercer Sector Audiovisual" irrumpe en la agenda política española', *Pueblos. Revista de Información y Debate*, 20, 21–23.
Miège, Bernard (2004) *L'information-communication objet de connaissance*, Brussels: De Boeck/INA.
Miguel de Bustos, Juan Carlos (1993) *Los grupos multimedia. Estructuras y estrategias en los medios europeos*, Barcelona: Bosch.
—— (2006) *Comunicación sostenible y desarrollo humano en la sociedad de la información*, Madrid: AECI.
Miller, Toby and Yúdice, George (2004) *Política cultural*, Barcelona: Gedisa.
Ministerio de Cultura (2006) *El valor económico de la cultura, 2000–2004*, Madrid: Ministerio de Cultura, Spain.
—— (2007) *Encuesta de hábitos y prácticas culturales en España, 2006–2007*, Madrid: Ministerio de Cultura, Spain.
—— (2008) *Anuario de estadísticas culturales 2008*, Madrid: Ministerio de Cultura, Spain.
Moragas, Miquel de and Prado, Emili (2000) *La televisió pública a l'era digital*, Barcelona: Pòrtic-Centre d'Investigació de la Comunicació.
Mosco, Vincent (2006) 'La economía política de la comunicación: una actualización diez años después', *CIC-Cuadernos de Información y Comunicación*, 11, 57–79.
Mosco, Vincent and Schiller, Dan (eds) (2001) *Continental Order?: Integrating North America for Cybercapitalism*, New York: Rowman and Littlefield.
Moulier Boutang, Yann; Corsani, Antonella and Lazzarato, Maurizio (2004) *Capitalismo cognitivo. Propiedad intelectual y creación colectiva*, Madrid: Traficantes de Sueños.

Murciano, Marcial (1992) *Estructura y dinámica de la comunicación internacional*, Barcelona: Bosch.
—— (2006) 'Las políticas de comunicación ante los retos del nuevo milenio: pluralismo, diversidad cultural, desarrollo económico y tecnológico y bienestar social', *Zer – Revista de estudios de comunicación*, 11(20), 371–398.
Olmos, Héctor Ariel (2008) *Gestión cultural y desarrollo: claves del desarrollo*, Madrid: Agencia Española de Cooperación Internacional para el Desarrollo.
Palma Martos, Mª Luisa (2003) *Una visión panorámica del sector de la edición en Andalucía*, Sevilla: Andalucía Comunicación/RD Editores.
Pascual, Jordi (2006) 'Exploring Local Policies for Cultural Diversity', in *VVAA Local Policies for Cultural Diversity (Report 1)*, Barcelona: UNESCO/Barcelona City Council/United Cities and Local Governments.
Pedro, Joan (2008) 'Evaluación crítica del modelo de propaganda de Herman y Chomsky', 2nd Conference ULEPICC-Spain 'Nuevos retos para la perspectiva crítica en Comunicación y Cultura', Barcelona, 28 November (article published in *Revista Latina de Comunicación Social*, 64, 2009).
Piedras, Ernesto (2004) *¿Cuánto vale la cultura? Contribución económica de las industrias protegidas por el derecho de autor en México*, México City: CONACULTA/Sogem/SACM/Caniem.
Población, José Ignacio and García Alonso, Pedro (1997) *Organización y gestión de la empresa informativa*, Madrid: CIE Dossat 2000.
Prado, Emili; Franquet, Rosa; Fernández Quijada, David; Ribes, Xavier and Soto, María Teresa (2006) 'Televisió interactiva. Simbiosi tecnològica i sistemes d'interacció amb la televisió', *Quaderns del CAC* (special issue), 1–115.
Quirós, Fernando (1998) *Estructura internacional de la información: el poder mediático en la era de la globalización*, Madrid: Síntesis.
Quirós, Fernando and Sierra, Francisco (eds) (2001) *Comunicación, globalización y democracia. Crítica de la economía política de la comunicación y la cultura*, Sevilla: Comunicación Social Ediciones y Publicaciones.
Rausell Köster, Pau (1999) *Políticas y sectores culturales en la Comunidad Valenciana*, Valencia: Tirant Lo Blanch.
—— (dir.) (2007) *Cultura. Estrategia para el desarrollo local*, Madrid: AECID/Instituto Interuniversitario de Desarrollo Local, University of Valencia.
Reig, Ramón (1998) *Medios de comunicación y poder en España*, Barcelona: Paidós.
—— (2001) *El éxtasis cibernético: comunicación, democracia y neototalitarismo a comienzos del siglo XXI*, Madrid: Libertarias Prodhufi.
Robins, Kevin (2006) *The Challenge of Transcultural Diversities: Transversal Study on the Theme of Cultural Policy and Cultural Diversity. Final Report*, Strasburg: Council of Europe.
Robinson, Jill (ed.) (2005) *Eurocult 21. Integrated Report*, Helsinki: Eurocult.
Rodríguez, Arantxa and Vicario, Lorenzo (2005) 'Innovación, competitividad y regeneración urbana. Los espacios retóricos de la *ciudad creativa* en el nuevo Bilbao', *Ekonomiaz-Revista Vasca de Economía*, 58, 262–295.
Rubim, Antonio A.C. and Bayardo, Rubens (eds) (2008) *Políticas culturales en Ibero-América*, Medellín: National University of Colombia.
Rullani, Enzo (2007) 'Arte y economía: la creación de valor en el capitalismo cognitivo', in VV.AA.: *Producta50*, Barcelona: YProductions Eds/Departamento de Cultura y Medios de Comunicación, Generalitat of Catalonia, 224–244.

Sánchez Ruiz, Enrique E. (2006) 'Industrias culturales, pluralismo y diversidad en América Latina', *CIC-Cuadernos de Información y Comunicación*, 11, 207–221.

Sánchez Tabernero, Alfonso (2000) *Dirección estratégica de empresas de comunicación*, Madrid: Cátedra.

Saperas, Enric (2007) 'La televisión digital y la configuración del escenario político', in Marzal, J. and Casero, A. (eds) *El desarrollo de la televisión digital en España*, A Coruña: Netbiblos, 185–195.

Schlesinger, Philip (2007) 'Creativity: From Discourse to Doctrine?', *Screen*, 48(3), 377–387.

Segovia, Ana I. (2006) 'Presentación: Cincuenta años de Economía Política de la Comunicación', *CIC-Cuadernos de Información y Comunicación*, 11, 7–10.

SGAE (Sociedad General de Autores y Editores) (2006) *Anuario SGAE de las artes escénicas, musicales y audiovisuales 2006*, Madrid: SGAE.

Shoemaker, Pamela J. and Reese, Stephen D. (1994) *La mediatización del mensaje: teorías de las influencias en el contenido de los medios de comunicación*, México: Diana.

Sierra, Francisco (2001) 'Privatizar el conocimiento: la comunicación y la educación, objeto de mercadeo en Europa', in Quirós, F. y Sierra, F. (coords) *Comunicación, globalización y democracia. Crítica de la economía política de la comunicación y la cultura*, Sevilla: Comunicación Social Ediciones y Publicaciones, 153–178.

Smiers, Joost (2006) *Un mundo sin copyright. Artes y medios en la globalización*, Barcelona: Gedisa.

Stolovich, Luis; Lescano, Graciela; Mourelle, José and Pessano, Rita (2002) *La cultura es capital*, Montevideo: Fin de Siglo.

Tomlison, John (1991) *Cultural Imperialism: A Critical Introduction*, Baltimore, MD: The Johns Hopkins University Press.

Torres, Juan (1985) *Economía de la comunicación de masas*, Madrid: Zero.

Towse, Ruth (ed.) (2005) *Manual de economía de la cultura*, Madrid: Fundación Autor.

Trejo Delarbre, Raúl (1996) *La nueva alfombra mágica. Usos y mitos de Internet*, Madrid: FUNDESCO.

—— (2006) *Viviendo en El Aleph. La sociedad de la información y sus laberintos*, Barcelona: Gedisa.

Tremblay, Gaëtan (1996) 'La sociedad de la información: del fordismo al gatesismo', in Ledo, M. (ed.) *Comunicación na periferia atlántica. Actas do I Congreso Internacional*, Santiago de Compostela: University of Santiago de Compostela.

UNESCO (United Nations Educational, Scientific and Cultural Organization) (2001) *Informe mundial sobre la cultura 2000–2001. Diversidad cultural, conflicto y pluralismo*, Paris: UNESCO/Mundi-Prensa.

—— (2005) *Convención sobre la protección de la diversidad de los contenidos culturales y las expresiones artísticas*, Paris: UNESCO.

—— (2009) *Segundo Informe Mundial. Invertir en la diversidad cultural y el diálogo intercultural*, Paris: UNESCO.

Vogel, Harold (2004) *La industria de la cultura y el ocio. Un análisis económico*, Madrid: Fundación Autor.

VV.AA. (2004) *La política cultural en España*, Madrid: Real Instituto Elcano de Estudios Internacionales y Estratégicos.

VV.AA. (2005) 'XXV aniversario del Informe MacBride: Comunicación internacional y políticas de comunicación', *Quaderns del CAC*, 21. Available at http://www.cac.cat/pfw_files/cma/recerca/quaderns_cac/Q21_ES.pdf.

Waterman, Peter (2006) *Los nuevos tejidos nerviosos del internacionalismo y la solidaridad*, Lima: National University of San Marcos.

Wolton, Dominique (2003) *L'autre mondialisation*, Paris: Flammarion.

Wyman, Oliver (2009) *Libro Blanco de los contenidos digitales en España 2008*, Madrid: Observatorio Nacional de las Telecomunicaciones y de la Sociedad de la Información (ONTSI), Ministerio de Industria, Turismo y Comercio, Spain.

Yúdice, George (2006) 'Las industrias culturales: más allá de la lógica puramente económica, el aporte social', *Revista Digital de Cultura de la OEI, Pensar Iberoamérica*, 10, 1–8.

Zallo, Ramón (1992) *El mercado de la cultura*, Donostia: Gakoa.

—— (ed.) (1995) *Industrias y políticas culturales en España y el País Vasco*, Leioa: University of the Basque Country.

—— (2002) 'Políticas culturales territoriales: una experiencia rica pero insuficiente', in Bustamante, E. (coord.): *Comunicación y cultura en la era digital. Industrias, mercados y diversidad en España*, Barcelona: Gedisa, 277–305.

—— (2007a) 'Las políticas culturales territoriales revisitadas', in Bustamante, E. (coord.): *Cultura y comunicación para el siglo XXI. Diagnóstico y políticas públicas*, Tenerife: IDECO/Cabildo de Tenerife, 215–258.

—— (2007b) 'La economía de la cultura (y de la comunicación) como objeto de estudio', *Zer – Revista de estudios de comunicación*, 12(22), 215–234.

Zurbano Irizar, Mikel (2005) 'Las regiones como sujetos de la economía global. Euskadi en la gobernanza multidimensional', *Ekonomiaz-Revista Vasca de Economía*, 58, 196–231.

2
The Political Economy of Communication: A Living Tradition

Vincent Mosco

Political economy is a living tradition in communication research, one that responds to changes in material conditions and to upheavals in intellectual life. This chapter demonstrates this by addressing five current trends in the political economy of communication, including the globalization of political economy research, a new turn in an enduring emphasis on historical research, a shift to alternative standpoints, especially feminism and labour, the transition from an emphasis on old media to new media, and expansion in political activism. None of these is an entirely new tendency; rather, each builds on existing tendencies which were often submerged beneath dominant trends in the field (Mosco, 2009).

The globalization of political economy

The political economy of communication has always included an important international dimension. For example, two founding figures, Dallas Smythe and Herbert Schiller, joined Armand Mattelart to assist the Chilean Government of Salvatore Allende to build a democratic media system. Moreover, research outside the developed core began as a response to the observation of media imperialism in the West. Nevertheless, on balance, most of the research in political economy had nationalist tendencies and distinct regional emphases. For example, the bulk of Smythe's major book *Dependency Road* addresses Canada's dependency on US media and asks why the Canadian nation state permitted this to continue for so long. Nationalism became an alternative to US media imperialism. Similarly, resistance to Western media domination across the developing world was met with calls for national resistance along the lines of the national liberation movements that had won independence for many nations after the Second World War. In addition to the tendency to focus on nationalist resistance to globalizing media, political economy developed specific regional tendencies that made it difficult for scholars to work together across their spatial and intellectual divides. Today, these regional differences have substantially diminished. Political economists from different regions are working together on common projects (Wasko et al., 2011), and it is no longer unusual to see research from one region taking up themes that were once prominent in another (Bhuiyan, 2014).

North American scholarship has made substantial contributions to political economic theory, once the primary emphasis of European research. This includes research on the integration of digital technologies into a capitalist economy (Schiller, 2014), the relevance of Marxian theory to communication scholarship (Fuchs and Mosco, 2012), and the application of autonomist theory to social movements that make use of new media (Dyer-Witheford, 2015). It is also just as likely that one would find concrete studies of media problems, once the focus of North American work, such as the commercialization of media and the decline of public media, featured prominently in European scholarship (Murdock and Gripsrud, 2015). Finally, while it is the case that scholars from developing societies are still concerned about issues of media imperialism (witness their involvement in the successor movement to the NWICO, the WSIS), there is just as much evidence that scholarship in the former Third World has taken a strong interest in the growth of political economic theory (Chakravartty and Zhao, 2008; Bolaño et al., 2012).

The process of globalizing political economy research is proceeding rapidly. Some of this is the result of the sheer movement of scholars, a development that has sped up over the last two decades. For example, the Canadian political economist Robin Mansell established a base for institutional political economy at the London School of Economics. Yuezhi Zhao (2008), who has provided the foundation for a political economy of China's media and telecommunications system, moved from that country to the USA and from there to Canada, establishing important connections among scholars in all three countries. One of her students, A. J. M. Shafiul Alam Bhuiyan, moved to Canada from Bangladesh and produced important work on political economy from the perspective of a postcolonial subject (2008). He has since returned to Bangladesh where he has written an important book on new governance and the global South. The Korean political economist Dal Yong Jin (2013) moved to the University of Illinois, Urbana, and worked with Dan Schiller to complete a dissertation on the political economy of telecommunications in South Korea. He has since joined Yuezhi Zhao and Robert Hackett to continue the historically strong presence of a political economy perspective at Simon Fraser University in Canada.

In addition to formal and informal movements of scholars across regions, universities with a strong political economy orientation have established an institutional base concentrating on international research. For example, the University of Westminster, where Nicholas Garnham helped to found the political economy perspective, has established, under the leadership of political economist Christian Fuchs, a major global research programme with particular strength in the study of digital labour and Marxist approaches to media studies. His colleague Daya Thussu, a scholar from India, has developed a programme to examine Indian media. Similarly, the political economist Colin Sparks, who was once based in the UK, has developed a strong research programme in Hong Kong.

At a more formal level, scholarly associations have been active in their support of global research. The IAMCR was founded in 1957 and, for many years, served as the only global academic society to support political economy research. The organization continues to advance political economic research with an international orientation. Under the leadership of its recent president, Robin Mansell, and through the hard work of political economy sections heads, including Janet Wasko, Graham Murdock and Helena Sousa, the IAMCR provides a genuine home to political economists worldwide. The establishment of the Herbert Schiller and Dallas Smythe awards to recognize the work of young scholars offers recognition and an incentive to continue the political economy tradition. In recent years the organization has advanced its leadership in critical communication studies and especially in political economy through the work of its president, Janet Wasko. In addition to creating the first permanent secretariat for the IAMCR in Montevideo, Uruguay, as well as its first executive director, Wasko has supported the work of the political economy section to create its own journal, *The Political Economy of Communication*. The general growth of academic journals has assisted the process of globalization, but specific examples have been especially helpful to political economy. Founded in 2002 by the political economist Yahya Kamalipour of Purdue University in the USA, *The Global Media Journal* has featured critical, especially political economic, research. By 2014 the journal had appeared in 18 different editions: African, American, Arabian, Australian, Brazilian, Canadian, Chinese, German, Indian, Malaysian, Mediterranean, Mexican, Pakistan, Persian, Polish, Portuguese, Russian and Turkish. In addition to content from practically everywhere in the world, the linguistic range assures a genuinely global character. Additionally, the Union for Democratic Communication, a US-based organization of critical scholars and media practitioners, has established *Democratic Communiqué*, a journal that strongly supports political economic research.

Aside from more research, has this process of global expansion made a difference to what political economists have to say? The primary difference is that current research addresses the profound integration of the global political economy and its media systems. Heretofore the focus was on how one (the USA) or just a handful (the USA plus the EU) of nation states and their own corporations dominated weaker states and their nascent economies, in the process of producing little more than dependency and underdevelopment. Today the emphasis is on the integration of corporations, states and classes across national, regional and even developmental divides (Martens et al., 2014). In the view of Chakravartty and Zhao (2008), this involves the creation of a 'transcultural political economy', which they document in a book containing contributions from primarily non-Western scholars.

Where once corporations, including those in the communication industry, were based in one country and moved through the world as an external force, today they are increasingly integrated into the fabric of several societies to the point where it is often difficult to determine their national identity. Operating as owners, partners and in strategic alliances with companies based in the host country, they have led political economists to shift from talking about the power of multinational corporations to addressing the rise of a worldwide transnational economy. Many of these companies originate in the West but the growth of other economies, especially the Chinese and Indian, render simplistic many of the standard models of Western domination. India, for example, which has traditionally been portrayed, quite accurately, as the victim of British and then general Western imperialism, now contains its own transnational firms that have integrated into Western economies. Conglomerates such as Tata, Infosys, WiPro and ICICI have strong bases in North America employing hundreds of thousands of workers, many of whom are eventually dismissed because, after training their own replacements, their jobs are outsourced back to India. They also train North America students as interns and operate their own outsourcing ventures throughout Latin America (Mosco and McKercher, 2008).

Political economic research has also documented the restructuring of public authorities, including nation states, regional blocs and global governance organizations. Furthermore, it has described their integration into the commercial sector to produce hybrids that blur the public–private distinction at every level of government activity. Again, it is no longer just a question of demonstrating how a large corporation 'captures' a government agency by getting it to steer policies and resources to big business. Rather, we are witnessing the thorough integration of both forms of power in a transnationalization of political authority (Schiller, 2014). As a result, intranational social class divisions, which once occupied the bulk of social class analysis in political economy, are now less significant than transnational class divisions that restructure networks of power across nations to link newly wealthy people in China, India and Russia to their counterparts in the USA and Europe. Indeed, any examination of the media elite is now incomplete and downright inadequate until it addresses those who wield media power in several nations. Consider, for example, the Chinese executives who own and operate Lenovo – what was once the personal computer arm of IBM, an icon of US dominance in the high-tech sector.

Much of this activity is aimed at establishing a new international division of labour with the communication industry at the forefront. By creating global labour markets and by making extensive use of communication technologies to carry out the restructuring process, transnational business gains the flexibility to make the most effective, least costly and therefore most profitable use of labour. Students of culture have spent a great deal of time charting the transnationalization of culture (Tomlinson, 1999; Lash and Lury, 2007). Much of this work has enriched what we know about the social production of meaning worldwide. But political economists and some students of culture are making up for a yawning gap in that research: the transnationalization of the labour that produces culture as well as the other material and immaterial products of contemporary society.

The global integration of corporate, government and social class structures is a work in progress. It is fraught with risks, tensions and contradictions. There is also considerable opposition, evidenced in the rise of social movements that have protested this development at meetings of international agencies such as the World Trade Organization (WTO) and other international bodies, such as the WSIS. Political economists have not only examined these developments but also taken praxis seriously and participated at the political and policy levels. In doing so they acknowledge the importance of the trend to transnationalize the political economy of communication. They also recognize the need to create transnational democracy and a genuine cosmopolitan citizenship.

A political economy approach to the history of communication

Research from the mid-1990s to the present has continued the trend to pursue historical analysis from a political economy perspective. More significantly, it has departed from more traditional forms of historical analysis in communication studies. Specifically, current political economy research demonstrates that media systems in place today are the result of a deeply contested history, involving not just duelling capitalists and their allies in government but also labour unions, citizens groups, consumer cooperatives, religious enthusiasts and social justice organizations of all stripes. McChesney (1993) firmly established the importance of this approach in his analysis of the battle for control over radio in the USA. Neither above politics, nor the privileged policy domain of a handful of elites, radio broadcasting was recognized early on as being crucial to democracy, and numerous social movement organizations used what power they had to democratize the medium. They did this by fighting for stations that trade unions, local communities and public interest organizations of all types could control for themselves. They also fought for citizen access to the airwaves to counter the dominant corporate control of broadcasting. And they worked to democratize the policy process by making the case for popular control over regulations that gave and took away licences, that assigned spectrum to services, and that established rules for the fair use of the medium. In essence, the struggle for radio was the struggle for democracy. More than the instrument of a handful of pioneers, or the esoteric magical diviner of the air, radio was embedded in the most significant political battles of the twentieth century, pitting supporters of the New Deal against the dominant conservative forces which generally held the upper hand in US politics (see also Starr, 2005).

Radio was a central instrument of what Denning calls 'the cultural front', a movement extending from the late 1920s to the early 1950s which provided the cultural energy for attempts to establish alternatives to the USA's traditional power structure led by big business (Denning, 1998). In addition to New Deal liberals, it included social democrats, socialists and some communists. It gained strength in the Great Depression and withered in the 1950s when business marshalled a massive counterattack, including the reactionary movement known as McCarthyism. Communication scholars writing history today from a political economic perspective are telling the detailed story of the media's role in the cultural front. Some have continued to enrich the story of radio. For example, Nathan Godfried (1997) examines the history of a Chicago radio station that was established and run by a labour federation representing unions in that city. Providing a voice for labour in a sea of commercial broadcasting was no easy task, particularly since many of the unions, whose members were also big fans of commercial stations, struggled to define a labour alternative. In the face of enormous commercial and business pressures, WCFL (for the Chicago Federation of Labor) was able to retain its unique character through the 1940s, providing both news and entertainment from a labour standpoint. Elizabeth Fones-Wolf (2006) describes the broader role of radio in the effort to build a democratic Left in twentieth-century America. She not only tells the story of several alternatives to commercial radio but also describes the battles that pitted labour and its allies against business in some of the central policy debates of the time. These included decisions about granting and renewing broadcast licences, determining the limits of station ownership, setting rules about acceptable content, and deciding precisely what should be the requirements to air diverse perspectives (see also Fones-Wolf and Fones-Wolf, 2007).

Political economy has also addressed the historical trajectories of other media, especially print journalism. For example, Tracy (2006) has written about the crucial role of the International Typographical Workers Union in battles to control the labour process and the introduction of new technologies in the printing industry. These culminated in a 1964 strike that shut down the newspaper business in New York City for four months. Drawing on interviews with the leader of the labour action, Tracy documents labour's once powerful voice in the media industry and assesses its strengths as well as its weaknesses, such as hanging on to a narrow craft ideology that ultimately contributed to muting that voice. My research with Catherine McKercher extends this view by telling the story of the battles between craft and class among communication workers throughout the history of US media (see also Mosco and McKercher, 2008).

As political economists who study media concentration have demonstrated, one of the ways in which business was able to defeat those calling for more democratic communication and press for a singular commercial form of media was through cross-ownership, or the purchase of multiple media located in a single community or region. But that also met with strong opposition from coalitions of citizen and labour organizations (Fones-Wolf and Fones-Wolf, 2007). The battle for control over Hearst-dominated media in San Francisco provides a stunning example of a company that refused to tolerate the slightest deviation from a conservative viewpoint in either print or broadcast media.

One can also find major recent examples that document the history of resistance in the telecommunications and computer industries. Countering the traditional great inventor, technicist and pro-corporate readings of AT&T's story, Venus Green (2001) examines the significant interplay of race, gender and class in the company's history. Dan Schiller (2007) recounts the struggles in the workplace and in policy-making circles that challenged business efforts to control the postal and telephone system. Pellow and Park (2002) take the analysis into Silicon Valley by telling the story of the struggles first of indigenous people, then of agricultural workers, and now of immigrant women who do the dirty hardware work and of more privileged but often exploited young software workers.

This is not just an American tale. Political economists north of the US border have also worked in this heterodox form of history. It is one of the truisms in countries with a national broadcaster such as the BBC or the Canadian Broadcasting Corporation (CBC) that such institutions provide a public defence against universal commercialism. But in her groundbreaking research on media history in Canada, Patricia Mazepa (2003, 2007) demonstrates that the story is significantly more complex. It also makes a difference to how we think about public media and what we do about it. Drawing on archival sources, Mazepa shows that the CBC developed not just to defend against commercial broadcasting crossing the border from the USA, but also to protect against alternative definitions of 'public' embodied in the media produced by immigrant, socialist and labour organizations in Canada which the national broadcaster generally ignored. In Canada, public broadcasting came to be associated with white settler media, mainly English, and a largely elite French version based principally in the province of Quebec. As a result, community and regional media developed by organizations outside the mainstream were not deemed to be fit for the CBC. Immigrant, socialist and labour media went up against both commercial media and the state. And the state often demonstrated far less tolerance and considerable eagerness to use its policy powers to undermine media emerging from outside the CBC and outside big private broadcasting. Mazepa's work not only uncovers the largely ignored story of media production and resistance from below; it also calls on scholars, especially those involved in the process of making broadcasting policy, to question the meaning of 'public' in public broadcasting. It also broadens that definition to incorporate genuine democratic alternatives and not just those that represent a white settler vision of Canada.

Writing about the history of journalism in Canada, McKercher (2002) charts the conflicts that erupted over the control of the labour process, the use of technology and the shape of the news. These were not simply established by those who owned the presses nor imposed by the changing technologies in the workplace, but arose from strikes and other labour actions as well. Several of these opened up spaces for workers and for those who wanted or needed a more diverse press. Many of them fell far short of success. But McKercher's historical work, like those of other political economists described in this section, offers a genuine alternative to the standard stories and, in doing so, gives back to social activists and workers the agency that is rightfully theirs (Mosco et al., 2010).

Standpoints of resistance

Historical research in the political economy of communication has begun to emphasize resistance and not just the admittedly important story of how the powerful dominate. The emphasis on resistance is increasingly generalized in research on the contemporary political economy, marking a shift in the central standpoint from a focus on capital, dominant corporations and elites to alternatives that draw from feminist and labour research. This marks a departure from a trend that has been a hallmark of political economy from the start: a focus on media concentration, on the erosion of content diversity, and on the standpoint of social class (Green, 1973; Bagdikian, 1992; Herman and Chomsky, 2002; Rice, 2008).

Recent research on the political economy of communication recognizes the importance of this work but argues in favour of a departure. One of the models for this type of thinking is feminist standpoint theory, which maintains that social science needs to be practised and society needs to be understood from the standpoint of women's rather than men's experience, as has been the case for so much of general social science. Developed by Hartsock (1999) in the early 1980s, feminist standpoint theory has flourished in the work of Harding (2003), Haraway (2003) and others who maintain that women's subordination provides a uniquely important basis for understanding an array of issues from the most general philosophical questions of epistemology and ontology to such practical issues as the appropriate social science techniques to deploy in research. The perspective has faced charges of relativism from inside and outside feminist scholarship (Haraway, 2003). It responds by asserting that feminist standpoint theory offers a genuine alternative to the equation of science and universalism with research by and about men, and an alternative to the reduction of feminist research to work that only documents the exploitation of women.

Feminist standpoint thinking has begun to influence research on the political economy of communication. One of the first major attempts to do so is contained in a collection by Eileen Meehan and Ellen Riordan. Meehan has made extensive contributions to political economy, most notably by extending the work of Dallas Smythe on the question of how the audience is made into a marketable commodity. In 2002, Meehan and Riordan produced *Sex and Money*, which gathered the work of leading feminists and political economists to address the relationships between these perspectives. Specifically, it describes how both political economic and feminist standpoints contribute to understanding capitalism at many different levels, including the personal, experiential, institutional and structural. For example, Balka's (2002) chapter on women's work in the telecommunications industry starts from the lived experience of women as they understand what she calls 'the invisibility of the everyday'. This includes how women experience the detailed measurement and monitoring of their work as well as their attempts to gain some control over it. Her description of this gendering process is connected to a political economic analysis of the industry which, in the region of Atlantic Canada which she studied, is undergoing intense change. Specifically, the shift from regulation in the public interest to a more intense commercial model leads companies to eliminate jobs and, using advanced technologies, impose tighter controls on those that remain (Balka, 2002). This gendering of political economy offers a rich reading of an experience that is all too often simplistically described as the inevitable consequence of technological change and global imperatives.

In their 2007 book *Feminist Interventions in International Communication*, Sarikakis and Shade take a further step to advance a feminist standpoint. This volume engages with central issues that political economists address but from a more explicitly feminist starting point. Like many political economic analyses, the book addresses power, technology, labour and policy, but it views them from the entry point of gender. For example, the globalization of the media industries is tightly connected to women's employment in media and new technology. In using a feminist standpoint, they enable us to rethink the study of international communication. Yes, traditional issues such as flows of news between rich and poor nations still matter. But international communication is also about policies for women's development, media production of pornography, media representations of HIV/AIDS and global campaigns to bring an end to this plague. It is also about the location of women in the new international division of labour, especially media and high-tech labour, and what women are doing about workplace exploitation. In essence, Sarikakis and Shade demonstrate that international communication is not gender blind; nor is it a field that simply describes a set of impacts on women. Rather, they and the contributors to their volume demonstrate how women can shape international communication, from production through employment to policy, and their book takes an important step by seeing all of these as women's issues.

Building on this research, Micky Lee (2006, 2007) and McLaughlin and Johnson (2007), among others, clear an enormous amount of ground in addressing political economic power from a feminist standpoint (Jin et al., 2014). Their work ranges from media, through telecommunications, and on to IT, from consumption to production, and from home to office (see also Huws, 2003; Mosco and McKercher, 2008, Chapter 2). There is also interesting work on feminist standpoint theory that spans political economy and cultural studies by examining how audience performances can be viewed as performances of power that defend or resist a dominant ideology (Atkinson, 2005).

This section concludes by taking up new departures in political economy research from a labour standpoint. Communication studies in general has done a more thorough job of addressing media content and audiences than it has communication labour. In recent years a genuine labour standpoint has begun to emerge (Fuchs, 2013; Huws, 2014). My work with Catherine McKercher demonstrates different dimensions of these expansions (McKercher and Mosco, 2006, 2007; Mosco and McKercher 2008), as does our work with Ursula Huws (Mosco et al., 2010). For us, while it is important to understand how corporate power, new technology and conservative governments are changing labour, it is equally important to determine what labour is doing about this. We identify two important developments. The first is the creation of labour convergence, which brings together trade unions from separate areas of the communication industries into one large union representing journalists, broadcasters, technicians, telephone workers and those employed in the high-tech world. Two major examples are the Communication Workers of America (CWA) and its Canadian counterpart the

Communications, Energy and Paperworkers Union (CEP). The development of integrated unions that span the converging media and IT industries provides the resources to better face the power of transnational business. The CWA demonstrated this by carrying out an effective action against the CBC when the national broadcaster locked out its workforce because it had refused to accept a shift to part-time labour and contracting out. Believing that a union which brought together high-paid performers and lower-paid technicians would not remain unified, especially one led by a union from the USA, the CBC locked out its workers, anticipating a rapid decline in solidarity. Using its financial resources and international networks, the CWA provided the support needed to carry on, and the workers not only demonstrated their solidarity across occupational and social class lines but were also able to enlist audiences to their side. After seven weeks, CBC management backed down. Other cases have not been so successful, but some progress has been achieved in the return of a One Big Union Movement, this time in the communication industry.

A second labour strategy is the formation of worker associations which emerge out of social movements that aim to address a significant problem. In his book *Cyber-Proletariat*, Nick Dyer-Witheford (2015) takes a social movement standpoint to address opposition to capitalism around the world today (see also Hackett and Carroll, 2006). He is especially focused on how social movements use new media to counter the transnational political economy. In this respect, the growth of what Marx called the General Intellect lives on in information-rich and media-savvy movements that resist and demonstrate alternatives to the status quo. McKercher and I have paid attention to this among workers who develop new movements and organizations in the world of informational or knowledge labour. We focus in particular on workers on either side of a major divide in the communication industry: technical employees, such as those who produce software (e.g. new code for computer systems), and cultural workers, primarily those who produce media content. The Washington Alliance of Technology Workers (WashTech) built a movement of contract computer workers that has achieved some success at Microsoft and has also been in the forefront of efforts to address the problem of outsourcing high-tech jobs to India and elsewhere (see also Brophy, 2006; Rodino-Colocino, 2007). Moreover, freelance writer organizations in North America represent the new *precariat* – people who work on a short-time, contract basis for media companies that pay low wages and provide few, if any, benefits. Labour activism among communication workers using the means of communication has gained traction internationally, as is evidenced by recent research on China (Yao, 2014) and India (Stevens, 2013).

Organizations like these are redefining the nature of the labour movement by rethinking trade unionism and by connecting their activities to wider political and social issues. Focusing on worker self-organization captures an enormous range of activities and problems that are simply not addressed in traditional research that concentrates on how capital exploits workers. Both are important, but it is time to restore the balance by describing the active agency of communication workers.

The transition from old to new media

Political economy has tended to pay considerable attention to describing and analysing capitalism, a system which, in short, turns resources such as workers, raw materials, land and information into marketable commodities that earn a profit for those who invest capital into the system. Political economists of communication have focused on media, information and audiences as resources and charted the ways in which they are packaged into products for sale. Many who make the shift from the study of old to new media emphasize the continuities between old and new media capitalism. For them, new media deepen and extend tendencies within earlier forms of capitalism by opening up new possibilities to turn media and audiences into saleable commodities. As a result, media concentration, commercialism, rich nation dominance over the global economy, divisions between information rich and poor, and militarism persist and grow (McChesney, 2013; Schiller, 2014). To paraphrase the title of one of Dan Schiller's books, new media may lead us to call it 'digital capitalism', but it is still capitalism and there is no doubt about which is the more important term (Schiller, 2000).

Within such a framework, social and technological change does take place, as new technologies expand the market and global governance becomes necessary, but it also creates problems for capitalism. What was once a largely national market for film and video products and audiences is now a global one, posing serious challenges for coordination. In such markets, what was once a largely national system of governance and regulation has proved to be inadequate. Global systems of governance are necessary if only to ensure the coordination of something as complex as the Internet address system. As a result we have a new alphabet soup of international organizations, such as the Internet Corporation for Assigned Names and Numbers (ICANN), which provides Internet addresses. However, such solutions create new problems as the

USA tries to protect its interests by controlling the ICANN, and many of the world's nations protest because they view it as little more than an extension of US power. Nevertheless, amid the changes, contradictions, opposition and conflict, there is a consistency in the central tendency to deepen and expand the capitalist market system.

In recent years, political economists have begun to emphasize discontinuities and departures from these tendencies. Hardt and Negri (2000, 2004), Lazzarato (1997) and Dyer-Witheford (2015) remain political economists because they are concerned about the power relations that mutually constitute the production, distribution and exchange of resources. However, as a result of the growth of new media, they view those power relations differently than do those who focus on continuities in capitalist relations. Their autonomist perspective, so named because it starts from the autonomy of the working class, maintains that capitalism is propelled by the energy and activity of those who work within it. From this perspective the focus needs to be placed on the self-activity and self-organization of what Hardt and Negri refer to as 'the mass', the vast majority of people typically viewed as exploited from other critical perspectives. Furthermore, the growth of communication and IT does not just serve capitalism; it significantly disrupts it. There are three major ways in which this happens.

Capitalism is based on the market and a system of private property. Both require legal controls that set limits on what people can do. Copyright, trademark and patent law constrain people's use of information and ideas that others own. Markets establish the value of products, including the information products that are increasingly prominent today. According to autonomists, the widespread availability of information and communication technology makes it very difficult for capitalism to preserve the legal regime of private property that historically limited flows of communication and information. It is now more difficult than ever to figure out what capitalism is doing when technologies challenge traditional ideas of production and consumption, use and exchange value. The ease of freely downloading music and video, of sharing files containing data, audio and video, and of copying material of all sorts, challenges the ability of capitalism to maintain and police its property and market regimes. Like the common lands that were once widely available until capitalism made them private property, cyberspace was once a more open space. But in order to make money it too needs to be turned into property, in this case the intellectual property of Microsoft, Google, Disney and the other commercial giants (Terranova, 2004). However, unlike the commons of old, cyberspace is difficult to fence in because it is a fundamentally immaterial resource.

For the autonomists, capitalism faces a second challenge. Although communication and IT provide it with the tools to manage and control large numbers of people from anywhere on the globe, these tools are also available to the masses, and at relatively low cost. For the autonomists, not only does technology challenge property and market rules but it enables people to disrupt the system just at a time when capitalism requires careful global coordination. For example, electronic social networking permits social movements to mobilize and coordinate their activities as never before. The vast expansion in the number of people who are skilled at producing disruptive software, who can hack and crack open seemingly secure programmes, creates critical problems for private property, markets and the overall ability of capitalism to maintain authority.

Finally, the autonomists concludes that the very immaterial labour that capitalism requires to carry out more and more of its work presents serious problems for maintaining control and discipline. Capitalism needs a highly educated workforce, but such a workforce is less likely to cede control over thought and ideas to management than did its blue-collar predecessors. Whether employed in developing software or at a call centre, knowledge workers are less likely to submit to rigid time and motion controls. And the very attempts to loosen rules and introduce a more playful atmosphere into the workplace lead to more questioning of the need for any rules, including those that determine who profits from labour. How do you manage a 'no-collar' workforce (Ross, 2004, 2009)?

Along with stressing discontinuities, recent political economy has taken a sceptical view of the enthusiasm that inevitably accompanies new media. This has been particularly important in historical work which demonstrates that much of what is considered new and revolutionary in new media was actually associated with every communication technology when old media were new. For example, Winseck and Pike (2007) demonstrate that convergence is as old as the telegraph, and that the promises and challenges we associate with the Internet were anticipated by that mid-nineteenth-century technology (see also Standage, 1998).

It is not just the social relations of capitalism that retain continuity; there is also nothing new about the hyperbole or mythologies that accompany today's media. Martin (1991) has described the promises associated with the telephone in much the same way. Whereas the telegraph was expected to bring about world peace, she documents the expectation that the telephone would end the exploitation of women because it would permit them to run a household *and* participate fully in society. Similar research has examined the Internet. Flichy's work *The Internet Imaginaire* (2007) views the Internet as more than just a tool or a social force. It also embodies a myth, by which he means a narrative containing both utopian visions of alternative realities and ideological discourses about how we should conduct our lives and organize society in a period marked by proliferating computer and communication networks.

This work is also important because it reflects a stepped-up interest among political economists to demonstrate the continuity between old and new media by engaging with culture. Drawing on the work of Martin and others, my book *The Digital Sublime,* Mosco (2014) demonstrates that the same promises made about the Internet have been made when old technologies, such as the telegraph, telephone, radio and TV, were new. World peace, gender equality, online education, racial harmony – all of these were once viewed as the inevitable consequences of these once new media. For believers, the Internet will realize all of these promises and more, including, in the work of MIT professor Raymond Kurzweil, an end to death as we know it. Ultimately, digital technologies imagine the end of history, the end of geography and the end of politics. Those who advance these views, I maintain, are doing something prominent throughout the history of 'new' media. They are invoking technology as an opportunity to achieve the sublime or the experience of transcending the constraints of everyday life (including time, space and social relations) to achieve a utopia beyond language. Once the province of art and literature (the sublime painting or poem), and of nature (e.g. the sublime Grand Canyon), the sublime is now to be achieved through technology and, increasingly, through communication technology. My 2014 book *To the Cloud: Big Data in a Turbulent World* deepens and extends the goal of building bridges between political, economic and cultural analysis.

Demonstrating continuity and a link to culture are important, but it is also important to return to political economy and document how all of this matters for the study of power. First, those who have made important contributions to studying the sublime do not pay enough attention to the connections between constructing the sublime and marketing, whether selling the latest computer, video game or political candidate. Visions of transcendence make for great advertising. Second, connecting new media to the end of history, geography and politics freezes into near inevitability and permanence the current political economy. The message is simple and powerful: there is no sense struggling over the control of transnational capital if there is no likelihood of ever creating an alternative. Finally, the sublime can mask the often banal world of everyday politics. New York's World Trade Center was to embody the sublime new world of informational capitalism that transcended old political relations founded in an industrial era, until the cataclysm of 9/11 when history returned with a vengeance. The seductive lure of the sublime can blind its seekers from the banal and terrible politics that lurks just around the corner. To correct these problems, I have examined the marketing, environmental, surveillance and labour implications of cloud computing and big data (Mosco, 2014).

The political economy of communication has also adjusted its recent focus to take up issues that are particularly important today. Among the major ones, copyright and intellectual property issues, surveillance and the tendency towards what some call a network economy are worth some comment.

From the time of Charles Dickens, who railed against what he considered the failure of the USA to pay royalties for his novels when they were distributed there in the nineteenth century, copyright has been a hot topic in debates around media. For media scholars today, including political economists, the debate has stepped up because new media make it easier to copy and share work under copyright. Bettig (1996; see also Bettig and Hall, 2003) has written about how business uses copyright to tighten its control, and Schiller (2014) and Zhao (2008) have studied the intellectual property challenge from China and other developing nations. Who will control intellectual property is one of the central questions facing political economy today.

So too is the threat of electronic surveillance. As Lyon (2007) and others have demonstrated, new media make it possible for governments and companies to monitor activities on an unprecedented scale. The so-called War on Terror has accelerated the spread of surveillance and legitimized activities that were once considered unacceptable violations of personal privacy. Political economists have addressed the extent of the problem and have also begun to document what can be done about it (Coleman, 2014).

Finally, as the work of the autonomists demonstrates, new media call into question traditional economic categories and the capacities of capitalist economies to control them. But political economists outside the autonomist orbit are also wondering about the challenge of new media to the understanding of economics. Specifically, should we begin to think about the emergence of a network economy and the need for a network economics to address it? Network economics argues that the value of goods shifts in a world of electronic networks. In particular, the worth of a product or service increases when others buy the same good or service, especially when the purchase connects people in a network (Mansell, 2004; Melody, 2007). New media are based on networks of cellphone users, Internet users, participants in social networking sites and so on. Traditional economics, it is argued, undervalues additions to the network because it does not take into account the geometrical expansion in the number of potential transactions that an addition to the network makes. The question for political economists is what this does to its conception of power. In other words: Is network economics also political economy?

Media activism

Praxis, or the unity of research and action, is a fundamental characteristic of a political economy approach. Most political economists of communication have been activists as well as scholars, involved in movements for media democracy, development communication, independent media and universal access, as well as with labour, feminist and anti-racist movements. The Union for Democratic Communication, which was created in the early 1980s, continues to bring together activist-scholars and media practitioners. The IAMCR provides a global forum for political economists, including those active in public policy work, such as its former president, Robin Mansell (2004–2011). Where once political economists such as Herbert Schiller and Armand Mattelart worked to make UNESCO a focal point to build the NWICO, politically active scholars are concentrating on democratizing the Internet through the international project WSIS.

Important as these developments are, one of the most significant advances in political activity has been the creation in 2002 of the Free Press by the political economist Robert McChesney (2007). The organization has been a focal point for the remarkably resurgent media reform movement in the USA that has brought together a diverse collection of public interest groups, including the Consumers Union, the Center for Digital Democracy, the Media Access Project and the Consumer Federation of America. These have joined with independent media organizations, such as Democracy Now!, a daily, national, independent news programme hosted by journalists Amy Goodman and Juan Gonzalez. Free Press has attracted enormous attention, including the support of well-known people such as Bill Moyers, Jane Fonda and the Revd Jesse

Jackson. It has sponsored an annual conference on media reform that has attracted literally thousands of people, including scholars, media activists, politicians and trade unionists. In the past, such meetings might have brought together at most hundreds of people, suggesting that we are observing a populist upheaval around the issue of media reform.

The upswell in the media reform movement can be attributed to the widespread view that the elimination of rules restricting media ownership, providing for some measure of content diversity, and limiting the prices that major cable, satellite and other media firms can charge consumers, has threatened what remains of media democracy, media quality and universal access to essential services. The loss of nearly hundreds of thousands of media jobs demonstrates for many the fact that media concentration is an enormous labour-saving project that is eroding the quality of journalism and what remains of its independence. To counter these tendencies, Free Press mobilizes activists, lobbies politicians and makes use of the media (including Bill Moyers' own public TV show) to press for alternatives. These include ending the concentration of old and new media in the hands of a few giant transnational firms, supporting content diversity and vigorous debate, and creating social policies that guarantee universal access to essential telecommunications and Internet services (McChesney, 2013).

Of particular importance is the fight to preserve 'network neutrality'. As pressure mounts on large media firms to increase profits, companies are tempted to restructure their networks to increase revenue. Specifically, they are creating a system of faster and slower 'lanes' on the information highway, reserving the faster lanes for higher-paying content providers, such as certain advertisers, or for those linked to the network service provider, such as its own subsidiaries. Traffic moves more slowly for those paying less and for competitors. One important consequence is that the websites of companies outside the mainstream, including alternative media sites, which do not have the funding to pay the premium for a fast lane, would only be available in lower quality. Responding to this threat, the media reform movement has fought for legislation and regulations that would preserve what has been the standard practice, with a few exceptions, of treating all content equally – with what amounts to one highway at one speed, delivering one standard of quality. Whatever the outcome of these specific struggles, it is evident that political economists have made a significant contribution to the overall resurgence of activism around major communication issues.

References

Atkinson, Joshua (2005) 'Conceptualizing Global Justice Audiences of Alternative Media', *The Communication Review*, 8, 137–157.

Bagdikian, Ben H. (1992) *The Media Monopoly* (4th edition), Boston, MA: Beacon Press.

Balka, Ellen (2002) 'The Invisibility of the Everyday: New Technology and Women's Work', in Meehan, E. R. and Riordan, E. (eds) *Sex and Money Feminism and Political Economy in the Media*, Minneapolis: University of Minnesota Press, 60–74.

Bettig, Ronald V. (1996) *Copyrighting Culture: The Political Economy of Intellectual Property*, Boulder, CO: Westview Press.

Bettig, Ronald V. and Hall, Jeanne Lynn (2003) *Big Money, Big Media: Cultural Texts and Political Economics*, Lanham, MD: Rowman & Littlefield.

Bhuiyan, A. J. M. Shafijiul Alam (2008) 'Peripheral View: Conceptualizing the Information Society as a Postcolonial Subject', *The International Communication Gazette*, 70(2), 99–116.

—— (2014) *Internet Governance and the Global South: Demand for a New Framework*, London: Palgrave Macmillan.

Bolaño, César; Mastrini, Guillermo and Sierra, Francisco (2012) *Political Economy, Communication, and Knowledge: A Latin American Perspective*, Creskill, NJ: Hampton Press.

Brophy, Enda (2006) 'System Error: Labour Precarity and Collective Organizing at Microsoft', *Canadian Journal of Communication*, 31(3), 619–638.

Chakravartty, Paula and Zhao, Yuezhi (eds) (2008) *Global Communication: Toward a Transcultural Political Economy*, Lanham, MD: Rowman & Littlefield.

Coleman, Gabriella (2014) *Hacker, Hoaxer, Whistleblower, Spy: The Many Faces of Anonymous*, London: Verso.

Denning, Michael (1998) *The Cultural Front*, London: Verso.

Dyer-Witheford, Nick (2015) *Cyber-Proletariat: Digital Labour in the Global Vortex*, London: Pluto Press.

Flichy, Patrice (2007) *The Internet Imaginaire* (trans. by L. Carey-Libbrecht), Cambridge, MA: MIT Press.

Fones-Wolf, Elizabeth A. (2006) *Waves of Opposition: Labor and the Struggle for Democratic Radio*, Chicago and Urbana: University of Illinois Press.

Fones-Wolf, Colin T. and Fones-Wolf, Elizabeth A. (2007) 'Labor Off the Air: The Hearst Corporation, Cross Ownership and the Union Struggle for Media Access in San Francisco', in McKercher, C. and Mosco, V. (eds) *Knowledge Workers in the Information Society*, Lanham, MD: Lexington Books, 1–18.

Fuchs, Christian (2013) *Digital Labour and Karl Marx*, London: Routledge.

Fuchs, Christian and Mosco, Vincent (eds) (2012) 'Marx Is Back – The Importance of Marxist Theory and Research for Critical Communication Studies Today (special issue)', *tripleC–Open Access Journal for a Global Sustainable Information Society*, 10(2), 127–632.

Godfried, Nathan (1997) *WCFL, Chicago's Voice of Labor, 1926–78*, Chicago and Urbana: University of Illinois Press.

Green, Mark J. (ed.) (1973) *The Monopoly Makers*, New York: Penguin.

Green, Venus (2001) *Race on the Line: Gender, Labor, and Technology and in the Bell System*, Durham: Duke University Press.

Hackett, Robert A. and Carroll, William K. (2006) *Remaking Media: The Struggle to Democratize Public Communication*, New York and London: Routledge.

Haraway, Donna (2003) *The Haraway Reader*, London: Routledge.

Harding, Sandra (2003) *The Feminist Standpoint Theory Reader*, London: Routledge.

Hardt, Michael and Negri, Antonio (2000) *Empire*, Cambridge, MA: Harvard University Press.

—— (2004) *Multitude: War and Democracy in the Age of Empire*, New York: Penguin Press.

Hartsock, Nancy (1999) *The Feminist Standpoint Revisited*, New York: Basic Books.

Herman, Edward S. and Chomsky, Noam (2002) *Manufacturing Consent: The Political Economy of the Mass Media*, New York: Pantheon.

Huws, Ursula (2003) *The Making of a Cybertariat: Virtual Work in a Real World*, New York: Monthly Review Press.

—— (2014) *Labor in the Global Digital Economy: The Cybertariat Comes of Age*, New York: Monthly Review Press.

Jin, Cao; Mosco, Vincent and Shade, Lesie R. (eds) (2014) *Critical Studies in Communication and Society*, Shanghai: Shanghai Translation Publishing House.

Jin, Dal Yong (2013) *De-Convergence of Global Media Industries*, London: Routledge.

Lash, Scott and Lury, Celia (2007) *The Global Culture Industry*, London: Polity.

Lazzarato, Maurizio (1997) *Lavoro immateriale: Forme di vita e produzione di soggettività*, Verona: Ombre Corte.

Lee, Micky (2006) 'What's Missing in Feminist Research in New Information and Information Technologies?', *Feminist Media Studies*, 6(2), 191–210.

—— (2007) 'On the Relationship between International Telecommunications Development and Global Women's Poverty', *The International Communications Gazette*, 69(2), 193–213.

Lyon, David (2007) *Surveillance Studies: An Overview*, London: Polity.

Mansell, Robert (2004) 'Political Economy, Power, and New Media', *New Media and Society*, 6(1), 96–105.

Martens, Cheryl; Vivares, Ernesto and McChesney, Robert W. (2014) *The International Political Economy of Communication: Media and Power in South America*, London: Palgrave Macmillan.

Martin, Michèle (1991) *'Hello, Central?': Gender, Technology, and Culture in the Formation of Telephone Systems*, Montreal and Kingston: McGill-Queen's University Press.

Mazepa, Patricia (2003) *Battles on the Cultural Front: The (de)Labouring of Culture in Canada, 1914–1944* (doctoral dissertation), Carleton University, Ottawa.

—— (2007) 'Democracy of, in and Through Communication: Struggles around Public Service in Canada in the First Half of the Twentieth Century', *Info*, 9(2–3), 45–56.

McChesney, Robert W. (1993) *Telecommunications, Mass Media and Democracy: The Battle for the Control of US Broadcasting*, New York: Oxford University Press.

—— (2007) *Communication Revolution*, New York: The Free Press.

—— (2013) *Digital Disconnect: How Capitalism Is Turning the Internet against Democracy*, New York: New Press.

McKercher, Catherine (2002) *Newsworkers Unite: Labor, Convergence and North American Newspapers*, Lanham, MD: Rowman & Littlefield.

McKercher, Catherine and Mosco, Vincent (eds) (2006) 'The Labouring of Communication. Special Issue', *Canadian Journal of Communication*, 31(3), 493–497.

—— (eds) (2007) *Knowledge Workers in the Information Society*, Lanham, MD: Lexington Books.
McLaughlin, Lisa and Johnson, Helen (2007) 'Women and Knowledge Work in the Asia Pacific: Complicating Technological Empowerment', in McKercher, C. and Mosco, V. (eds) *Knowledge Workers in the Information Society*, Lanham, MD: Lexington Books, 249–266.
Meehan, Eileen and Riordan, Ellen (eds) (2002) *Sex and Money: Feminism and Political Economy in the Media*, Minneapolis: University of Minnesota Press.
Melody, William (2007) 'Cultivating Knowledge for Knowledge Societies at the Intersections of Economic and Cultural Analysis', *International Journal of Communication*, 1, 70–78.
Mosco, Vincent (2004) *The Digital Sublime: Myth, Power, and Cyberspace*, Cambridge, MA: MIT Press.
—— (2009) *The Political Economy of Communication* (2nd edition), London: Sage.
—— (2014) *To the Cloud: Big Data in a Turbulent World*, Boulder, CA: Paradigm Books.
Mosco, Vincent and McKercher, Catherine (2008) *The Laboring of Communication: Will Knowledge Workers of the World Unite?* Lanham, MD: Lexington Books.
Mosco, Vincent; McKercher, Catherine and Huws, Ursula (eds) (2010) *Getting the Message: Communications Workers and Global Value Chains*, London: Merlin.
Murdock, Graham and Gripsrud, Jostein (eds) (2015) *Money Talks: Media, Markets, Crisis*, London: Intellect.
Pellow, David N. and Park, Lisa Sun-Hee (2002) *The Silicon Valley of Dreams*, New York: New York University Press.
Rice, Ronald E. (ed.) (2008) *Media Ownership*, Creskill, NJ: Hampton Press.
Rodino-Colocino, Michelle (2007) 'High-Tech Workers of the World, Unionize! A Case Study of WashTech's "New Model of Unionism" ', in C. McKercher and V. Mosco (eds) *Knowledge Workers in the Information Society*, Lanham, MD: Lexington Books, 209–227.
Ross, Andrew (2004) *No Collar*, Philadelphia, PA: Temple University Press.
—— (2009) *Nice Work If You Can Get It. Life and Labor in Precarious Times*, New York: New York University Press.
Sarikakis, Katrherine and Shade, Leslie Regan (eds) (2007) *Feminist Interventions in International Communication: Minding the Gap*, Lanham, MD: Rowman & Littlefield.
Schiller, Dan (2000) *Digital Capitalism*, Cambridge, MA: MIT Press.
—— (2007) 'The Hidden History of US Public Service Telecommunications, 1919–1956', *Info*, 9(2/3), 17–28.
—— (2014) *Digital Depression*, Urbana and Chicago: University of Illinois Press.
Standage, Tom (1998) *The Victorian Internet*, New York: Walker and Company.
Starr, Paul (2005) *The Creation of the Media*, New York: Basic Books.
Stevens, Andrew J. R. (2013) *Call Centers and the Global Division of Labor: A Political Economy of Post-Industrial Employment and Union Organizing*, London: Routledge.
Terranova, Tiziana (2004) *Network Culture: Politics for the Information Age*, London: Pluto.
Tomlinson, John (1999) *Globalization and Culture*, London: Polity.
Tracy, James F. (2006) ' "Labor's Monkey Wrench": Newsweekly Coverage of the 1962–63 New York Newspaper Strike', *Canadian Journal of Communication*, 31(3), 541–560.

Wasko, Janet; Murdock, Graham and Sousa, Helena (eds) (2011) *Handbook of Political Economy of Communication*, New York: Wiley-Blackwell.
Winseck, Dwayne and Pike, Robert (2007) *Communication and Empire: Media Power and Globalization, 1860–1930*, Durham, NC: Duke University Press.
Yao, Jianhua (2014) *Knowledge Workers in Contemporary China: Reform and Resistance in the Global Publishing Industry*, Lanham, MD: Lexington Books.
Zhao, Yuezhi (2008) *Communication in China: Political Economy, Power, and Conflict*, Lanham, MD: Rowman & Littlefield.

Part II

Cultural or Creative Industries?

3
Intellectuals and Cultural Policies

Philip Schlesinger

This chapter considers the relationship between intellectuals and cultural policies, in particular in the role played by various categories of 'expert' in the production of the official discourse on creativity that now occupies the conceptual high ground and has effectively displaced – or at least obscured – the discourse on the cultural industries.[1]

First, as Nicholas Garnham (2005) has pointed out, the discourse relating to creativity is an offshoot of that about the information society. In the UK, the Labour Party – responsible for introducing creative industries policy – has been profoundly influenced by neoliberalism. This means that in the field of communications the political parties largely share the same ideas about the importance of international competitiveness and, where feasible, the need for deregulation.

Second, the issue of the information society – or knowledge society – has been developed at an intellectual level. The intervention of Daniel Bell (1974), who noted in the early 1970s the formation of a new postindustrial knowledge-based class structure, was instrumental in the evolution of the intellectual field. We can trace various lines of filiation of this mode of thinking. For example, note some of the continuities in the work of the sociologist Alvin Gouldner (1979), who identified a 'new class' of intellectual, and the invocation of the 'creative class' currently proposed by the economist Richard Florida (2002, 2005).

What interests me in particular is the relationship between the level of general ideas and the implementation of public policies. I would like to illustrate my argument by reference to my national context and own research. The community that is influential and active in the field of transforming ideas into practical policies – the 'policy community' – is not that large because the costs of entry into the debate – the conceptual and empirical investment necessary – are rather high. In order to have an influence it is not sufficient just to gain access to the disciplinary field surrounding cultural policies: the weight of one's contribution depends on the structural position one occupies, which is to say that it depends on being recognized by those holding political power and one's proximity to it. This is why there are very few providers of influential ideas. It is clear, moreover, that the government of the day has its own preferences when it comes to selecting useful ideas for its projects. This brings us to the need to construct a political sociology of intellectuals concerned with the production of 'official' discourse.

Cultural policies

Cultural policies are formed at the crossroads of the political and the cultural, between various modes of practice and experience, and the highly institutionalized form of the state. This is why cultural policies are territorialized and predominantly developed in the national or state context. We do need to differentiate between state and nation. However, considering the impact of the globalization of culture and communication, and given that national borders have become rather permeable, the possibility of a complete sociocultural closure is fairly limited, even in autocracies. For this reason, academic research cannot focus solely on the national state. Projects termed 'national' must therefore take into account both the external environment and each country's internal imperatives.

Broadly understood, cultural policy is a compendium of individual public policies on the media, communications, heritage and the arts – although it also may extend to policies on education and science. This does not mean that each of these is coherently connected to each of the others. Quite the contrary: policy development is not always a rational linear process

In fact, the process of public policy formation and implementation is inherently likely to be sidetracked. To understand what this means, we first have to bear in mind that the dominant contemporary official understanding of culture – and therefore of cultural policies – is closely tied to the economy and to the pluralism of most contemporary societies. Moreover, what we understand by culture is also constantly being delineated by tensions between profitability and aesthetic value, as well as framed by the highly permeable borders between the public and the private, between creativity and banality, and so on.

In this sense, as the distinguished sociologist Zygmunt Bauman (1992) has highlighted, culture and 'intellectuals' are profoundly connected.

According to him, intellectuals make up a new and crucial layer of expertise, one that first formed during the Enlightenment and that has emerged in parallel with the idea of culture conceived as a distinct space with characteristics of its own.

Initially, Bauman has argued, intellectuals were legislators who in effect articulated the ideology of the new order, rejecting diversity and backwardness, spurred by the desire to centralize political and cultural life. However, with the failure of each and every epistemological certainty in the postmodern era, the legislative role has given way to interpretation. This is a far more modest role, which consists in finding, understanding and recounting the diversity that exists in the huge number of local cultures – including the nation.

This is why intellectuals now have minimal social relevance, says Bauman. They talk above all about themselves, and work in universities and other cultural and scientific institutions. Although they have the consolation of being able to communicate with their peers and earn a salary at the same time, they are essentially disconnected from political power.

Bauman's thesis is brilliant, but he is wrong. Its most insightful aspect is this: that with the collapse of the traditional order, the cultural sphere has emerged as a space for action – that is to say, something that needs to be managed and administered. It is the cultural sphere that stands at the heart of intellectuals' concerns. However, my recent empirical research (Schlesinger, 2009a) suggests just the opposite: that the legislative impetus remains strong in some intellectual quarters and disciplines. In addition, states have not yet abandoned hegemonic projects pursued and articulated in the name of the nation, just as governments do not always respect the complexity existing in contemporary societies. In short, Bauman's perspective does not allow us to propose an active role for intellectuals in the evolution of cultural policies.

For his part, Theodor Adorno (1991) takes another point of view regarding the role of experts and expertise. For him the majority of intellectuals are, to use his expression, 'servile', and not much can be expected of them. We find ourselves in a fallen contemporary world, dominated by a cultural industry that is fed by mass consumption and that in turn creates a cultural scene of 'eternal similitude'.

Moreover, for Adorno, the idea of administered culture is repugnant – and worse still if it is administered by public authorities – since he regards culture as being constituted by the so-called 'critical impulse'. That is to say, it functions precisely in counterpoint to or contrast with the practice of administration. In spite of this, however, he believes that it is possible for a cultural policy to be self-critical and for expertise to be used 'for the protection of cultural matters from the realm of control by the market' (Adorno, 1991, p. 89). There is a need, therefore, to protect high culture not just from the operations of the administration but also from the ignorant tastes of an uneducated *demos*.

Now, Adorno has chosen the 'least bad' solution, since along with the administration of culture there is a discretionary space in which those cultural experts capable of critical judgment could make good decisions. In this way they would have a legislative function.

This perspective is relevant to my current line of research regarding the role played by experts in the public debate on creative industry policy in the UK. The problem is that intellectual legislation can be a source of disappointment. No doubt what is happening in the UK would be a negative affair for Adorno, because it confirms, against his principles, the importance of the market in the cultural sphere.

Comparison

Each public policy undeniably has its own history. It is embedded in its own institutional context, which is why when thinking about formulating or implementing cultural policies we cannot disregard the functioning of government ministries, arts councils, communications regulators and other cultural agencies.

Although all countries face global trends – and, in the context of the EU, the equivocal process of Europeanization – national contexts tend to be very different from one another. It is true that we live in a framework of international governance – which is more or less effective, depending on the global balance of forces – and that the idea of classic national sovereignty has been overtaken, but no one can deny that the international system continues to be constituted by states.

In that sense a comparison of the public policies of states and nations may prove very fruitful, providing that the state or national specificity is not eliminated. The problem is that the act of comparing entails a logic that minimizes particularity in pursuit of comparable elements. This is why it is necessary to highlight the differences and similarities deemed essential, because only in this way, by facing up to the limits of a comparative analysis, can we arrive at the cultural and social fabric, at the materiality of difference.

The particularity of each political context thus raises an interesting question: To what extent can we transfer public policies and solutions from one context to another? There can be no doubt that ideas travel, but they do not do so without a certain baggage. Besides, they are susceptible to interpretations shaped by the contexts of reception.

In the case of the UK, where the discourse of creativity has been produced in precise conditions over the course of a decade, it is highly interesting to examine the question of its exportation and transferability. Moreover, the recent evolution in the country's public policies on communication and its cultural policies raises a series of questions about the creative industries, or the 'creative economy', their new label.

The UK

The UK is a state made up of different nations. Due to the devolution of powers to Scotland, Wales and Northern Ireland, the internal differentiation of the British state – that is to say, the growing distinctiveness of the smaller nations in relation to England – is causing institutional variations as well as differences in public policies themselves.[2] For this reason it is necessary to take into account another comparative level – the one existing within the state.

Since the beginning of the century and until very recently, it was not difficult to find differentiated public policies for culture, broadcasting, telecommunications and so on. However, technological change in the UK has gradually effected the growing integration of the audiovisual sector and that of communications. In addition, the increasing use of the label 'creative content' shows how accelerated digitization is bringing about the convergence of sectors that in the past were clearly distinguished from one another. It is not always easy to distinguish communication policies from cultural policies.

In this wider context, 'creativity' has established itself as a hegemonic term in our current debate, closely linked to the idea of innovation in trade, education and science. In the context of globalization, the policy of creativity has become an integral part of a discourse of national renewal – both at the UK level as well as that of the UK's devolved nations. When that official discourse is analysed, its exponents can be seen to resort rhetorically to the idea that it is an evidence-based policy – in other words, they tend to demonstrate its rationality (Schlesinger, 2007).

However, underlying the search for facts, beneath the rationality of policy, there is also a credo: a belief associated with a particular vision of the world in which the economic exploitation of creativity is the key to achieving global success. This belief also involves an anthropology of human capabilities, based on the idea of *Homo economicus*.

In addition, it is important to acknowledge that cultural policies have two key intertwined aspects: the applied and the symbolic. The latter is based on the imaginary of the national community and has to do with the image projected by a public policy. In the case of creativity in the UK, it was initially an image of rupture, innovation, youth and renaissance, which began to permeate public discourse from 1997, in the shape of 'Cool Britannia' in the early days of Prime Minister Tony Blair's period in office. Now, nearly two decades on, we have another much more ostentatious and at the same time more banal imaginary: that of acting as a global cultural hub, capable of influencing trends in cultural production and consumption in the international market.

The stages

It was in 1998 that the new policy was launched. The New Labour government set up a working group with the aim of producing a cartography of the creative industries for the Department of Culture, Media and Sport (DCMS). Remarkably, since then the resulting work, entitled the *Creative Industries Mapping Document* (DCMS, 1998), has been an important benchmark for contemporary debate not only in the UK but in many other countries.

The official definition – clearly quite durable – is the following: that the creative industries have their origin in 'creativity, skills, individual talents... which have a potential for wealth and job creation through the generation and exploitation of intellectual property' (DCMS, 1998, p. 3).

In reality, this is no more than a pragmatic list, but for many it has proved to be an ineluctable starting-point for discussion. Rather than a true conceptualization of the creative industries, it is an officially designated cluster of chosen sectors – namely, 'advertising, architecture, art and antiques, design, fashion, cinema, interactive software, music, performing arts, publishing, software, television and radio' (DCMS, 1998, p. 3).

In sum, the creative industries have been defined by two fundamental characteristics: they are conceived as activities based on individual creativity in terms of their ability to generate intellectual property – which is exportable – along with the exploitation of these selfsame activities as a basis for wealth and job creation. In that sense the UK definition is economistic, since the communicative and symbolic functions of a culture – as well as the generation and communication of ideas – are interesting only because they have use-value. In other words, culture is displaced by creativity. Thus the conception of the 'creative' industries constitutes a break with the idea of the 'cultural' industries. This has significant consequences for public policies.

To all this it must be added that the discourse of the creative industries is embedded in the discourse of the knowledge economy. The approach is individualistic and seemingly democratic because, according to the doctrine, all individuals can be conceived as creative subjects. Ostensibly, then, creativity is a quality equally present in all of us. But, as Antonio Gramsci (1971) once observed, the fact that all can use their intellectual capabilities does not mean that they all therefore have the function of intellectuals.

The seductive power of this new anthropology of creativity is strengthened in the technological age of user-generated content. For example, all those individuals who can now access technological resources are able in principle to produce content for the Internet, most notably for most, distributing messages through social media. However, this does not mean communicative equality. Barriers remain in respect of quality, extent of circulation, impact and profitability, among many others. The democratizing image of communication technologies is thus strongly linked to the persuasive power of the new doctrine of creativity, which in turn constitutes a break with the ideas of 'originality' traditionally associated with creative artistic production.

The key idea of the current UK doctrine of creativity is to maximize the economic impact of the 13 industrial sectors identified. As we can see, this concept represents a distinct stage beyond cultural industries policy – an approach initiated in the 1980s. Indeed, the list of selected industries combines formerly separate sectors – communication and the arts – to which information and communication technologies have been added. Accompanying the doctrine of creativity, there is an underlying ideological current: the apotheosis of business innovation as a model for all other practices, along with the need to develop human capital, trained – ideally – to a high level of skill.

It is important to point out that the DCMS's intervention brokered two crucial ideas that have continued to influence UK public policy and that of other countries. On the one hand there is the conception of the UK as a competitive nation facing the challenge of the BRICS countries (Brazil, Russia, India, China and South Africa). On the other is the belief that state intervention is necessary and legitimate to ensure the wellbeing of 'UK plc'.

Empirical research

The evolution of the UK's national policy highlighted the importance at an early stage of a particular segment of intellectuals – those working in New Labour think tanks. Such bodies typically produce an expert discourse geared towards the fields of politics and the media, thereby participating in a day-to-day ideological struggle. Indeed, the New Labour think tanks were set up with the aim of waging a war of positions in the struggle for hegemony at the level of ideas.

The importance of think tanks in today's UK political culture lies in the fact that they are in charge of mediating ideas and disseminating public policy proposals in the public sphere; they are driven by a clear intention to produce political effects – that is, they seek to influence the policy domain. Thus they are themselves actors within the wider media field.

This type of activity touches on the question of the role of expert government advisors in our societies. The political role of such experts has been important since the early twentieth century, since those close to power possess a structural advantage: they are able to both influence politicians and public policies, and position ideas and launch debates onto the public agenda.

In the case of New Labour, as previously in the case of the Conservative Party, think tanks have functioned not only as efficient ideological laboratories but also as producers of political talent. Important prime ministerial advisors, senior civil servants, two culture secretaries, one trade and industry secretary and one foreign secretary all came to power following a period of training in think tanks. Similarly, other key figures have moved between the BBC and Ofcom (the communications regulator) and government.

While the UK has occupied a key place in developing the discourses on creativity, the idea of the creative industries has also been widely disseminated throughout the world. The United Nations Conference on Trade and Development's (UNCTAD's) *Creative Economy Report 2008* and its successor versions have contributed to the globalization of the discourse.

The Creative Economy Programme

From 2005 onwards we can trace the creation of elements in the new public policy through a series of official reports initiated by Gordon Brown, who at the time was chancellor of the exchequer, later becoming prime minister in succession to Tony Blair.

The Cox Report (HM Treasury, 2005), chaired by the design expert Sir George Cox, proposed as its central line of argument the exploitation of the nation's creative skills and the establishment of closer ties between business, universities and cultural creators. Along with this it invoked the importance of innovation as a mediator between creativity and design. The substance of the report was, to use Pierre Bourdieu's (1977) expression, a *doxa* shared by the authors of other reports of this type. The underlying beliefs thus consisted of economic nationalism, the affirmation of the role of the state and of public agencies in global competitiveness, and the need to transform business and organizational culture into a creative culture for all.

I do not wish to multiply the examples, but it is instructive to acknowledge that the same ideas penetrated the field of education, not only at university but also at secondary school level. The thinking of Prof. Ken Robinson (1999), who propounded the need to develop creativity in the school context, has been highly influential since the late 1990s. The basic concept is that the specific skills acquired at school might ensure a student's personal success in the so-called knowledge economy. For its part, the Department for Education – in close collaboration with the DCMS – promoted the Roberts Report (Roberts, 2006) on the nurturing of young people's creativity. According to ministers and their advisors, in order to establish a global hub of creativity, it was necessary to mobilize the UK's young creative talent. To do this they proposed forging connections between selected secondary schools and the creative industries.

A significant moment came with the launch of the Creative Economy Programme (CEP) in 2005 by the DCMS in conjunction with the Department of Trade and Industry (DTI) and with the support of the Treasury. In a statement that was almost a declaration of faith, the culture secretary pronounced that 'every industry must look to become a creative industry, in the broadest sense of the word' (Jowell, 2005).

The CEP, in typical New Labour fashion, was initiated by working groups that produced reports on particular issues: access to funding, training and skills, diversity, technology, testing and analysis. Leaving aside any discussion of the detail, it is important to be aware of the conceptual effort involved first in identifying and characterizing a creative economy and second in trying to draw out the main implications.

Much of this conceptual work was undertaken by experts outside the DCMS: advisors, consultants and, of course, think tanks. Two important steps should be noted.

First, a leap was made from a mere list of creative industries to an attempt to conceptualize the creative economy. That is to say, after years of operating with a more or less arbitrary and non-differentiated list of creative industries, the CEP experts suggested grouping the industrial sectors into three categories: production, services and arts. At the same time, a group inside the DCMS agreed that, in fact, there were no adequate or reliable data on the creative industries. Ironically, this happened after years of insisting that the 'creative sector' had an economic importance equal to that of the financial sector.

Second, in a more radical step, a first elaborate conceptualization of the 'creative economy' was finally produced. This came in the report *Staying Ahead: The Economic Performance of the UK's Creative Industries*, published in June 2007 and written by members of the Work Foundation with the sponsorship of the Secretary of State for Culture, Media and Sport. The title of the report, *Staying Ahead*, reflects the widespread obsession with competitiveness: the desire to maintain the cultural and linguistic advantages already gained by the UK.

It is also relevant to note the publication, just a few months before *Staying Ahead*, of the significant report written for the European Commission entitled *The Economy of Culture in Europe* (KEA European Affairs, 2006). The main author of this study observed in a discussion that the use of the word 'culture' was not fortuitous. Clearly, at that time, the label 'creativity' was not acceptable to the European Commission as a mobilizing idea. Notwithstanding the terminological differences, there was a conceptual convergence between the two reports regarding the fundamental role fulfilled by culture in the generation of wealth.

According to *Staying Ahead* (Work Foundation, 2007), we need to radically rethink the functioning of the economy, reimagining it as a figure composed of concentric circles. In this new model, the cultural fields – the fruit of expressiveness – are at the core, followed by the cultural industries, then the creative industries and finally the rest of the economy. It is an invitation to imagine that the fundamental dynamic of the economy might come from 'cultural creativity'. This project and its imaginary are actively seeking adherents around the globe.

In the UK, however, as elsewhere, this particular framing of the creative economy has sometimes been met with scepticism and resistance, even within government. The DCMS's project encountered reservations on the part of the DTI and the Treasury. In fact, even within the DCMS, the Work Foundation vision was not accepted because it was considered too radical and critical of current public policies, in a clear example of the limits to the influence of think tanks when civil servants oppose a proposal.

The *Creative Britain: New Talents for the New Economy* report (February 2008) subsequently produced by the DCMS turned out to be a compilation of public policies without any underlying integrative or strategic conception. In some respects, this was the last of a particular sequence of reports, and in many ways it marked the high watermark of official thinking regarding the creative industries, as attention subsequently shifted into addressing the impact of the digital revolution and the key role of intellectual property in the creative economy. By that stage, in any case, as the groundwork had been done, the set of concerns outlined above had become so naturalized in the dominant discourse that it easily made the transition, post-New Labour, into the everyday framing of policy by the Conservative-Liberal Democrat Coalition government that took office in May 2010.

Notes

1. This chapter was originally written in Spanish in 2008 as a plenary lecture for a hispanophone readership, and it was later revised for publication in 2010. The present text is a lightly revised version of the chapter published in Luis A. Albornoz (ed.) *Poder, Medios, Cultura: Una mirada crítica desde la economía política de la comunicación* (Buenos Aires: Paidós, 2011). Both expository and critical in intent, this contribution was above all meant to convey to an international readership some of the background of the well-known UK contribution to the creative economy debate. Faced with its unexpected and republication in English translation, the choice has been either to try to update and develop what has been said or to leave it largely as it is and smooth the inevitable wrinkles that are evident after such a lapse of time. As much of the detail will be unfamiliar to some readers, and the overall argument doubtless unknown to even more, I am content to let this chapter speak for itself. It reminds us of how we have arrived at where we are now. For those who wish to read it, my subsequent work on this theme is readily available. See, for instance, Schlesinger (2009b), Schlesinger and Waelde (2012) and Schlesinger (2013).
2. The referendum on Scottish independence held on 18 September 2014 was the catalyst for wider recognition of fundamental faults in the UK's wider constitutional framework. How these will, or will not, be resolved is another matter.

References

Adorno, Theodor W. (1991) *The Culture Industry*, London: Routledge.

Bauman, Zygmunt (1992) *Intimations of Postmodernity*, London and New York: Routledge.

Bell, Daniel (1974) *The Coming of Post-Industrial Society*, London: Heinemann Educational Books.

Bourdieu, Pierre (1977) *Outline of a Theory of Practice*, Cambridge: Cambridge University Press.

DCMS (Department of Culture, Media and Sport) (1998) *Creative Industries Mapping Document*, London: Department for Culture, Media and Sport.

—— (2008) *Creative Britain: New Talents for the New Economy*, London: Department of Culture, Media and Sport.

Florida, Richard (2002) *The Rise of the Creative Class*, New York: Basic Books.

—— (2005) *The Flight of the Creative Class*, New York: Harper Collins.

Garnham, Nicholas (2005) 'From Cultural to Creative Industries: An Analysis of the Implications of the "Creative Industries" Approach to Arts and Media Policy Making in the United Kingdom', *International Journal of Cultural Policy*, 11(1), 15–29.

Gouldner, Alvin (1979) *The Future of Intellectuals and the Rise of the New Class*, London: The Macmillan Press Ltd.

Gramsci, Antonio (1971) *Selections from the Prison Notebooks*, London: Lawrence & Wishart.

HM Treasury (2005) 'The Cox Review of Creativity in Business: Building on the UK's Strengths', London: HM Treasury.

Jowell, Tessa (2005) Keynote Speech at the Creative Economy Conference, 5–7 October, London. Available at www.egovmonitor.com.

KEA European Affairs (2006) *The Economy of Culture in Europe*, prepared for the European Commission, Directorate General for Education and Culture, Brussels. Available at http://ec.europa.eu.

Roberts, Paul (2006) *Nurturing Creativity in Young People: A Report to Government to Inform Future Policy*, London: Department of Culture, Media and Sport.

Robinson, Ken (Chairman) (1999) *All Our Futures: Creativity, Culture and Education*, Report of the National Advisory Committee on Creative and Cultural Education, London: DCMS/DfEE.

Schlesinger, Philip (2007) 'Creativity: From Discourse to Doctrine', *Screen*, 48(3), 377–387.

—— (2009a) 'Creativity and the Experts: New Labour, Think Tanks and the Policy Process', *The International Journal of Press/Politics*, 14(1), 3–20.

—— (2009b) 'The SNP, Cultural Policy and the Idea of the "Creative Economy" ', in Hassan, G. (ed.) *The Modern SNP: From Protest to Power*, Edinburgh: Edinburgh University Press, 135–146.

—— (2013) 'Expertise, the Academy and the Governance of Cultural Policy', *Media, Culture & Society*, 35(1), 27–25.

Schlesinger, Philip and Waelde, Charlotte (2012) 'Copyright and Cultural Work: An Exploration', *Innovation: The European Journal of Social Science Research*, 25(1), 11–28.

UNCTAD (United Nations Conference on Trade and Development) (2008) *Creative Economy Report 2008. The Challenge of Assessing the Creative Economy towards Informed Policy-Making*, Geneva: UNCTAD.

Work Foundation (2007) *Staying Ahead: the Economic Performance of the UK's Creative Industries*, London: The Work Foundation.

4
Cultural Industries, Creative Economy and the Information Society

Gaëtan Tremblay

A decade has passed since Tony Blair's New Labour popularized the notion of 'creative industries', an expression that some analysts and commentators do not hesitate to use as a substitute for the concept of cultural industries. Advocates of an economic strategy based on developing 'creative industrial sectors' have gradually started talking of a 'creative economy'. Taken up by technocrats from several countries, and even by the UN, this approach has rapidly spread. In April 2008 the United Nations Conference on Trade and Development (UNCTAD) published a document aimed at measuring the degree of development of the creative economy in all regions of the world: *Creative Economy Report 2008. The Challenge of Assessing the Creative Economy: towards Informed Policy-Making*.

As Garnham (2005) and Schlesinger (2007) have amply demonstrated, the origin of the concept of 'creative industries' is essentially political. It serves as a description of the desire to reposition the UK economically in an increasingly globalized world, and is an attempt to identify those sectors on which to base the new competitiveness of the UK economy *vis-à-vis* its international competitors. Since it was first formulated in the late 1990s, the creative industry approach has shown a distinguishing strategy: 'The pursuit of a creativity policy became a national project, "branding" the UK as at the global cutting-edge' (Schlesinger, 2007).

The use of this concept would spread rapidly through technocratic and academic circles. A large number of symposia and reports would

---

A first version of this chapter was published in 2008 in the Canadian edition of *Global Media Journal* 1(1) under the title 'Industries culturelles, économie créative et société de l'information'.

contribute to its national and international dissemination; and this distinguishing strategy was widely shared because, as UNCTAD fervently claims, creativity is a characteristic of every human being, and all societies are equally endowed with it.

In a globalized world, where standardizing forces are powerfully present, the economy of creativity would appear to lead us in one sense towards a new international division of labour founded on the cultural specificities of each country and even each region. The economic policy of creativity combines harmoniously with the cultural policy of diversity. This approach inevitably asks questions of scholars interested in the cultural industries, since these appear to be included in the notion of 'creative industries', despite the vagueness of its definition. What does this new creativity-based paradigm mean for the analysis of cultural and media industries? How are these creative sectors defined? What characterizes this so-called 'creative' economy? Where does it fit with other attempts to grasp the contemporary economy, also recently referred to as the 'information economy' or 'knowledge economy'? Is it necessary to revise the culture industry theory formulated by the Frankfurt School in the post-war period, then taken up again in the 1970s and further developed by scholars of communication science?

This chapter analyses the available data and the arguments surrounding these issues. After reviewing the broad lines of the culture industry theory, we locate this 'new model' in relation to the various attempts to name and interpret the changes affecting industrial societies since the end of the Second World War: from Daniel Bell and Alain Touraine's 'post-industrial society', to UNESCO's 'knowledge society'. We then move on to a critical examination of the definitions and assessments of the creative industries. Finally, we try to interpret the underlying reasons for promoting this new version of the information society ideology.

Culture industry theory

The expression 'culture industry' was coined by Theodor W. Adorno and Max Horkheimer ([1947] 1974) in response to the threats posed by the application of industrial reproduction techniques to the creation and mass dissemination of cultural works. In two radio lectures given in 1962, Adorno revealed that in their early research he and Horkheimer used the term 'mass culture' and then later abandoned it in favour of the expression 'culture industry' to avoid any implication 'that it is a matter of something like a culture that arises spontaneously from the masses themselves, the contemporary form of popular art. From the latter the culture industry must be distinguished in the extreme' (Adorno, 1964).

It is important not to lose sight of the context of the origin of the expression. In 1947, Adorno and Horkheimer proceeded to carry out a critical analysis of the standardization of contents and the predominant pursuit of the effect resulting from the application of industrial reproduction techniques to cultural creation. As Adorno (1964) clearly states, the analysis did not specifically address production processes:

> Thus, the expression 'industry' is not to be taken too literally. It refers to the standardization of the thing itself – such as that of the *Western,* familiar to every moviegoer – and to the rationalization of distribution techniques, but not strictly to the production process.

Immediately after the Second World War, Adorno noted that cinema was one of the few sectors of cultural production in which capital investment and the division of labour attained an advanced form. Many other sectors were still characterized by craft production, in which the individualization of the work still retained its full importance.

The concept of culture industry took shape, then, in a context marked by the emergence of the mass media, as an attempt to critically analyse the standardization of contents and the pursuit of the effect which – according to the Frankfurt School theorists – was at the antipodes of what a work of art essentially is.

For the theorists of the Frankfurt School the application of industrial methods in the field of culture would lead to the death of art. While this current of thinking still has its adherents, the expression 'cultural industries' – which became widely used during the 1970s and 1980s – no longer necessarily evokes that catastrophic prospect. After all, it can hardly be argued that the meteoric development of the cultural industries since the last quarter of the nineteenth century has been accompanied by the disappearance of creative work in the different sectors of artistic practice. On the contrary, never have the conventions and canons of artistic creation been as frequently reconsidered as since the end of the nineteenth century, and new languages of expression have appeared as never before in history since the beginning of the Industrial Revolution. If we think about the field of painting alone, for example, we observe that since the beginning of the nineteenth century, new approaches and schools have followed on from one another at an accelerated pace: Impressionism, Fauvism, Cubism, Abstractionism, Constructivism, Surrealism, Hyperrealism, Pop Art and so on. While it is true that cultural mass production has developed considerably, it is no less true that creative pursuit has developed in parallel. Not only has art not disappeared since the advent of industrialization but it has witnessed a renewed ebullience, so much so that we might ask whether industrialization has not in fact stimulated creativity.

When the concept of the 'cultural industries' emerged towards the end of the 1970s, the context had, of course, evolved profoundly. New media were seen to develop, with TV at the forefront, and there was a marked emphasis on the commercialization of culture. The connotations of the term 'culture industry' changed. First it was used in the plural – 'cultural industries' – before the singular, and referred to a multiplicity of economic sectors rather than a single process. Second, the catastrophic emphasis – the end of artistic creation – and nostalgia faded to give way to a more economic-style analysis. Finally, attention came to focus mainly on production processes.

The work of Huet et al. (1978) presents the research studies conducted since the early 1970s, which mark a shift in focus on the subject. Flichy (1980), for his part, is representative of the new direction taken in the area of research. The attitude of outrage towards the invasion of industrial methods into the field of culture gave way to detached sociological observation: although mythologized to some extent, artists do not live outside of this world and they are subject to the social and economic adversities that characterize the society in which they evolve. The task of scholars was to clarify the particularities of capitalist economic expansion in this new field of valorization. Nevertheless, the critical perspective had not changed; what had changed was the problematic framework: it had gone from being ethical-philosophical to socioeconomic.

The project carried out by Huet and his colleagues was two-fold. It aimed, first, to demonstrate that the field of culture and communication is not exempt from the basic rules of capitalist economics; and, second, to identify the particularities that occur in the commercialization and industrialization processes of the various productive sectors that can and must be distinguished – including amateur photography, new audiovisual products, recordings and editions and so forth.

Situating himself in this tradition that prioritized the analysis of production processes, Flichy proceeded to investigate industrial structures and the strategies used by actors from the different branches of the audiovisual sector, in which he discerned two broad types of organization of production and circulation: product production and flow production. Some years later, Miège et al. (1986) took up this distinction and systematized it into a typology of logics that structure the culture and communication sector. The works of Bustamante and Zallo (1988), Miguel de Bustos (1993) and our own (Tremblay, 1990; Tremblay and Lacroix, 1991) were to complete this systematization effort.

A report published by UNESCO (1982), following a meeting held in Montreal in 1980, proposed the following definition of cultural industries:

> Generally speaking, a cultural industry is held to exist when cultural goods and services are produced, reproduced, stored and distributed on industrial and commercial lines, that is to say on a large scale and in accordance with a strategy based on economic considerations rather than any concern for cultural development.
>
> (UNESCO, 1982)

According to Ramón Zallo (1988), the UNESCO definition presents two difficulties. First, it is subjective, since it refers to the intention of producers and distributors, who are only interested in the economic aspects of production, at the expense of cultural value. Numerous film-makers and producers of TV programmes, among others, would disagree with such a formulation. No one can doubt the existence of both cultural and economic motivations. It is the presence of capital and of the mechanization and division of labour, and not the intentions of the creators, which determines whether a production is industrial in nature or not. Second, mass production appears to exclude the mass dissemination of a work from the field of industrialization. To put it another way, when it comes to culture, industrialization can make use of two forms of distribution: the reproduction of individual copies from an original (manuscript, master, zero copy, etc.) and dissemination via the appropriate networks of a single copy able to be captured by thousands of receivers.

Dissatisfied with the UNESCO definition, Zallo put forward another definition of cultural industries, aimed at coherently organizing the set of activities and products resulting at the same time from a creative work, a process of capital valorization and mass consumption, and which, unlike other products, fulfil an ideological and social function:

> Cultural industries are here understood to mean a set of industrial branches, segments and ancillary activities that produce and distribute goods with symbolic content, designed through creative work,

> organized by self-valorizing capital and ultimately aimed at consumer markets, with an ideological and social reproduction function.
>
> (Zallo, 1988)

In an attempt to consider the diversity of the cultural industries and the varying degree to which they have been integrated into commercial and industrial logics, we have proposed a definition of cultural industries that distinguishes commercialization from industrialization, at the same time as it highlights the progressive nature of the industrialization process and emphasizes the capitalist relationship between cultural workers and the products they create:

> Cultural industries can therefore be defined as the continually evolving set of cultural production and exchange activities subject to the rules of commercialization, in which industrial production methods are developed to a greater or lesser degree, but in which work is increasingly organized according to the capitalist model of a dual separation between the producer and their product, between the tasks of creation and execution. This dual process of separation results in an increasing loss of control by workers and artists over the fruits of their labour.
>
> (Tremblay, 1990)

This definition insists on the fact that the processes of commercializing and industrializing culture are not finished, and that they are constantly undergoing profound transformations. In particular, culture is being extended, deepened and reorganized, as we shall see further on, becoming integrated into the information and communication sectors. The definition also recognizes that this is a specific economic field comprising activities that are still very heterogeneous. It is necessary to explain, therefore, what that specificity and heterogeneity consists of.

Scholars usually acknowledge that the cultural industries display characteristics that when considered individually may be found in other industrial sectors, but when considered together are only to be found in this sector whose particular profile they collectively make up. Zallo (1988) divides them into three groups: (a) the importance of creative work; (b) the requirement to constantly renew products; and (c) the random nature of the demand. We could also mention: (d) a certain non-elasticity of demand; (e) a greater variety of forms of labour remuneration in comparison with other industrial sectors; (f) a dual articulation between the hardware and content industries; and (g) the particularities of consumption in the area of culture (Miège et al., 1986; Tremblay, 1990).

Any cultural work, even if it is produced industrially, involves a degree of creative work at the outset. However, in spite of advances in IT, the creation process is still a long way from being mechanized. This is a random process that is impervious to systematization and control, even if a certain division of labour and monitoring mechanisms have developed in some economic sectors – as in cinema and TV, for example. Given the difficulties of integration into the industrial logic that the creative process faces, large firms often prefer to leave that part of the production process in the hands of smaller companies, with the inherent risks that this implies. The importance of creation in the production of cultural works has another implication. It gives rise to the setting up of publishing and production houses whose main functions consist in establishing an interface between creators and industries, and editing the content of the selected works.

The market for culture requires constant and accelerated product renewal. Of course, there are certain works – termed 'classics' – that enjoy a long life, but the majority of cultural products experience rapid obsolescence. Most books, CDs, films and TV programmes have a very short life. Due to the fact that culture is a never-ending process of redefining meaning, cultural productions must constantly face the demands of novelty and renewal.

Moreover, the market for culture is constantly unpredictable, which results in highly random demand. Despite the advances in opinion polls and marketing techniques, public tastes are hard to predict. It is possible to invest millions of US dollars in a film or TV series without having any guarantee of how the public will react to it. Of course, cultural entrepreneurs implement strategies to combat this uncertainty – creating a *star system*, developing and testing pilot programmes or reproducing tried and tested formulas – but they only manage to partially offset the risks inherent in the random nature of the demand.

The demand is uncertain but it is also relatively non-elastic. This point refers to the fact that cultural consumption depends on the amount of both time and income available. While the amount of time devoted to leisure, in general, and to the media, in particular, has increased significantly since 1945, it is also true that it reached its maximum level quite some time ago (Pronovost, 1996). Cinema and theatre admissions or the consumption of TV programmes do not depend only on price but are also subject to time available. This means that a reduction in prices does not necessarily translate, as it does in other economic sectors, into in an increase in consumption, and that an increase in cultural and media offerings does not usually give rise to an increase in the total consumption time, but instead increases the competition between products from different cultural sectors.

It should also be noted that the form of labour remuneration favoured in capitalist industries, the wage, is not as widespread across the cultural industries. Payment of a monthly salary was expanded, of course, to many technical, manufacturing and management jobs, but the particularities that underpin the creative process mean that other formulas are employed, such as economic remuneration in the form of royalties or fees (Lacroix, 1990). It can be stated too that the current trend is towards a reduction in regular employment – and consequently in salaries – in favour of underemployment or the so-called 'self-employed' work.

The cultural industries also have the particularity of simultaneously needing media devices and contents. Strictly speaking, the cultural industries as such are those related to content: production and distribution of books, newspapers, CDs, programmes, films, radio or TV broadcasts, and so on. The media device industries – such as the manufacturing of TVs, video players, cameras, disc readers, disc pressing or book printing – are little different from manufacturing industries, like the automobile or household appliance industries. However, in the field of culture, the evolution of the media device and content industries are closely linked. The two are too interdependent to allow a theory of cultural industries to be separated from the media device industry. For example, the particularities and capabilities of transmission networks, video compression techniques, high-definition TV or the digitization of signals are all phenomena that condition the design and production of content.

Finally, cultural consumption is distinguished by the fact that it does not necessarily involve the appropriation of an individual copy by the consumer; besides, the act of consumption does not necessarily destroy the work. Consumption in the field of culture is more of a question of access – availability – and of sharing than of individual material appropriation. This characteristic enables a two-fold form of commercialization and industrialization: the first is a matter of material reproduction; the second involves the use of communication networks.

The availability of cultural products occurs in different forms, which reflect the relationships between content and media device. In some cases, consumers are offered an individual copy of the work – when a CD, book or newspaper is sold, for example. In other cases a single work is disseminated on a mass scale, as in the case of radio and TV broadcasting. A third possibility is the circulation of a reduced number of copies accessible via a limited number of specialist points on payment of an entry fee. Flichy (1980) proposed calling the production and distribution processes that characterize the first and third forms the editorial model and those that characterize the second form the flow model. However, the widespread use of personal recording devices later came to complicate this bipolar typology. With a level of quality that comes close to that offered by manufacturers, consumers can produce their own copies of a distributed product with increasing ease. A digital player recording a digital piece of music, for example, can produce a similar result to that of a compact disc. Here we have a curious situation in which industrial reproduction encourages the participation of consumers equipped with reproduction devices – a quite singular case of industrialization that poses specific problems (e.g. with regard to the payment of copyright fees).

The information society and the creative economy

The idea of an 'information society', which dates back four decades now, emerged from the continuous efforts undertaken in the post-Second World War period to interpret the structural changes that disrupt advanced industrial societies. From the late 1960s on, some economists, sociologists and other scholars acquired the belief that North American and Western European societies were undergoing profound transformations that were taking them into a new phase of economic development. The sociologists Touraine (1969) and Bell (1973) are regarded as the forerunners of such thinking on the emergence of postindustrial societies, but the economist Fritz Machlup (1962) preceded them when it came to demonstrating the importance of knowledge and education in the functioning of twentieth-century economies, presented by Touraine and Bell as among the main elements that define postindustrial societies. Indeed, according to these theorists, the societies that emerged in the 1950s in the USA, Germany and Japan, and some years later in Canada and other countries of Western Europe, are characterized essentially by:

- the growth of the service sector, which replaces the manufacturing sector as the main area of labour concentration;
- the centrality of information and knowledge as factors of production;
- the increase in productivity, thanks to innovation;
- the emergence of new technical elites and new principles of social stratification.

The 'information society' gradually imposed itself as the most commonly used term among a set of more or less equivalent labels that were competing with each other: knowledge society, postmodern society, society of abundance, consumer society, network society, informational capitalism, digital capitalism and so on. No doubt 'information society' won out over the other names proposed because it appeared to be, on the one hand, more encompassing than those that refer more specifically to economics and, on the other, more ideologically 'neutral' than those with neo-Marxist connotations.

The numerous visionaries of the information society include authors who have achieved considerable renown, such as the economists Marc Porat (1977) and Jeremy Rifkin (2000), the futurologist Alvin Toffler (1980), the essayist Howard Rheingold (2000) and the sociologist Manuel Castells (1998, 1999a, 1999b), who provided a masterful synthesis with his trilogy on the information age.

There are several versions of information society model, which diverge and even contradict each other on more than one point. For Rifkin (2000), for example, the advent of the network society led to a widespread commercialization – 'hypercapitalism' – based less on ownership, production and the market than on access, marketing and consumption. For Castells (1998, 1999a, 1999b), however radical the change, it is no more than a new form of capitalism: 'informational capitalism'. For his part, Rheingold (2000) places the emphasis on creativity and the world of the virtual; and the legal scholar Lawrence Lessig (2004) fights for freedom of access. Nevertheless, regardless of the various emphases and differences in these multiple incarnations, the information society model has been formed around a core of values that serve both as a basis and as an aim: the horizontality of relations in a network organization; the unlimited potential of digital technology; freedom of creation and access; internationalism; diversity of viewpoints and cultures; knowledge sharing; and democratization.

The postindustrial society model, according to those who invented it, was geographically and historically situated: it was the birthright of the more industrially advanced societies in North America, Western Europe and Japan. And it was situated in a temporal continuity, in which the traditional rural model was succeeded by an urban industrial model and, finally, a postindustrial model. For its part, the information society model is presented as the heir to the postindustrial model, of which it is the most precise and highly developed formulation. But it is not geographically circumscribed: all the countries on the planet, regardless of their level of development, are invited to subscribe to it, as proclaimed at the World Summit on the Information Society (WSIS) organized by the UN and the International Telecommunication Union in 2003 and 2005. The information society is not just a stage of development but an objective to be reached. Of course, even superficial observation reveals inequalities in equipment, access and financial and human resources. These inequalities are obstacles on the path to the information society that demonstrate the possibility or the existence of a 'digital divide', which must be prevented or eliminated.

The information society model is proposed as a global vision of the changes under way. To an extent it is presented as the culmination of two patterns of categorizing social evolution: one very anthropological and the other more socioeconomic. The first, starting from a criterion that is sociocultural in nature, establishes a succession that includes primitive myth-based societies, tradition-based societies, modern societies built on the principles of rationality and postmodern societies that rest on the relativity of value systems. The second system emphasizes the structural patterns of economic organization: from harvest to agriculture, industrialization and then, finally, postindustrialization. The information society thus appears to be an attempt to amalgamate postindustrial and postmodern society. A consequence of the considerable progress made on transport and communication-related issues, it is seen as inaugurating a new model of economic production, social regulation and cultural life.

The creative economy model is in line with the theories developed to explain the changes that have characterized advanced industrial societies since the mid-twentieth century. The concepts of technological change (particularly those resulting from digitization), innovation, information, networks, knowledge and life-long learning, always retain a prime role. This model demonstrates the same synthesizing intention:

> This concept of 'creative economy' is gaining ground in contemporary thinking about economic development. It entails a shift from the conventional models towards a multidisciplinary model dealing with the interface between economics, culture and technology and centred on the predominance of services and creative content.
>
> (UNCTAD, 2008)

Obviously, the centrality of 'creation' and 'creativity' proves to be something of a novelty.

In the conclusions to a work on cultural industries and the information society published in a series of monographs in *Current Sociology* in 1997, Jean-Guy Lacroix and I affirmed the emblematic and paradigmatic value of information, culture and communication industries in the development of contemporary capitalism. Those tempted to see a prefiguring of the creative economy will on reading this extract note that the dissemination of the characteristics of cultural production that we observed was not limited to just the linear projection of 'creativity':

> The information and cultural industries, given the real or potential growth potential they show or that we expect, are perceived as the main engine of economic development for the future 'information societies'. These are presented, in the official discourse, as the standards and models to follow in order to overcome the current crisis. They are the 'leading-edge' sectors that will ensure the revitalization of the entire economic fabric. In this sense, we can talk of the paradigmatic and emblematic value of these industries. But we see also other meanings for this value.
>
> It increasingly spreading its law towards the sectors of culture, information and communication, the commercial and industrial logic is looking to conquer new social spaces. The integration into the commercial and industrial logic of sectors of activity with such particular characteristics is, through a boomerang effect, causing a series of transformations in the way other sectors of the economy function, not to mention the functioning of capitalism itself. In addition to generalities about the new information economy and the aberrations in the replacement of capital by knowledge, we believe it is necessary to carry out a detailed analysis of the extent to which the current reorganization of the economic sphere is leading, at least in part, to a greater integration of culture, information and communication into the capitalist universe. The skills now required of workers and the new working conditions imposed on them in various sectors of the economy are strangely similar to those that have long dominated in the culture and communication sectors: creativity, product quality, flexibility and versatility, imagination and a significant degree of novelty, but also job precariousness. Can it be deduced that at that same time that capitalism is integrating cultural and communication activities into its logic, it becomes 'contaminated' by what characterizes them? Are the collective forms of labour organization currently emerging inspired by the cultural sector? Could it be that salaried work, the typical form of Fordism so characteristic of capitalism might in the era of Gatesism be giving way to more precarious

pay formulas typical of the cultural sector? Is it therefore necessary to interpret the process of commercialization and industrialization of culture and communications as a complex dialectical movement that at the same time includes: 1) the integration of cultural and communicational activities into the commercial and industrial sphere; 2) a redefinition of the rules of production resulting from this integration; 3) the spreading of cultural sector characteristics to the majority of economic production as a whole; and 4) a dilution, concomitant to that spread, of the specificity and density of the fields of culture and communication?

(Lacroix and Tremblay, 1997)

Evaluation and criticism of the creative economy

Creation is a human activity whose inner workings remain mysteriously hidden; and creativity[1] is a potentiality that is universally distributed but little known.[2] Clearly, the multiple definitions of the creative industries seek to regroup the activities in which creativity plays a prime role. This is no simple task, since these activities extend far beyond the artistic and cultural sectors. The *Creative Industries Mapping Document* (*CIMD*), published by the UK's Department for Culture, Media and Sport in 1998 and updated in 2001, lists as many sectors traditionally identified as cultural – cinema, music, radio, TV, performing arts and publishing – as other sectors, less recognized as being cultural, in which creativity is deemed to be an essential component: advertising, architecture, crafts, design, fashion, videogames, software and the antiques trade. Why restrict the list to these areas? The reasons are not clear. For their part, the authors of the UNCTAD report, who acknowledge the existence of a multiplicity of definitions, willingly concede that the creative economy is broadly speaking a subjective concept and its definition a work in progress. The list of activities included in the UNCTAD report is significantly different from that of the *CIMD*.

If the definition of the field of creative industries includes, but goes beyond, the cultural industries, then taking into consideration the economic weight of the different activities leads to an even greater dissociation between the two universes. As can be seen in Figure 4.1, the 'Software & Computer Services' and 'Design' sectors account for a much greater proportion of GDP than the sum of 'Publishing', 'Television & Radio', 'Music', 'Film & Video' and 'Performing Arts'. In fact, the activities not traditionally identified with the cultural industries make up over 65 per cent of the total income of the creative industries.

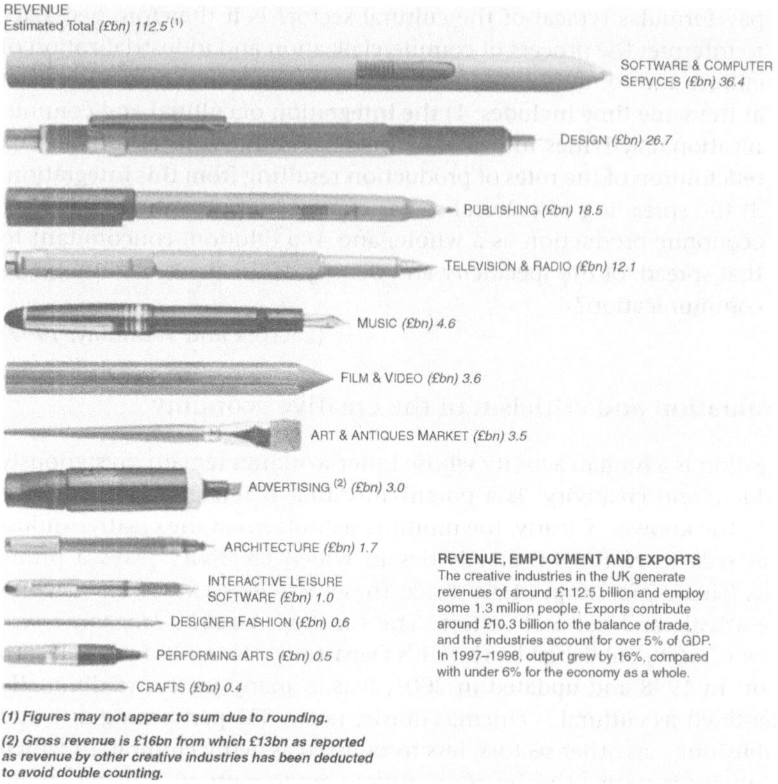

Figure 4.1 Creative industry sectors according to the *CIMD*
Note: The original figure is in this link – see page number 10: https://www.gov.uk/government/uploads/system/uploads/attachment_data/file/183544/2001part1-foreword2001.pdf.
Source: *CIMD* (UK, 2001, p. 10).

Consequently the cultural industries account for scarcely a third of the creative industries.

The inclusion in the same universe of cultural and other industries, such as 'Software and Computer Services' and 'Design', presents a dual advantage. On the one hand, it allows all the activities concerned to benefit from the prestige that surrounds the work of artists; on the other, it makes it possible to achieve an exceptional business volume and growth rate, attributable mainly to the world of software and that of videogames. The much-vaunted creativity can thus be proclaimed to be the main engine of the economy.

Lumping together various activities under the umbrella of the creative industries has another advantage: it extends the demands made by the cultural industries with regard to intellectual property recognition and regulatory intervention by the state in all the activities involved. As Nicholas Garnham (2005) points out, the creative industries approach enables an alliance to be formed between the huge industry of IT and media producers and small cultural producers and creators with the aim of strengthening copyright protection.

> In the *Mapping Document* the term 'creative' was chosen so that the whole of the computer software sector could be included. Only on this basis was it possible to make the claims about size and growth stand up. However this inclusion had two valuable policy consequences for the interests involved. It enabled software producers and the major publishing and media conglomerates to construct an alliance with cultural workers, and with small-scale entrepreneurs, around a strengthening of copyright protection.
>
> (Garnham, 2005)

The last section of the UNCTAD report, dedicated to the initiatives to promote the creative economy, does not hesitate to take up arguments that are usually invoked to justify the intervention of public authorities in artistic and cultural matters.

From the creation of a new sector, that of the creative industries, we rapidly moved on to the proclamation of a new economy, the 'creative economy', in which creative activities and products play a key role. It was thus claimed, somewhat tautologically, in the UNCTAD report (2008) that 'the creative industries are at the heart of the creative economy'. In order to demonstrate that US society had become an information society, Porat (1977) added some data on different job categories labelled as 'information processing'. Effectively this meant that statisticians, journalists, telephonists, teachers, scientists, computer specialists and others were classified under the same title. It is clear, however, that although all of these occupations are related in some way to information, they are quite different from one another.

The evaluation of the creative industries rests on a use and interpretation of statistical data that is even more dubious. The surprising (read aberrant) results arrived at by the authors of the UNCTAD report in their attempt to assess the size of the creative economy throughout the world

Table 4.1 Major exporting countries of creative products (2005)

Exporting countries	**All creative industries (in millions of US dollars)**
China	61,360
Italy	28,008
Territory of Hong Kong, China	27,677
USA	25,544
Germany	24,763
UK	19,030
France	17,706
Canada	11,377
Belgium	9,343
Spain	9,138

Source: Taken from UNCTAD (2008, pp. 260–263).

eloquently illustrate this point. Two examples are immediately apparent. First, the data used to identify the top ten countries that stand out due to the weight of their creative economies place China first on the list, by a long way (Table 4.1). It is not a matter here of challenging the creativity of the Chinese, which is no doubt equal to that of any other people on Earth, but rather of questioning the production and interpretation of the data on which such a conclusion is based. Did China and the territory of Hong Kong in fact export creative products worth more than the total of the values for the USA, Germany, the UK and France in 2005?

Observing other data (Table 4.2) allows us to understand why China ranks first among exporting countries in the creative economy.

The products traditionally considered as cultural, classified under the heading of 'Visual arts', 'Publishing', 'Music' and 'Audiovisual' (Table 4.2), do not account for more than about 25 per cent of all world exports, while 'New media' does not account for more than 3.59 per cent. Let us remember here that the category of 'Software & IT services', a different but related category to that of 'New media', was at the top of the *CIMD* list of UK exports.

Those products classified in the 'Design' category are the ones that make up the bulk of world exports of creative products, with a proportion close to two-thirds. However, this is a complex category that groups together no less than 139 different codes. The authors of the report adopted a relatively broad definition to identify creative products:

Table 4.2 Exports of creative products by economic groups in 2005 (in millions of US dollars)

	World total	Developed economies	Developing economies	Transition economies
All creative products	335,494	196,109	136,231	3,154
	100%	**100%**	**100%**	**100%**
Arts and crafts	23,244	9,118	13,881	137
	6.93%	**4.70%**	**10.19%**	**7.74%**
Audiovisual	664	592	55	2
	0.20%	**0.31%**	**0.04%**	**0.16%**
Design	218,173	112,595	102,413	1,735
	65.03%	**58.14%**	**75.18%**	**64.16%**
Music	14,924	13,424	1,412	63
	4.45%	**6.86%**	**1.04%**	**3.09%**
New media	12,035	6,471	5,508	50
	3.59%	**3.30%**	**4.04%**	**3.03%**
Publishing	44,304	36,593	6,567	1,096
	13.21%	**18.68%**	**4.82%**	**14.59%**
Visual arts	22,149	15,651	6,395	71
	6.60%	**8.00%**	**4.69%**	**7.22%**

Source: Taken from UNCTAD (2008, pp. 252–259).

> Given the complexity of making clear distinctions and defining the borderline between a creative good that is exclusive and mass production, between handmade and machine-made, between decorative and functional, etc., this exercise of compiling statistics for creative goods includes all the creative goods with the above characteristics since they fall under the criteria of the UNCTAD classification of 'the cycle of creation, production and distribution of a tangible product with creative content, economic and cultural value and a market objective'.
>
> (UNCTAD, 2008)

In response to this approach, we may legitimately ask what is hidden by the statistics produced by the different states and to what extent they might confuse creation with reproduction. If we take into consideration the relocation of Western companies in search of cheaper labour in recent decades, we may doubt the statistics used to measure creativity in the UNCTAD report. Should we consider mass reproductions, with or without a licence, of designs created elsewhere to be 'creative products'? If that is the case, then the very notion of the creative economy loses all meaning.

Table 4.3 The largest exporting countries of audiovisual products (2005)

Exporting countries	Audiovisual products (in millions of US dollars)
Canada	318
Italy	160
UK	29
USA	28
France	21
India	16
Mexico	11
Korea	10
Australia	10
Romania	9

Source: Taken from UNCTAD (2008, pp. 260–263).

Let's look at another surprising example of the results obtained by UNCTAD in assessing the weight of the creative economy: exports of audiovisual products. One would expect to find the list of exporting countries to be headed by India, the USA, Brazil, Mexico or Nigeria. Well, in fact, this is not the case. According to UNCTAD, Canada is the biggest world exporter of audiovisual products (Table 4.3). The surprise is even greater when we consider the amount of money at stake: in 2005, Canada apparently exported eleven times as many audiovisual products than the USA. When we know that Canadian screens are dominated by US movies, there is reason to be surprised. In fact, these statistics can only be understood if we take into account the movies and TV series that the Hollywood majors shoot in Canadian cities (Toronto, Montreal and Vancouver), attracted by competent and cheap technicians and advantageous tax measures. In the Canadian trade balance, these foreign productions, filmed on its soil, are counted as exports. While the statistics are correct from a solely economic standpoint, they are deceptive from a cultural standpoint, and questionable when used to measure the creative economy.

In the two examples given above, that of China in the case of design and that of Canada in the case of the audiovisual sector, the volume of exports can be attributed more to advantageous conditions of production – essentially cheap labour and accommodating tax regimes – than to the country's 'creative' capacity in the sector in question. The UNCTAD statistics clearly assess the capacity for reproduction rather than creativity. Paradoxically, they provide a much better illustration of the extent of an economy of reproduction rather than the emergence of a creative economy.

As a result, the model of creative economy developed in the UK can hardly be applied as is to all the countries on the planet. While it is correct to state that creativity is a human quality that is equally shared out, it is unclear that it is at the basis of economic development in all parts of the world. In fact, the definitions and statistics mentioned do not measure the same thing.

Why then seek to extend this model to the whole planet? What are the interests that motivate such an undertaking? Let us recognize the goodwill expressed, in the commotion of the WSIS in Geneva (2003) and Tunis (2005), regarding efforts to put an end to the digital divide existing between nations and to adopt the Convention on the Protection and Promotion of Diversity of Cultural Expressions (UNESCO, 2005). The desire to extend the creative economy model to the whole of the planet is part of this same ideological universe. But irrespective of good intentions, this initiative also aims to extend and strengthen the recognition of intellectual property and encourage different types of government to respect the payment of copyright – a strategy of inclusion designed to enforce the rules of the game even in those countries that reproduce much more than they create.

Conclusion

The data from the successive editions of the UK's *CIMD* (1998, 2001) and the UNCTAD report (2008) show that the cultural industries play a relatively limited part in the value of the so-called 'creative industries'. In the case of the *CIMD*, software and IT services constitute the driving force of the creative industries; in the case of the UNCTAD report, design fulfils the role of growth engine. Nevertheless, art and culture are at the heart of this ideological construction. Invoking creativity makes it possible to build bridges towards cultural activities, whose integration adds lustre and legitimacy to the creative industries as a whole. Above all, forging closer links with the cultural industries makes it possible to demand the same economic specificities that analysis has enabled us to pinpoint over the last four decades, and insist on the same protective interventions that the public authorities have implemented for years in the artistic and cultural sectors.

The notion of creativity also relates to innovation, a value central to the information society theories that make up the dominant general framework for interpreting the social change currently under way. While this operation appears to endow artists and cultural producers with a privileged status in these knowledge societies, it comes at the price of some misunderstanding, because the creativity and innovation imagined by their ideologues, technocrats and politicians are of a much more scientific than artistic and cultural order.

The ideological operation is therefore completely and ostensibly coherent, provided that we do not worry about satisfying abstract notions and are unconcerned about whether it conforms to reality. We have seen how different groups of actor, from software multinationals to small cultural producers, can find a common interest in pursuing strategic objectives, particularly with regard to intellectual property. But, from a scientific standpoint, what does this approach contribute?

A rigorous analysis does not take long to demonstrate the fragility of the ideological construction. At the theoretical level, the concept of the creative industries contributes absolutely nothing to the work on the cultural industries. Quite rightly, the importance of creation had already been recognized. And the extension of the models developed to explain the specificities of cultural production and dissemination to other activities – such as design, fashion or software – is not undertaken convincingly. A practical demonstration would therefore be necessary before trying to implement the same public protection and promotion measures enjoyed by the cultural industries in the creative industries.

Perhaps, as we suggested at the time (Lacroix and Tremblay, 1997), it would be useful and fruitful to investigate the dissemination of certain characteristics of the cultural sectors to the general economy in which they are embedded. But such an operation would require going further than mere labelling, carrying out a rigorous analysis of the conditions of creation, production and dissemination. The advocates of the creative industries do not appear to be remotely interested in research of this type.

From an empirical point of view, the literature on the creative industries is not at all convincing. Various economic activities require a creative form of work in some way. Why then take some sectors more into consideration than others? The selection criteria are not explicitly stated, the definitions are vague and the data used do not allow us in any way to assess the real economic value of creativity in the sectors involved.

Some will be pleased by the replacement of the cultural industries with the creative industries, as well as by the proposal to extend public authority intervention to new sectors of activity linked to digitization. They will see in the extension of the very logic of the cultural industries to the most dynamic sectors of the economy, based on the use of digital technologies, a 'culturization' of the economy, a return of the political – in other words, the end of a strictly 'economistic' vision of human affairs. Taken as a model to imitate, the cultural industries would see their social role recognized, their economic contribution valued, their state backing strengthened. Creativity – they would say – means to give power to imagination! This hypothesis, which rests, on the one hand, on the blind acceptance of methodologically dubious results, postulates, on the other hand, a non-existent ideological consensus. With regard to the role of the state, the UNCTAD document is at the antipodes of the UK's *CIMD*; while the former refers to the argument of meritorious goods and public service, the latter is content to recall the importance of education and respect for copyright.

From another standpoint, the amalgamation of the cultural and creative industries poses a potential danger: the dilution of the specificity of the cultural industries and the weakening of the arguments in favour of public authority intervention. For example, the concepts of public service and meritorious goods, already quite badly treated by neoliberalism in recent decades, run the risk of losing all credibility if attempts are made to extend their application to domains such as fashion or videogames. Once they have been discredited by unjustified demands, it will be increasingly difficult to fall back on these arguments to legitimize state intervention in the area of broadcasting, artistic production and cultural services. In short, it could ultimately result in a further integration of the cultural industries into the capitalist logic, rather than a problematic 'culturization' of the economy.

Notes

1. Advocates of the creative industries and the creative economy favour the use of the term 'creativity' over that of 'creation', giving the impression that they consider these terms to be interchangeable. The former alludes to a quality, a potentiality; and the latter makes reference to a process, a design and production activity. Substituting the former for the latter is to confuse potentiality with reality. This fashion inevitably reminds us of the enthusiasm some years ago for using the term 'interactivity' to evoke a potentiality of technology rather than actual interactions. Certainly, it is easier to discern possibilities than to analyse facts.
2. An earlier version of this section appeared under the title 'Creative Statistics to Support Creative Economy Politics' (see Tremblay, 2011).

References

Adorno, Theodor W. (1964) 'L'industrie culturelle', *Communications*, 3, Paris.

Adorno, Theodor W. and Horkheimer, Max ([1947] 1974) *La raison dialectique*, Paris: Gallimard.

Bell, Daniel (1973) *The Coming of Post-Industrial Society: A Venture in Social Forecasting*, New York: Harper Colophon Books.

Bustamante, Enrique and Zallo, Ramón (eds) (1988) *Las industrias culturales en España. Grupos multimedia y transnacionales*, Madrid: Akal.

Castells, Manuel (1998) *La société en réseaux. L'ère de l'information I*, Paris: Fayard.

—— (1999a) *Le pouvoir de l'identité. L'ère de l'information II*, Paris: Fayard.

—— (1999b) *Fin de millénaire. L'ère de l'information III*, Paris: Fayard.

Flichy, Patrice (1980) *Les industries de l'imaginaire: pour une analyse économique des médias* (2nd edition 1991), Grenoble: Presses Universitaires de Grenoble.

Garnham, Nicholas (2005) 'From Cultural to Creative Industries. An Analysis of the Implications of the "Creative Industries" Approach to Arts and Media Policy Making in the UK', *International Journal of Cultural Policy*, 11(1), 15–29.

Huet, Armel; Ion, Jacques; Lefèbvre, Alain; Miège, Bernard and Peron, René (1978) *Capitalisme et industries culturelles* (2nd edition 1991), Grenoble: Presses Universitaires de Grenoble.

Lacroix, Jean-Guy (1990) *La condition d'artiste: une injustice*, Montreal: VLB.

Lacroix, Jean-Guy and Tremblay, Gaëtan (1997) 'The Information Society and the Cultural Industries Theory', *Current Sociology Trend Report*, 45(4), 1–154. Available at http://csi.sagepub.com/content/45/4.toc.

Lessig, Lawrence (2004) *Free Culture*, New York: Penguin Press.

Machlup, Fritz (1962) *The Production and Distribution of Knowledge in the United States*, Princeton, NJ: Princeton University Press.

Miège, Bernard; Pajon, Patrick and Salaün, Jean-Michel (1986) *L'industrialisation de l'audiovisuel. Des programmes pour les nouveaux médias*, Paris: Aubier.

Miège, Bernard and Tremblay, Gaëtan (1999) 'Pour une grille de lecture du développement des techniques de l'information et de la communication', *Sciences de la société*, 47, 9–22.

Miguel de Bustos, Juan Carlos (1993) *Los grupos multimedia, estructuras y estrategias en los medios europeos*, Barcelona: Bosch.

Porat, Marc U. (1977) *The Information Economy: Definition and Measurement*, Washington, DC: Department of Commerce, USA.

Pronovost, Gilles (1996) *Sociologie du temps*, Brussels: De Boeck.

Rheingold, Howard (2000) *The Virtual Community: Homesteading on the Electronic Frontier*, London: MIT Press.

Rifkin, Jeremy (2000) *The Age of Access: The New Culture of Hypercapitalism*, New York: Putnam.

Schlesinger, Philip (2007) 'Creativity: From Discourse to Doctrine?' *Screen*, 48(3), 377–387.

Toffler, Alvin (1980) *La troisième vague*, Paris: Denoël.

Touraine, Alain (1969) *La société post-industrielle*, Paris: Denoël.

Tremblay, Gaëtan (ed.) (1990) *Les industries de la culture et des communications au Québec et au Canada*, Quebec: Presses de l'Université du Québec/Télé-Université.

—— (2011) 'Creative Statistics to Support Creative Economy Politics', *Media, Culture & Society*, 33, 289–298.

Tremblay, Gaëtan and Lacroix, Jean-Guy (1991) *Télévision: la deuxième dynastie*, Quebec: Presses de l'Université du Québec.
UK Department for Culture, Media and Sport (1998) *Creative Industries Mapping Document*, London: Department for Culture, Media and Sport, UK.
—— (2001) *Creative Industries Mapping Document*, London: Department for Culture, Media and Sport, UK.
UNCTAD (United Nations Conference on Trade and Development) (2008) *Creative Economy Report 2008: The Challenge of Assessing the Creative Economy Towards Informed Policy-Making*, Geneva: UNCTAD.
UNESCO (United Nations Educational, Scientific and Cultural Organization) (1982) *Cultural Industries. A Challenge for the Future of Culture*, Paris: UNESCO.
—— (2005) *Vers les sociétés du savoir*, Paris: UNESCO.
Zallo, Ramón (1988) *Economía de la comunicación y la cultura*, Madrid: Akal.

5
Creativity versus Culture?

Enrique Bustamante

The wave of 'creative industries' and all their multiple variables has seemed unstoppable in recent times. Enthusiastically promoted by the mass media, euphorically supported by right-wing neoliberal governments but also by quite a few social democrat administrations, endlessly built and rebuilt by a legion of trade consultants, though not without the blind complicity of certain opportunistic academic researchers, 'creativity' and its economy appear to have firmly and permanently established themselves as the new universal engine of development. One might even think that creativity had so far been absent from the evolution of humanity and that it had suddenly become the yardstick for every kind of progress imaginable.

The signal for the globalization of this 'new' economy seems to have come from the 2008 report by the United Nations Conference on Trade and Development (UNCTAD), as the impetus to internationalize what had until then been just an 'Anglo-Saxon' or, to be more precise, a Labour Party and above all British affair. At the hard core of this international expansion one might find the same consultants and authors who have made the leap from the UK market to the EU (KEA, European Affairs, 2006 report on the economy of culture in Europe) and then to the global scale. But this reading, although verifiable to some extent, would imply a conspiratorial interpretation that cannot be sustained in the complex dynamics of present-day society.

More reasonable and interesting is the reflection made by some authors on the change in the relationship between political power and intellectuals, which has shifted in our era from the scientific and academic milieu to the largely economistic and neoliberal world of consulting and think tanks (Schlesinger, 2008). But it should be noted that part of the university and academic world, certainly already stripped of prominence and downgraded in its critical function, now accompanies this and many other similar fashions, indiscriminately accepting appointments with consultants, prophets and gurus, and acritically jumping on the bandwagon of market trends – a perspective that calls for an updating of the research into the role of intellectuals in our society and, in particular, their critical function with regard to political and economic power.

The meteoric advent and capillary spread of this new creative trend are nevertheless impressive and can only be explained by the logic of acceleration imparted by the Internet. In Spain, for example, several regions that for decades had not even considered real studies or strategic plans on culture have commissioned studies or reports on the creative industries. These include the report *Industrias creativas*, by the European Business and Innovation Centre of Navarre, which forms part of the *Sectoral Ideas for the Twenty-First Century Series* (CEIN-Navarra, 2008), and the study sponsored by the Economic and Social Council (CES) of the Canary Islands, whose report and corresponding conferences concluded that the role of the public sector 'proves fundamental in supporting culture, by facilitating the liberalization of trade flows and avoiding all kinds of barriers that can hinder these flows' (CES-Canary Islands, 2009). On the other side of the Atlantic, too, there are numerous initiatives, such as the conversion of the prestigious Observatory of Cultural Industries (OIC) of the city of Buenos Aires into the Observatory of Creative Industries (also OIC), right at the time of Mauricio Macri's neoliberal government's coming to office in the city. The OIC now provides an endless stream of trivial and unconnected news items over the Internet, yet sponsored the first report on the city's 'creative economy' – with the support of the Ministry of Economic Development, through the significantly named Office of Creative Industries and Foreign Trade. And from Colombia comes news of the launch of a guide to producing regional mappings of the creative industries, with official support and the collaboration of the British Council. This is a small sample of the impact the 'new creative wave' has had among Ibero-American institutions. A multitude of local consulting firms has already sprung up to meet this demand.

All these documents and conferences bring together varying versions of the concept and its limits: some identify creative and cultural industries as synonyms; others identify culture with creativity or else just relate it to the economic concept of innovation; others still differentiate and single out culture as a minor subsector within the broader creative industries, whose variable borders never cease to expand, from design to advertising to creative R&D, to 'recreational' sectors, from hardware – networks, equipment – to IT software, to digital services of all kinds, including popular festivals. This is in line, moreover, with the UNCTAD (2008) definitions of 'any economic activity producing symbolic products with a heavy reliance on intellectual property and for as wide a market as possible'. Ultimately, as Schlesinger (2008) says, this term 'is not a true conceptualization of the creative industries but rather an official grouping of a few selected sectors'.

The topic that seems to be enjoying the greatest success in the university milieu is that of creative cities, coinciding with the dissemination of Richard Florida's books, which have been the subject of numerous congresses and seminars in Madrid and Barcelona – for example, in autumn 2009, where the term was taken to cover unforeseen domains, from music, cinema, literature or comics; and the city, to the city as a place to live, commute and do business or the city that is enterprising and innovative in industry, trade and economics. Not to be left behind, the Municipal Council of Cáceres and its right-wing government organized the Creative Cities Congress 'in the imagination society', where the mayoress – from the Partido Popular – affirmed the need for cities to have 'a dream'. This was a tough demand to make of the broad narrative of Spanish municipalities, plagued in recent years by waves of corruption cases, where a more apt economic concept might be that of 'destructive creativity' (see Mehlum et al., 2003), applied by economists to refer to situations in which mafia and parasites 'become more efficient at rent extraction', laying waste in the process to the productivity and sustainability of the economic system as well as the development of its societies.

The microterritorial context is, moreover, protected by international institutions. Following in the footsteps of the UNCTAD and the European reports, the Brussels Commission thus proposed that 2009 be declared European Year of Creativity and Innovation. For its part, the World Intellectual Property Organization (WIPO), which met in Geneva in October 2007, devoted its international conference to the creative industries, inextricably linked to copyright (see the final report by the Ibero-Latin-American Federation of Performers (FILAIE), 2007). And UNESCO itself, allegedly committed to implementing the Convention on the Protection and Promotion of the Diversity of Cultural Expressions (UNESCO, 2005), has demonstrated a willingness to revise the statistics on cultural exchange – hitherto scarcely representative, since they mix hardware with cultural content (see Buquet, 2008) – to protect the creative industries (see UNESCO/Global Alliance for Cultural Diversity, 2006). Given the sample of statistical results from the UNCTAD report, whose import–export balance in practice puts the mere assembly of equipment and products of all kinds before cultural creativity and its added value, a revision of UNESCO's statistical methodology is a pretty risky and unpredictable challenge.[1]

In conclusion, it can no doubt be stated that the 'creativity wave' that is washing over us is unstoppable and will enjoy resounding success for some time. In the context of the currently hegemonic conceptions of culture, this triumph does not have too great an importance. In terms of national accounts and employment, it will serve to unduly inflate the statistics on culture and the economy, just as the reports on the information economy did in the 1960s, by Fritz Machlup, and in the 1970s, by Marc Porat, among others, which exaggerated the weight of information in the economy. As in the case of 'everything-is-information', who could oppose 'everything-is-creativity' or humans beings being creative since the Neanderthals?

Also, as on that occasion, the concept of the 'creative economy' is so ambiguous and changeable that is can encompass all the industrial and commercial interests present in each institution or country. It is doubtful therefore that it may be of any practical utility even in industrial policies, beyond the legitimization of aberrations that have already been occurring, such as the inclusion by some governments of budgets to support theme parks and even water parks as part of the amount earmarked for culture, or the industrial and commercial bias of the reduced cultural policies. With regard to the statistics that come under this fluid concept, they will lack any firm empirical basis and will hardly be able to serve as tools on which to base public policy or private strategies.

In short, the fashion of the creative industries will pass in a few years, and once it has been exhausted it will probably be replaced by new advertising slogans. It is not dangerous in itself; the danger instead lies in its redundant and legitimizing effects in relation to longstanding trends: the dissolution of culture in the economy; the swing towards trade and profit within regulation and cultural policies; and the conception of diversity as a natural market effect, a process that had already been occurring for years and whose most notable consequences I will address further on. But in order to examine these consequences in depth it is necessary to review the terminological battles that have been taking place for at least three decades.

Cultural industries versus entertainment, creativity and 'digital content'

In an earlier text (Bustamante, 2009) I outlined in detail the opposing characteristics of the contemporary theory of culture and the cultural industries when compared with terms in vogue in different contexts and periods, such as 'entertainment industries' – a classic and enduring success in the USA – or others that are fleetingly fashionable and quickly outdated, such as 'information hypersector', 'copyright industries', 'intangible services' and 'digital content industry'. I will not repeat this argument therefore but will summarize the main conclusions here as a matter of course.

I began by recalling the genealogy of the concept and the development of the theory of the cultural industries to emphasize that both were from the outset characterized by being as pragmatic – in recognition of the industrial and commercial nature of their object – as they were empirical, on the basis that it was only by analysing reality that it could be known and changed, without ever losing their critical orientation on the most negative outcomes of capitalism. I pointed to the numerous studies on the capitalist concentration of the cultural industries – and its negative consequences for pluralism and diversity – on their value in terms of redistribution and participation in a capitalist society, on the defence of citizens/consumers, which culminated in the international recognition of the right of access to culture. I also briefly summarized the elements that distinguished classical culture from the cultural industries, as well as the deep ties that united them and that made up a specificity irreducible from the rest of the economy. In short, I situated the study of contemporary culture within the framework of political economy, since it easily overcomes the numerous errors and deviations – mediacentrism, eurocentrism – of the functionalist theory of communication.

This review of the terms that have been successively used as an alternative to 'cultural industries' is also revealing. First, that of entertainment industries, originating in the field of consulting but also established in the US university system for three decades at least, whose politically correct perimeters – never contemplating the erotic or pornographic content industry, despite its importance – mixes culture and the cultural industries with a variety of activities that have no more in common than the goal of 'entertainment' and their only vision as a business, without any compassion for the specificity of culture, without any role for the public sphere. As complementary versions there was the expansion to 'entertainment and leisure' by some societies of authors – such as the General Society of Authors and Publishers of Spain – or the fixation with 'copyright industries' (WIPO, Organisation for Economic Co-operation and Development (OECD)), whose undisguised aim was to focus exclusively on payment of copyright – to producers – forgetting and marginalizing culture that has fallen into the public domain or any cultural creation not subject to rights.

More recently we have seen the name 'content industries', presented by some of the media as denoting 'digital content', to better mark the allegedly absolute break between analogue and digital culture. Here, in view of the considerable range of empirical and critical studies conducted by cultural industry theory on the transformations in culture in terms of digital devices and networks – the catalysation of commercialization, concentration and transnationalization – with general restructuring of the culture of a single original into a cultural industry centred on mass reproduction, the name is elevated to 'digital content industries' – as though cultural content had not coexisted in digital networks and long done battle – over investments and efforts, monetary and consumer time budgets – with analogue content, as though creativity were born of networks and devices. From the insane perspective of these artificial cut-off points in the history of culture, the analyses of coexistence and struggle have been interpreted selectively by some new authors as the 'marginalization' of the role of digital culture.

By placing all the emphasis on the technological nature of the hardware (digital) and establishing that complete caesura between two worlds (this and the analogue one), some analysts at the same time legitimize the fusion of networks and software with 'content', and within that content they merge culture with any other commercial service originating on the Web, be it communicative (telebanking, tourism-related, pornographic) or simply relational (chat rooms, forums, search engines, prescribers). This is something similar to what was done by the fleeting advocates of the 'information hypersector', who, as is the case at present with the champions of the field of 'immaterial or intangible' services – usually telecommunications operators or big IT groups – sought to assimilate culture into networks and devices, cultural content into the container, so as to better reduce national and international regulations to the single rule of business and commercial competition. In short, digitization and digital conversion were pretexts for destroying any protection of democratic pluralism, any defence of the citizen. This is hardly a fortuitous confusion when one thinks about the fact that the EU tradition – in both the parliament and commission – has for two decades been precisely the rigorous defence of different regulation for networks and for cultural content, a differentiation that has begun to be eroded in recent years, as demonstrated by the text of the latest Television without Borders Directive of 11 December 2007.

However, the meteoric expansion of that sparkling new category of 'creativity industries', which tends to give rise to many other outgrowths (creative economy, creative firms, creative workers, creative countries) amicably intertwines with the entertainment, copyright and digital content industries in an amalgam of concepts that have a great deal in common and are therefore able to coexist and reinforce one another:

- Culture is subsumed into the general world of the economy, industry and trade, amputated of its social, solidarity and democratic facet. There is no place therefore for community culture, or for public service, or for a non-profit third sector.
- Citizens are regarded merely as participants in that economic endeavour, in relation to technology and in the service of companies, or as mere consumers. There is no room for unfettered creation, or for free exchange, and less still for the right to culture for all peoples and individuals.
- The concentration of culture and communication in the hands of large business groups does not constitute a serious threat to democratic pluralism and creative diversity but rather a great opportunity to defend 'our' culture and identity – national champions. Far from needing anti-trust regulation to protect us, what is advisable, in the best-case scenario, is a precaution *a posteriori* to safeguard competition from 'abuse of a dominant position'.
- Copyright is considered to be an inescapable rule that is to be defended with every weapon available – WTO sanctions, international regulations, legal sanctions, the pursuit of consumers – and likened to unlimited capitalist ownership in times and forms, without ever questioning the prices or abusive practices to which it gives rise, and without accepting even a minimal adaptation to the digital age.
- Given the economic weight, whether direct or indirect, of culture, public policies are passed on from ministries responsible specifically for culture to departments of trade and industry, which have little sympathy for the role of debut works, collective and associative cultures and non-patentable or exportable innovations.
- In the international arena, a tacit version of the free flow of trade once again predominates, aimed not only at creating wealth – all countries exporting creative products or services to one another – but also at ensuring its 'diversity', in terms of market. Neither exemption nor cultural exception have any meaning under this reign of

> free trade, where cultural cooperation – support for the presence in the world of industrially weaker cultures, egalitarian exchange and a real capacity for choice on the part of users – remains limited to the mutual sale of symbolic products. The UNESCO Convention on Diversity would thus become a mere diplomatic protocol of good intentions.

As I have written elsewhere,

> in fact, most of the texts devoted to defending these 'creative industries' (and the 'digital content' industries), mix together very heterogeneous elements in varying doses: they insist on individual (and not collective) effort, their combination with the new digital technologies (not social interactions), their immediate exploitation in terms of patents (without questioning copyright but instead reinforcing it), large organizations (and not small and medium-sized enterprises), their necessary enrichment with management techniques, their export projection (and not horizontal cooperation among cultures and peoples).
>
> (Bustamante, 2009)

In short, in contrast with the cultural industries, the creative industries – like the entertainment industries at another time, like the digital content industries – have rid themselves of any cultural and democratic complex and are exclusively geared towards the market and short-term profitability. And when they point to their value in terms of the 'social inclusion' of users, they are referring exclusively to their role as connected and permanently active consumers, ignoring the multiple digital divides between social sectors, between genders, between migrants and between sociocultural capabilities, which are now conspicuously pronounced on a national as well as international scale, even in the most developed countries.

From conservative utopias to the defence of creativity in diversity

Earlier I pointed out the link that seems to connect the new mythologies on digital culture with the long history of conservative utopias on the information society: the ever-revived and renewed promise of a user who is at last active, which would enable an abrupt cut-off to be made from the history of technologies and the mass media. And the quasiprophecy of a 'new culture, new communication' which radically breaks with the social history of communication through the promise of an end to monopolies, of free and full activity by the consumer, through the illusion of a flow of total diversity thanks to the simple logic of technology and the market.

This is not the place for an analysis of the long history of mythologies on the information society, which has developed in particular since the post-Second World War period, and been vigorously relaunched every so often in the 1960s, 1980s, 2000s – from Daniel Bell to Alvin Toffler and Yoneji Masuda, from Zbigniew Brzezinski and John Naisbitt to Nicholas Negroponte and Bill Gates. Numerous authors have already analysed this succession of falsely utopian discourses aimed at imposing a conservative ideology of resignation, of the end of ideologies and history due to the absolute reign of the market (Sfez, 1988; Proulx, 1992; Breton, 1995; Mattelart, 1999). And it was Patrice Flichy in particular who best analysed the resurrection of such myths centred on the advent of the PC and the Internet in 1970s California, in an eclectic mix between the individualistic anarchism of the period and the savage market ideology – a true anarchocapitalism – of the IT entrepreneurs (Flichy, 2001). In our historical analysis of this ideological succession, we concluded not only that scientists had been replaced by disseminators, and the latter by managers and success consultants, but also and above all that techno-utopias had been supplanted by market utopias, in which technological determinism (technology as the sole engine of social transformation) was superseded by simple market dynamics – in turn as an engine of technological innovation. The present ideological basis has become much simpler than in the past and can be summarized in the equation:

$$\text{technology} + \text{market} = \text{happiness}$$

As I wrote a few years ago in my study on these trends,

> Without doubt, these thirty years of 'conservative-utopian' thinking play a promotional role in creating demand and manufacturing a market that mythological thinking always satisfies. But a synthetic view of this long chain of private utopias and official actions or reports, in mutual collaboration, demonstrates a potency that reaches much further, and that is aimed at ensuring the maintenance and reproduction of a set of central myths: power as a mere technique; the primacy of freedom over equality; the horizontal interconnection

> between citizens (social relations reduced to mere communication); freedom of communication-trade as a new imperialist 'human right' in relation to all the others; the harmonious articulation between individual behaviours and collective interest in the network market (the new invisible hand).
>
> (Bustamante, 2002)

The 'new religion' with ministers, industrialists and scribes as its chief priests, the 'new social contract' incarnated in the networks, are thus no more than the perfect realization of the market through IT, the neoliberalist dream without any cracks. Having abandoned the libertarian and countercultural concomitances, this discourse has become so hegemonic as to constitute an authentic example of one-way thinking, not only in the field of information and its technologies, but in all social domains; no longer from just the economic but also from the social and cultural perspectives. And not only does its imperial role subordinate the old ideals of progress, of emancipation through education and culture, of social equality, but it completely replaces them with the new paradigm of communication.

Following the depression brought about by the Internet crisis of 2001, the emergence of the so-called Web 2.0 from 2006 has proved to be a moment of renewal for the prophecies and wonders spoken about culture and communication. And it appears to be no accident that the flood of gurus and prophets that has surrounded the expansion of social networks, with their promises of permanently active users (prosumers, viewers) and of a new leap for humanity ('collective intelligence', 'the alchemy of crowds') should coincide with the explosion of this 'new' creativity; or that the renewed promises of maximum spontaneous diversity through the market should be disseminated above all from platforms such as *Wired*, which always proclaims the 'teachings' of Töffler, such as the widespread but never verified theory – prophecy – of Chris Anderson's 'long tail'. (But that is another story that is beyond the limits of this chapter.)

In the final analysis, and after having assimilated this long narrative, far from absurdly opposing humanity's evident 'creativity', we should fly the flag for it with a few small qualifications:

- Cultural creativity is taught: it is imperative therefore to reintroduce a universal education – from primary school – based on culture and the arts, the cultural industries and the media, capable of forming critical users; and training for creators, which along with technology and management teaches the social and mutually supportive role of artists.

- Cultural creativity is a social virtue, it belongs to communities, social groups, peoples. It is therefore vital to protect shared cultural heritage, promote its appropriation and revitalization on the part of citizens, and foster its dissemination.
- Cultural creativity is a crucial feature of a true democracy, as an essential vector of participation in collective decision-making, in the future project that necessarily involves a – regional, national and international – political space. It thus requires public support policies, and an expanded concept of public service capable of making quality culture available to all citizens via every network and device.
- Cultural creativity requires permanent pools of innovation that are frequently found among creators and social groups, in small and medium-sized enterprises, in minority and underprivileged communities. Cultural and industrial public policies should centre on support for these reservoirs of creation and renewal, which are often anti-market and anti-establishment.
- Cultural creativity is damaged by the cloned culture led by the big multimedia and transnational groups, which on account of their merely commercial dynamics are geared towards economic censure and the endless repetition of successful formulas. There is a need for strict and vigilant anti-trust regulation to defend the diversity of creativity in production and distribution.
- Diverse cultural creativity is penalized by an antiquated and unfair commercial copyright system which freezes innovation, favours reiteration and discriminates against citizen-users. It is necessary to renew and reformulate this original social pact according to which legitimate remuneration for creators had to be reconciled with the universal right of access to culture and communication.
- Cultural creativity is born of intercultural diversity and genuine exchange between cultures because it cannot fail to be global in our current age. It requires horizontal cooperation between peoples, with support for those cultures that are the weakest from the industrial and commercial standpoint.

Note

1. As reported in several international news bulletins, the UNESCO Institute for Statistics (UIS) is currently carrying out a review of the Framework for Cultural Statistics (FCS), which will lead to a complete update of its methodology in

which special attention will be given to the creative industries. The UIS has already asked the London School of Economics, the University of Leeds and the Burns Owens Partnership (a UK private consultancy specializing in cultural statistics) to review the intellectual framework underlying the FCS and to identify indicators that might be applied in the national system of official statistics of all UNESCO member states.

References

Breton, Philippe (1995) *L'utopie de la communication. Le mythe du village planétaire*, Paris: La Découverte.

Buquet, Gustavo (2008) 'El comercio internacional de bienes y servicios culturales. Crítica a la metodología implementada por la UNESCO', *Telos - Cuadernos de Comunicación e Innovación*, 77, 41–46.

Bustamante, Enrique (2002) 'Sociedad de la Información: el reinado de las utopías conservadoras', *Tram(p)as de la comunicación y la cultura*, 1(4), 7–12.

—— (2009) 'De las industrias culturales al entretenimiento. La creatividad, la innovación… Viejos y nuevos señuelos para la investigación de la cultura', *Diálogos de la comunicación*, 78, 1–25.

CEIN-Navarra (Centro Europeo de Empresas e Innovación de Navarra) (2008) *Informe. Industrias creativas*, Noáin: CEIN-Navarra/Asociación Navarra de Empresas Laborales/Asociación Cederna-Garalur.

CES-Canary Islands (Economic and Social Council (CES) of the Canary Islands) (2009) 'La relevancia y el impacto de las actividades creativas y culturales en la economía canaria', capítulo V del *Informe anual 2009 del Consejo sobre la situación económica, social y laboral de Canarias en el año 2008*, Las Palmas de Gran Canaria: CES-Canary Islands.

FILAIE (Federación Iberolatinoamericana de Artistas, Intérpretes o Ejecutantes) (2007) 'Informe FILAIE sobre la Conferencia Internacional de la OMPI sobre la propiedad intelectual y las industrias creativas', Geneva, 29–30 October 2007, FILAIE.

Flichy, Patrice (2001) *L'imaginaire d'Internet*, Paris: La Découverte.

KEA, European Affairs (2006) 'The Economy of Culture in Europe', Study Prepared for the European Commission (Directorate General for Education and Culture). http://ec.europa.eu/culture/library/studies/cultural-economy_en.pdf.

Mattelart, Armand (1999) *Histoire de l'utopie planétaire. De la cité prophétique à la société globale*, Paris: La Découverte.

Mehlum, Halvor; Moene, Karl and Torvik, Ragnar (2003) 'Destructive Creativity', *Nordic Journal of Political Economy*, 29, 77–84.

Proulx, Serge (1992) 'De l'utopie sociale à l'idéologie de la communication', *CinémAction – Les théories de la communication*, 63, 219–224.

Schlesinger, Philip (2008) 'Discurso de la creatividad: políticas e intelectuales' (keynote lecture), IV Pan-American Conference on Communication: 'Industrias de la creatividad: creatividad, industrias culturales y desafío para los comunicadores', Santiago de Chile: Mayor University.

Sfez, Lucien (1988) *Critique de la communication*, Paris: Seuil.

UNCTAD (United Nations Conference on Trade and Development) (2008) *Creative Economy Report 2008: The Challenge of Assessing the Creative Economy Towards Informed Policy-Making*, Geneva: UN/UNCTAD.

UNESCO (United Nations Educational, Scientific and Cultural Organization) (2005) *Convention on the Protection and Promotion of the Diversity of Cultural Expressions*, Paris: UNESCO.

UNESCO (United Nations Educational, Scientific and Cultural Organization)/Global Alliance for Cultural Diversity (2006) *Comprender las industrias creativas. Las estadísticas como apoyo a las políticas públicas*, Paris: UNESCO.

Part III

Cultural Consumption from a Critical Perspective

6
Studying Cultural Behaviours, Consumptions, Habits and Practices

Armand Mattelart

The political economy of communication and cultural studies

First of all, I want to touch on the tension that grew up between two 'enemy brothers' during the 1980s and 1990s: cultural studies in its UK incarnation (there being other modalities), and the political economy of culture and communication. I refer to them as 'enemy brothers' since the two were born of convergent projects, only later to become distanced from one another. There was a consensus that emerged with cultural studies in the 1970s (if we take forerunners into account, it began in the 1950s); political economy would later position itself as a new force in the late 1960s and early 1970s. Both cultural studies and political economy sprang from a critique of functionalist sociology, and its instrumental perspective on the media and the receiver, as well as its propensity to leave the media outside the structure and silence of the structural determinations that affect both the media and their receivers. The critique of functionalist sociology also targeted its methodology, which focused on the study of manifest content, as though the relationship were a transparent one. Counteracting that view, political economy and cultural studies united in insisting on the centrality of ideological processes, ideology, subtexts and secondary meanings. Another point shared by both schools in their early days was the break with the reductionism of orthodox Marxism built on the antinomy between economic base and culture, infrastructure and superstructure: a view of culture as a reflection of the material base. The critical standpoints of Raymond Williams, E.P. Thompson and, later, Stuart Hall (Hall et al., 1980) were in line with the assumptions that prevailed during the setting-up of the project of the political economy of communication and culture, whether it was in North America in the late 1970s, Latin America in the early 1970s or Europe at the end of that same decade, each with its own cultural and sociopolitical specificities.

In the early days, neither cultural studies nor the political economy of communication and culture was particularly interested in audiences or reception. The reason was that, following Marx's thinking, production and consumption were accepted as forming an indissoluble whole. Nevertheless, I would refute the assertion that political economy and cultural studies did not deal with the field of reception at an early stage. On the one hand, in cultural studies we find the work of Richard Hoggart,[1] one of the only founding fathers of cultural studies not to claim Marxist affiliations, and even to criticize the fervour of the young scholars who proclaimed themselves to belong to that tradition. On the other, it is important to point out that it was from the perspective of political economy that the first study on audiences during a revolutionary process was carried out: the research by Michèle Mattelart and the Argentinian Mabel Piccini on TV and the popular strata in the shanty towns of Santiago in 1972, during a period of growing class conflict in Chile (Mattelart and Piccini, 1974). This was a study that cannot be understood without appreciating the need that gave rise to it: to draw up an alternative policy on the production of fiction for public TV.[2]

Towards the autonomization of culture

What I propose to do first is to show how the culturalist perspective has gradually permeated ways of approaching communication and culture (Mattelart and Neveu, 2002, 2004). Broadly speaking, we could describe the 1970s as the period in which both political economy and cultural studies began to mature; it was a decade marked by problems of social change, inequalities and asymmetric relations relating to the issue of power. During the following decade a drastic change took place. As the savage deregulation of social solidarity systems progressed, the imperative of a discourse of identities and differences overtook the discourse of the principle of equality as the primary goal of political action.

It is not possible, however, to approach those days of the 1980s in antonymic terms, for their defining feature was that they were marked by a heuristically qualitative leap in the understanding of communicational and cultural processes, but also by ambiguity and ambivalence. Restoring the hitherto widely marginalized perspectives of social relations as communicative interactions, what Michèle Mattelart and

I have termed 'the new paradigm of the fluid and of postlinearity' no doubt opened the door to new objects of research, new methods and new theoretical references. What could then be glimpsed was the reticular view of social organization in networks, the attention to mediations and negotiations, the return to the subject, intersubjective links and the rituals of daily life. At the same time, the 'paradigm of the fluid' introduced doubt and contradiction into the critical field. To make myself clear I will cite what Michèle Mattelart and I wrote at the dawn of this new paradigm in the book *Penser les médias* (1986), the US edition of which appeared six years later under the title *Rethinking Media Theory*:

> The great contribution of the new paradigm of the fluid is precisely to have challenged the smooth and unilateral certainty of the categories and paradigms that had long dominated critical thought. Along with its merit, however, we must point out the ambiguities of the progress thereby made possible. And we must also be quick to recognize that the ambiguity itself have some merit, because it allows us to gain a better grasp of the polysemic character of reality and the actors who embody it.
>
> (Mattelart and Mattelart, 1992, p. 58)

In our formulation itself it is possible to perceive the difficulty of expressing the duplicity of this phenomenon.

When it comes to ambiguity and ambivalence, the so-called 'deregulation' years, or rather the years of hegemony of the law of market self-regulation, have more than fulfilled all the promises, beyond what was foreseen and foreseeable. The triumph of 'active reception' as the new common sense, brought about by what has been dubbed 'the ethnographic turn', which took place during the second generation of cultural studies, is a brilliant and lasting example (and is still valid) of the effects of this deregulation in the critical arena.

It is true that prior to this process of focusing on audiences, cultural studies had another focus: confinement to the text as a means of ideological analysis, which can be interpreted as the first sign of tension between the political economy project and that of cultural studies. It is this first focus that explains the fact that as early as 1979, the moment when the project of political economy of communication was formalized in the UK, in the second issue of the journal *Media, Culture & Society*, established that same year, Nicholas Garnham (1979) should have harshly criticized what he called 'the idealist autonomization of the ideological level', which according to him made cultural goods appear as mere carriers of messages, leaving aside the question of the existence and functioning of the cultural industries and the question of a social world organized by their producers and their mechanisms. The ethnographic turn went much further. It abstracted itself not only from the existence and functioning of the cultural industries and their producers but also from the problem of ideology. Quite simply it left aside the text. And indeed, in the period dominated by the ethnographic turn, there would be no study that analysed ideology, the subtexts of the cultural products watched by the much studied audiences. Such an absence is thus tantamount to renouncing a founding concept. This 'omission' of 'content' implies that the 'resemanticization' of televized or other messages by audiences takes place in a world freed from the inherent weight of the material character of the production of a cultural order. It is in these cases that it becomes possible to measure the distance separating the ethnographic project from the project of cultural materialism developed early on by Raymond Williams, whom I consider to be a precursor of both critical political economy and cultural studies. Williams has not ceased to insist on the need to articulate the material, the economic and the ideological on three analytically distinct but interconnected levels within concrete social practices (Garnham and Williams, 1980).

Indeed, the underlying logic of the mainstream of studies on the uses and practices inspired by the paradigm of active reception has been that of autonomizing the question of the culture of social, economic and technical determinants, of industrial and financial strategies, as well as the geopolitical stakes. This isolation within the social microcosm has affected studies on the reception of cultural products, beginning with TV productions 'with a global ambition', such as *Dallas* and *Dynasty*. Consider, for example, what seems to me the most extreme study in this sense: the one on the soap opera *Dallas* conducted by Ien Ang (1985), who under the pretext of the freedom of TV viewers to produce their own meaning from what they have seen, denies the need for communication policies.[3] This culturalism, this autonomy in culture, has also wreaked havoc in the research on the social uses of new technologies, as evidenced by the *dérives* of many of the studies on the topic in France and Quebec, countries that are nevertheless pioneers in this area.

The universe of the 'citizen-consumer'

It is not possible to analyse theories without taking into account their effect on reality. One of the first effects in the theoretical field of ethnographic tropism has been to enable bridges to be built between traditions that until the 1980s ignored each other and were considered to be epistemologically incompatible, such as in the case of the convergence of cultural studies and studies on uses and gratifications – or negotiated reading. Another of the effects is that of having encouraged the articulation of the interests and objects of so-called academic research with the demands of administrative research or that originating from the industry of marketing.[4]

The culturalist perspective has also accompanied the mutation of the ideology of the international institutions responsible for culture – and communication – related issues. In this regard it is interesting to observe how UNESCO's orientation has gradually changed. In the 1970s, a time of debates on unequal exchange, the cultural industries, the processes of financial and economic concentration of the media and communication policies, this agency was close to the vision of political economy, but it has progressively tended towards an alliance with anthropology – and not with just any anthropology but with a revised and corrected version – and with the acritical sector of cultural studies. As proof we have UNESCO's famous report on culture (UNESCO, 2000): in it there is no representative of the political economy of communication and culture; all representatives are from cultural studies, or from an anthropology that, in my opinion, has a very shortsighted view of structural problems, being centred on theories of cultural globalization that pay little attention to geoeconomics and geopolitics. This dissociation of culture from economics within UNESCO now results in a total dissociation between the idea of cultural policy and communication policy. At present it is impossible in UNESCO to address the problem of financial and economic concentration.[5] The self-censorship in this area is such that in the history produced by the institution itself of the path it has taken in relation to issues of cultural diversity, there is no mention of the debates on media diversity that took place in the 1970s (Stenou, 2003).

From a strictly ethnographic observation of the ways of using products and artefacts, distinguished simply as 'resistances', there has been a slide towards cultural relativism. The ethnographic perspective has been made to say what cannot be said on the sociological level: to deny the existence of the asymmetrical relationship on a global scale. In short, the absolute transparency of the interface between supply and demand. The denial of the power relations between cultures and communication systems has led to the replacement of the theory of cultural imperialism, denounced in my opinion without much epistemological precaution and in a decontextualized manner, by a theory on the link between the global and the local. The management term 'glocalization' was even adopted. It is here that the representation of the consumer intertwines with a theory of cultural globalization, which involves adhering to a model of global integration based on neoliberal reason and on the divine laws of the self-regulated market, presented as something neutral. In this view of the world and its evolution, there is no salvation beyond the project of reordering the global world as it is and as it will remain. This ideological position harbours a paradox, because by abstaining from questioning this structuring framework, by sterilizing the very notion of globalization and its genealogy, by becoming an accomplice to a particular globalization project that is promoted as being universal, culturalism has only aligned itself with the linear model, climbing the stairway of history, as conceived by the most classical political economy. The autonomization of culture in relation to economics and geopolitics culminates in the assimilation of the globalization model as the last rung on the ladder, the unsurpassable horizon of human evolution. Instead of history, what emerges is a perpetual present. This explains why, for those who have rejected this long-term view of the internationalization of capitalism, the process of globalization began just two or three decades ago. Ultimately, the neutralization of the hegemonic global process explains the use they make of the concept of 'citizen-consumer', which seems to me aberrant. This cultural neopopulism involves subscribing to dogmas that equate the freedom of commercial expression with the freedoms that establish the status of citizen and puts democracy on a level with the global democratic marketplace, to use the expression sanctioned by the globalized elites.

This view of the 'citizen-consumer' goes hand in hand with the thesis on the decline of the nation state and the emergence of a world defined as 'complex, diffuse volatile and interactive' (I am reintroducing these adjectives, which of course are not mine), a world of such headless and ungraspable deterritorializations that all traces of power evaporate. Consequently, the decline is not only that of the state but of everything relating to the public administration of communication and culture. The rhetoric on cultural globalization, the mainstream, has erased the nation state from the map of the problem of mediation and of the actors in the communication process. This is also interesting for the purposes of reality, since it is a thesis shared by postmodern theories and treatises on global management. But history also wreaks its revenge and, through a strange and curious irony, this myth of the disappearance of the nation state was refuted so blatantly by the economic and financial crisis that broke out in September 2008, and it reaffirmed the state's role of economic intervention and as guarantor of the collective interest.

What is worrying about the *dérives* of culturalism, particularly in the 1980s and early 1990s, is that it has led to the abandoning of all the proposals of critical theory on the practice and practitioners of cultural and communicational devices, precisely as imagined by someone as polyphonic as Michel de Certeau. The concept of 'domination' and 'dominated', which still formed part of his vocabulary, has been erased from the cognitive map. If we read Michel de Certeau with intellectual honesty, we will see – as Michel Foucault (1975) did when he analysed 'networks of discipline' – that his studies on 'networks of antidiscipline' are intimately related to a theory of power, even in those situations in which citizens express their own ability to use in a different way what the programmer programs, to use Certeau's expression. The very notion of programming is inseparable from the principle according to which the society where citizens attempt to resist through their way of using the products imposed by a dominant productive and social order is a society where individuals are increasingly reduced to a calculation, to a measurement, and managed as such (Certeau, 1980). The approach of antidiscipline networks complements that of discipline networks.

To conclude my reflection on this wave produced by the ethnographic turn, which has introduced quasireligious views of the active status of audiences, I will again quote a passage extracted from *Rethinking Media Theory* which enables me to segue neatly to the second part of my exposition. In 1992, Michèle Mattelart and I warned against the risk that might be run with a univocal, one-dimensional view of the return to the subject and the receiver:

> All these developments [the turn of the return to subject and receiver] can be understood and experienced only with reference to the reconciliation with pragmatic humankind and the happiness of pragmatic humankind spoken by Kant, and which signifies, no doubt, the recognition of the needs of concrete individuals, but also the beginning of infinite negotiations – not only endless but without finality, because they are born just at the point where utopias end.
>
> (Mattelart and Mattelart, 1992, p. 54)

The social demand of the citizen-subject

Since its foundation, the political economy of communication and culture has attempted to recover the portion of social utopia included in any project that is critical of the existing order and that escapes the confines of the institutional and commercial logic of supply and demand. That said, nothing could be further from my view than to credit political economy alone with the building of a new body of theory. The building of another vision, different from the logic of supply and demand, is, and will be, the result of diverse and multidisciplinary perspectives. In this sense I think that political economy has delineated a broad area of reflection by insisting on the need to link research to social demand and social needs. This is the only way to escape the ambiguity raised by the title 'Studying cultural behaviours, consumptions, habits and practices', which ultimately is a trick title since it is fraught with ambiguity and prompts me to take a stance on these issues.

The figure that has oriented the field of political economy of communication studies since its foundation is clearly not that of the consumer *vis-à-vis* the supply of cultural products or technological gadgets but rather 'social demand'. I have put this concept in quotation marks because I am aware of just how controversial it is. This 'social demand' emanates from citizen-subjects, and not from citizen-consumers, arranged in a configuration of asymmetric relationships in a game of hegemony/counterhegemony. The notion of 'social demand' is not a given; it is a permanent construction. If I had talked of 'social demand' during the decades of desertification in critical thinking, many would have been immediately sceptical of my proposal, but the context has changed. The concept of 'social demand' combines with and refers, between the lines, to a project of society, a utopia of social emancipation.

Every critical project involves an insurrectional creed, an insurgency. The paradigm of the active participation of the citizen – a central point of social demand – in building a counterhegemony through the appropriation of cultural and communicational mechanisms is at the heart of the political economy of communication and culture project. The mobilization and social struggles that characterized the first moments of political economy's gestation have resulted in the following idea that comes from Bertolt Brecht, one of the only left-wing intellectuals to take the lead in developing a thinking on the dialectic between producer and consumer in a medium: transforming the audience into an actor and producer (Brecht, [1932] 2003). This utopia of giving back the word to those who have no voice was valid for both popular communication projects and those involving a popular education based on the dialogic relationship between teacher and learner. The need to think about the alternative in terms of communication policies and the active participation of citizens have formed part of the problems addressed by political economy since its founding moment.

In this regard it is interesting to recall the first sources of insurrection in Latin America, during the 1960s and 1970s, against the development model endorsed by the functionalist theories in their diffusionist variants. There was a critical unanimity with respect to the conception of the citizen as a consumer or client, reflected in the positions of those who worked on the processes of agrarian reform (Beltrán, 1976), on literacy campaigns (Freire, 1970) or on birth-control policies – an issue that led me to further explore the sociopolitical challenges of communication. In these three fields, the question of the relationship established between 'diffuser' and 'consumers' was what provided the impetus for thinking, from various perspectives, about social demand as an alternative to vertical forms of communication.

In other social formations, such as that of France, what was decisive in the gestation of the first generation of political economy's theorizations on the idea of social demand coupled with that of participation was the critique of 'social engineering', which reduced social demand for new technologies to solvent demand and research on uses and users to experiments aimed at pushing back the 'thresholds of acceptability' for these technologies (Mattelart and Stourdzé, 1985).

The notion of 'social demand' is inherent to a question that has gradually been taken up again with the crisis of contemporary civilization: What are the fundamental social needs? Since the beginning of this millennium, a new configuration of historical subjects has highlighted the process of maturation on the reflection of social demand through the integration of alternatives to the private patrimonialization of culture, the media, information and knowledge. This is a reality that was demonstrated in the international negotiations in which alternative projects of society have served as a contrast in debates about the status of culture, information, communication and knowledge within the new world order. Such is the case of the discussions about cultural exception and cultural diversity in the audiovisual sector, where it has been observed that the epigones of a cultural diversity that is likened to the broadening of the range of products offered in the market for cultural goods or technologies were opposed by those who defended the principle of a cultural diversity anchored in qualitative rationality in relation to creation, which advocates a special status for cultural production with respect to free trade. Thus they opposed the notion of cultural diversity based on the idea of abundance, the multiplication of the supply of TV channels and programmes. In these debates, therefore, the question has emerged of the citizen-subject, which had disappeared from the political landscape in the last two decades of the last century.

Principles, rights and modes of intervention

Gradually there has evolved a body of theory inseparable from the building of strategies of action. A new generation of committed, if not militant, scholars has emerged and draws on the support of logistics, new forms of agora and exchange via networks.[6]

This gestating body of theory gives rise to two principles. The first is the exercise of the rights to communication; this is related to the debate about the democratization of the media and networks in the 1970s, right at the time when the project of political economy of communication and culture was being born in various places. The way of approaching the problem of rights to communication does not merely entail critically adopting these precedents but rather, in contrast with what occurred during that period, the current reflection on the right to communication is accompanied by the contributions of a new generation of specialists in public law, who call into question the essentialist view of human rights. And for this reason they put forward the need to expand existing rights, update them and, at the same time, think up others in order that they all meet contemporary social needs. In this regard I would like to pay tribute to Joaquín Herrera Flores, who died in 2009 in Seville, and whose works on the reinvention of human rights are mandatory references for any democrat. His thinking can be summed up in the following words: human rights are the rights of all to participate in the transformation of society; it is only through this participation that the individual can build their human dignity (Herrera Flores, 2008).

The second principle involves a philosophy on general wellbeing, what is called the common good. I believe there is a growing conviction that the common good should be considered as universal. This is what is meant by the philosophy of common public goods; all these assets to which persons and peoples should be equitably and freely entitled, and which for this reason must be removed from the logics of patrimoniality or of private appropriation. This principle motivates citizen mobilizations not only in relation to the communication of knowledge but also with respect to health, living matter, the environment, water, computer programs and the distribution of broadcasting frequencies. All these domains should be governed by the rules of public service. Along the same lines, there is a reincorporation within critical thinking – and it is important that there should be – of the debate about public service.[7]

The above principles give rise to forms of intervention and declamation. A first form of collective intervention is the criticism of the actions of the hegemonic media. The idea is that the citizen's gaze and freedoms in relation to the media are not givens but are instead constructed through citizen counterbalances. This translates into the multiplication of oversight committees and critical observatories on information, culture and cultural policies or knowledge society-related policies. The attraction of these observatories, which are increasing in number mainly in Latin America – although these initiatives are also slowly beginning to have a presence in Europe – is that they show that there is no single formula, there are many, and this is due to the fact that they are related to specific social and media contexts. What I find interesting is that it is a reflection that leads to the need for a broad alliance with regard to the reading of the media and to forms of action as a response. They are not simply organizations with the right to criticize on account of having academic ability but rather their action also involves reflecting on the participative process in this criticism (Albornoz and Herschmann, 2008).

A second form of intervention is the field of action of everything related to the democratization of communication. It seems to me that there is now a convergence on the need to undertake a multilevel reflection on the transformation of the media: the idea of perennializing the third sector, the need to consolidate a public service (or create it where it does not exist) that is not the transmission belt for the voice of the state, the commercial private sector's obligation to be consistent with the authorization granted to it to use a common public good – the spectrum of frequencies. The new laws on audiovisual services in Argentina, the pressure for reform in Mexico and the reflection taking place in Brazil all bear witness to how much progress has been made on this such strategic an issue for democracy.

All these thoughts, principles and modes of intervention are paths towards the collective construction of the idea of social demand and social needs, and are fundamental, being guided by the awareness of an asymmetrical relationship in the world which is permeating every aspect and level of social relations.

Critical firewalls

The current crisis favours the deepening of reflection on social demand. I do not share the conviction held by the newspapers and constantly announced that we are emerging from the crisis. I believe this is a systemic crisis, which is to say that capitalism cannot manage to rebuild itself as a system. Like Immanuel Wallerstein (2009), I am convinced that we are in an era in which new territories of reflection and action are opening up for those who think in terms of alternatives in response to a deregulated world. This is important, and the proof is that many utopias of social emancipation are making a comeback – for example, there is increasing discussion of the social economy, of the caring economy, of the need to subordinate the economy and finance to fundamental human needs and so forth. There is a set of marginalized forms of thinking that are re-emerging and making themselves heard. They are not prescriptions but they are indications.

All this accumulation of critical action and thinking about a new type of society had been buried by the neoliberal globalization model, which believed that it had reached the final rung of history. The reflections on satisfying basic human needs and the survival of the ecosystem are central questions that are related to the damage caused by a productivist system whose basic unit is ultimately the consumer-consumerist. In this area, a completely different perspective of questioning can be seen from the one that existed in the 1980s and 1990s. New territories are beginning to open up for the utopia of knowledge-sharing rooted in the philosophy of rights to communication and of common goods.

Who would impose the rules of the game in a society where there was a sharing-out, a commonwealth of knowledge? It is a recurring question. Either we are content to argue in favour of the intervention of public authorities and the economic role of the state until another crisis arises, or we commit ourselves to the founding principle of popular sovereignty and the primacy of the political, which involves new forms of organization and joint decision, with the aim of making a qualitative leap in terms of citizen participation in all the main issues facing society and its future.

This is a cardinal aspect, since it relates to the issue of knowledge-power. Those of us who work in research and teaching are key players – although often in a very precarious manner – for the future producers of the knowledge society (Sierra Caballero, 2006), and I do not think that we have sufficiently questioned what it means to redefine our social contract with the citizenry as a whole. This is a fundamental question that underlies the whole embryonic body of theory that is emerging and is attempting to provide a response. It is a vital issue, since we are in a period in history where the modes of hegemony become producers of knowledge, and these producers can repeat the mechanisms of hegemony of previous cognitive monopolies. The key is to approach the problem without populism on the basis of a lucid reflection on the need to drastically change our status within the knowledge society to adapt it to the new realities of democracy. In this sense it is important to activate firewalls to counter all the discourses enthralled with the knowledge society. These critical firewalls are needed in order to establish a knowledge economy and society that does not reproduce the power structure and power relations that have marked the development of industrial society.

Moreover, the knowledge economy and society are also an economy and a society in which the general intellectualization of work and consumption runs the risk of becoming so normalized as to reduce the mechanisms of social control. The failure of this democratic renovation would mean the rise of new forms of authoritarianism. The increasing investment made by so-called democratic societies in control technologies – in the workplace and public spaces – raises suspicions about what this new world and its new language would be like. The imperatives of national security and of the War on Terror have ultimately accelerated this tendency, which is not a recent creation and has been turned into a necessity.

'We're moving toward control societies that no longer operate by confining people but through continuous control' (Deleuze, 1995, p. 174), observed the philosopher Gilles Deleuze in *Pourparlers* (1990). The model for running society came from the management model. What has happened is that there has been a transposition of the management model to all units and institutions, such as education with the Bologna Plan. Deleuze's was a very astute intuition, very similar to that of William Burroughs in the 1970s. Since the era in which Deleuze proposed the concept of a 'society of control', the control has intensified; we need only look, for example, at how the idea of the reification of work has progressed and the way the worker is viewed.[8]

The novelty with regard to the so-called information society is that in recent years it has revealed its darkest side (Mattelart, 2010). What can be observed today is an art of governing built on traceability, the monitoring of persons and goods. There is an attempt to establish a new normality based on what I call actuarial reasoning – that is to say, on the ability to identify the probability of a certain behaviour, to anticipate it by constructing categories of behaviours on the basis of statistical frequencies via the proliferation of intrusive technologies and the crossing of files with data banks for eminently practical purposes related to areas as varied as consumption, education, criminal justice, health and immigration. The systematic exploitation of the personal data of Internet users for the purpose of establishing profiles with the help of search engines is just one example.

The risk of this compulsion towards the recording of the population lies in negating the citizen-subject by reducing them to an individual who is measured, calculated and inserted into the norm. Or in the words of one of Foucault's disciples, 'The dream of a new science of humankind would be to succeed in combining Internet connections, DNA test results and certain consumer behaviours. The mystery of human nature would then be exhausted' (Ewald, 2008) – all in the service of eminently practical aims. Whether we like it or not, this is one of the dynamics that moves our society. Without vaunting the effectiveness of the artefacts for assuring the social and productive order, the observation about the quantitative and qualitative leap taken by traceability devices makes us think of the dystopian, anti-utopian worlds of total control imagined by Franz Kafka, Evgeny Zamiatin, Aldous Huxley and George Orwell. The difference is that present-day democratic societies and their modes of social control no longer live in the era of industrial, Fordist or totalitarian society; they exist in a time of post-Fordist society, a society dominated by the flexibility, fluidity and transparency of digital and Web technologies. Earlier technologies existed in the age of energy machines, a symbol of the ideology of infinite progress; later ones are fed by the sources of the ideology of communication without limits. The technodeterministic belief in the magical power of communication and networks that has accompanied the years of deregulation and wild speculation – while repeating the promise of the global information society as a new version of the Athenian agora – is the same one that has naturalized the painless dissemination of intrusive technologies in postindustrial societies. If the exception to the rule of law is now tending to become the rule in contemporary democracies and managing to pass itself off as normal, it is because it is concealed by the belief, which is firmly rooted in the collective thinking, about the power of technology to solve society's problems.

To conclude, I will take the liberty of quoting the phrase that serves as a conclusion to the book *Theories of Communication: A Short Introduction*, which I wrote with Michèle Mattelart:

> The age of the so-called information society is also that of the production of mental states. It will be necessary to rethink the question of freedom and democracy. Political freedom cannot be reduced to the right to exercise one's will. It also lies in the right to control the process whereby that will is formed.
>
> (Mattelart and Mattelart, 1998, p. 156)

Notes

1. Hoggart's work *The Uses of Literacy: Aspects of Working-Class Life with Special References to Publications and Entertainments* (London: Chatto and Windus, 1957) has now become a classic.
2. In the late 1970s these researchers had participated in the first study to cover both the ownership structure of the media and press discourses. See Mattelart et al. (1970).
3. See also Ang (1990).
4. The contributions by Schlesinger (Chapter 3), Tremblay (Chapter 4) and Bustamante (Chapter 5) refer to the development of the ideology of the 'economy of the creativity' and the diversion of cultural studies, which is closely related to the diversion and occupation of a field such as design, within the many avenues of cultural studies.
5. A former assistant on my research team, which formed part of the committee for drawing up the Convention on Cultural Diversity of 2005, dared to raise the problem of business concentration (it was not present and it was a fundamental element of cultural diversity), but the response was that the issue should not be dealt with in a section of cultural policies and intercultural dialogue. This example demonstrates that intercultural dialogue obscures many issues.
6. I usually provide a corrective to this statement, telling young researchers who embrace the critical perspective and commit themselves to alternative actions and practices that they form part of the minority of minorities who now think in a different way and attempt to imagine a different world.
7. A thread of Ariadne links the notions of 'public service' and common public good. It must be remembered that as early as 1874 the concept of 'public service' was a cause of division among the members of the First Workers International, with some focusing on strategies for taking over the state and others preferring to pledge their commitment to the multiplication of public service organizations run directly by the 'Commune' and mutual organizations.
8. The large number of suicides in the French company France Telecom, one of the icons of public service, is proof of the fact that control, using old and new methods, is a real problem.

References

Albornoz, Luis A. and Herschmann, Micael (2008) 'Ibero-American observatories in the sectors of information, communication and culture: a brief history', *Media, Culture & Society*, 30(5), 723–734.

Ang, Ien (1985) *Watching Dallas: Soap Opera and the Melodramatic Imagination*, London: Methuen.

—— (1990) 'Culture and Communication: Toward an Ethnographic Critique of Media Consumption in the Transnational Media System', *European Journal of Communication*, 5, 239–260.

Beltrán, Luis Ramiro (1976) 'Alien premises, objects and methods in Latin American communication research', *Communication Research*, 3(2), 107–134.

Brecht, Bertolt ([1932] 2003) 'Teorías de la radio (1927–1932)', *Revista Eptic Online*, 5(2), 5–16 [extracted from B. Brecht (1973) *El compromiso social en Literatura y Arte*, Barcelona: Península].
Certeau, Michel de (1980) *L'invention du quotidien 1. Arts de faire*, Paris: Union générale d'éditions 10–18.
Deleuze, Gilles (1995) *Negotiations: 1972–1990*, New York: Columbia University Press (original: *Pourparlers*, Paris: Minuit, 1990).
Ewald, François (2008) 'Voici venue l'ère du contrôle généralisé', *Enjeux. Les Echos*, 1 February, Paris.
Foucault, Michel (1975) *Surveiller et punir*, Paris: Gallimard.
Freire, Paulo (1970) *Pedagogía del oprimido*, México: Siglo XXI.
Garnham, Nicholas (1979) 'Contribution to a political economy of mass-communication', *Media, Culture & Society*, 1(2), 123–146.
Garnham, Nicholas and Williams, Raymond (1980) 'Pierre Bourdieu and the sociology of culture: An introduction', *Media, Culture & Society*, 2(3), 209–223.
Hall, Stuart, Hobson, Dorothy; Lowe, Andrew and Willis, Paul (eds) (1980) *Culture, Media, Language*, London: Hutchinson.
Herrera Flores, Joaquín (2008) *La reinvención de los derechos humanos*, Valencia: Atrapasueños.
Mattelart, Armand (2010) *The Globalization of Surveillance. The Origin of the Securitarian Order*, Cambridge: Polity.
Mattelart, Armand and Mattelart, Michèle (1992) *Rethinking Media Theory: Signposts and New Directions*, Minneapolis, MN: University of Minnesota Press.
—— (1998) *Theories of Communication. A Short Introduction*, London: Sage.
Mattelart, Armand; Mattelart, Michèle and Piccini, Mabel (1970) 'Los medios de comunicación de masas. La ideología de la prensa liberal en Chile', *Cuadernos de la realidad nacional*, 3 (special edition), Santiago de Chile: Centro de Estudios de la Realidad Nacional, Catholic University of Chile.
Mattelart, Armand and Neveu, Erik (2002) *Los* Cultural Studies. *Hacia una domesticación del pensamiento salvaje, Ediciones de Periodismo y Comunicación*, 20, La Plata: National University of La Plata.
—— (2004) *Introducción a los estudios culturales*, Barcelona-Buenos Aires: Paidós.
Mattelart, Armand and Stourdzé, Yves (1985) *Technology, Culture and Communication: A Report to the French Minister of Research and Industry*, Oxford: Elsevier Science Publishers.
Mattelart, Michèle and Piccini, Mabel (1974) 'La televisión y los sectores populares', *Comunicación y Cultura*, 2, 3–75.
Sierra Caballero, Francisco (2006) *Políticas de comunicación y educación. Crítica y desarrollo de la sociedad del conocimiento*, Barcelona: Gedisa.
Stenou, Katérina (2003) *UNESCO and the Issue of Cultural Diversity: Review and Strategy, 1946–2003*, Paris: UNESCO.
UNESCO (United Nations Educational, Scientific and Cultural Organization) (2000) *World Culture Report 2000*, Paris: UNESCO.
Wallerstein, Immanuel (2009) '2008: el fallecimiento de la gloalización neoliberal', *La Jornada*, 16 February, México.

7
New Approaches for New Sociocultural Practices

Micael Herschmann

This chapter assesses the extent to which the theoretical-methodological 'circuit of culture' approach developed by Stuart Hall (Du Gay et al., 1997; Escosteguy, 2009) sets out fundamental contributions in the building of an extended and necessary research agenda for communication researchers,[1] especially for those committed to studying the dynamics and complexity of cultural habits and practices.

It should be stressed that, in spite of identifying key references in the work of Stuart Hall and Raymond Williams for the ideas developed here and in my research, the aim of this chapter is not to present a romantic or idealized perspective of the British cradle of cultural studies. While, on the one hand, I identify 'advances' when referring back to this protocol, on the other hand, we have to recognize that the world has changed in recent decades, presenting new challenges that call for the articulation of new forms of knowledge – the development of an interdisciplinary perspective – and the adaptation of the analytical tools available.

As Kellner (1998) suggests, the adoption of the theoretical-methodological 'circuit of culture' protocol put forward by Hall, articulated to an interdisciplinary perspective that specifically brings cultural studies and political economy closer together, may provide researchers with better conditions for meeting the challenges of research in the complex contemporary world.

> I am advocating a political economy approach that does not merely read texts as examples of capitalist ideology or that of the ruling classes, but instead takes into account a multiplicity of types of representation, which include class, sex, race, ethnicity, nationalism, etc., when analyzing the production of texts. I would like to explain that

> economic analysis [of the political economy of communication] can complement and enrich the readings of cultural studies and that textual analysis and that of political economy are not, therefore, antithetical.
>
> (Kellner, 1998)

Kellner underlines the fact that these fields of study can play complementary roles. While, on the one hand, studies on political economy have always displayed great skill in analysing production and distributions systems, as well as their linkages and tensions with power and capital, on the other hand, the works undertaken by cultural studies have always shown themselves to be adept at analysing the cultural processes of receiving and constructing meaning among audiences and consumers. Kellner thus champions the construction of an interdisciplinary agenda that can build what he calls a 'political economy of culture'.

Criticisms, limitations and alternatives for research

A number of authors rightly criticize the trend within academia towards excessively favouring consumption, reception or audience in recent decades. They condemn what they refer to as 'cultural populism' (Mattelart and Mattelart, 1997; Ferguson and Golding, 1998; Mattelart and Neveu, 2004). Some point to the tendency to overestimate consumer sovereignty, a growing overvaluation of the idea that consumers today can have significant influence in shaping the media output offered to them. In that respect, they criticize studies that relativize the power of media production, particularly in the present day, when we are witnessing a concentration of production that tends to standardize opinions and culture. In other words, such studies would appear to underestimate the fact that there is a certain harmony between supply and demand in the globalized world. Some researchers even claim that 'consumer sovereignty' is a myth that needs to be deconstructed: the precariousness of labour relations and the intensive exploitation of human capital demonstrate the difficulties of creating a more balanced world within present-day capitalism.

However, even those authors who take a more sceptical view with regard to the possibilities of insubordination in today's world recognize in their works the important role played by certain counterhegemonic forces, pointing out that these movements and/or social networks play a significant part in the criticisms of and calls for changes in the global order.

There are a number of important questions to be asked in this regard: how to study the abovementioned forms of activism, or even the new sociocultural practices, while evaluating their potentialities without repeating past mistakes; how to research the social in a critical way – that is to say, without developing a naive or limited perspective; how to become fully immersed in the micro- and the social without losing sight of the macro-aspects of reality, without overlooking the more structural aspects of the functioning of globalized capitalism; and how to approach strategies for hegemony-building, and for reproducing relations of power and capital in research on counterhegemonic networks.

It is in this sense that I suggest taking as an alternative theoretical-methodological approach to these problems the proposal of working with 'circuits of culture' or 'cultural circuits', a notion developed by Hall and elaborated on the basis of the connected concepts of encoding/decoding (Du Gay, 1997; Du Gay et al., 1997). I justify this option insofar as the aforementioned proposal integrates the spaces of production and reception/consumption, thereby weakening the premise of the 'relative autonomy' between them. The relationship between culture and economy is increasingly interconnected: it is a phenomenon that cannot be ignored given the growing move on the part of transnational corporations to monopolize the cultural space.

Thus the adoption of this theoretical-methodological approach implies the need to work with a fairly broad research agenda that covers topics more commonly addressed by cultural studies or the political economy of communication. This more global perspective would allow researchers to critically consider various crucial moments and spheres of social life (Williams, 1992; Hall, 2005).

Hall considered 'cultural circuits' to be a highly significant concept which, when used appropriately in a research agenda, would enable various significant moments in the dynamics of social life to be analysed in a coordinated manner (Hall, 2005). In other words, this concept would, in his opinion, enable the analysis of

> linked but distinct moments – production, circulation, distribution/consumption, and reproduction. This would be to think of the process as a 'complex structure in dominance', sustained through the articulation of connected practices, each of which, however, retains its distinctiveness and has its own specific modality, its own forms and conditions of existence.
>
> (Hall, 2005)

On the basis of cultural circuits, Hall sought to build a research model that, on the one hand, did not focus specifically on one stage – of either production or consumption – and, on the other hand, was not linear like the traditional sender–message–receiver research model. It is the combination of the stages, articulated in a particular way, that enables them to be understood.

> You have to remember what a circuit is. It doesn't matter where on the circuit you start, as you have to go the whole way round before your study is complete. What is more, each part of the circuit is taken up and reappears in the next part. So having started with representation, representations become an element in the next part, that is, of how identities are constructed. We have separated these parts of the circuit into distinct sections, but in the real world they continually overlap and intertwine in complex and contingent ways. However, they are the elements which taken together are what we mean by doing a 'cultural study' of a particular object.
>
> (Du Gay, 1997)

This theoretical-methodological framework proposed by Hall does not, then, abandon the founding postulates of UK cultural studies. Economic relationships and changes are not absent from the work of either Hall or Williams: on the contrary, their presence is continually assumed through the supposition of cultural materialism. However, changes in the economic sphere are understood through their effects on the subjects' fields of experience, the relationships lived out: through 'global ways of life' or the 'constitutive social processes that create different and specific ways of life'. Broadly speaking, in this type of approach, culture is regarded as a space of protest and conflict, and also of consensus and social reproduction (Williams, 1992).

It is worth pointing out that Hall takes up the concept of 'articulation', which denotes the interweaving of things, as a useful idea for explaining the relationships between the symbolic (cultural) and the economic. Yet the concept of articulation does not simply describe a combination of forces – as may appear at first glance – but rather a hierarchical relationship. Thus this articulation of forces has been associated with the idea of 'structures in dominance', at least during a certain period of his thinking (Hall, 2005).

Operating in the gap between the textual and the social, Hall's work often tends to be seen as centring merely on the discursive. However, Hall himself opposes the current trend towards the textualization of cultural studies and his own inclusion within a perspective of that type. Taking into account not only his own explanations but also his theoretical output, it may be concluded that Hall's analysis places emphasis on cultural, symbolic and discursive practices; that issues of power and politics must be and always are embedded within representations; and that, although textuality is central, it is not sufficient for an understanding of culture. There are signs, then, that Hall is not satisfied with forms of analysis that ignore the materialities of power and inequality.

Thus, without abandoning this sphere of action, the cultural circuit theoretical-methodological model offers the possibility of constructing an object of study that includes culture as one aspect of the social practices that make up social formations. That is to say, research that adopts this protocol can be guided by an understanding of how cultural processes become effective in the articulation of a social whole. In that vein, in addition to the premise of articulation between the various moments that make up the circuit of culture, one of its advantages is that it incorporates the regulation stage, in which power takes up a central position and the action of the subject comes to be regarded in relation to the various processes of social control, which are absent from most studies that limit themselves to reception or production.

Developing the expanded research agenda

Working with the circuit of culture theoretical-methodological approach would thus enable a degree of progress to be made in research efforts, in spite of the fact that it is not always easy to work within an interdisciplinary perspective – articulating tools of economics, history, anthropology and sociology with communication – or in a complementary manner with quantitative and qualitative data, or with information gathered from primary and secondary sources. What is proposed is to preserve the dynamics of the process of production and reception, as well as a necessary correspondence between them, while nevertheless admitting that it is in the production phase that the message is created – that is to say, the starting point for the meaning-building process. In the conditions of production, institutional structure, production routines and the interference of professional ideologies are just as important as the social environment. The aim, therefore, of those research studies that have adopted this protocol is, on the one hand, to highlight the mechanisms of reproduction and subjugation present in contemporary society, and, on the other hand, to reflect on the ability of certain individuals or social networks to react, define or elaborate alternative proposals to the existing social order (Certeau, 1994).

In my recent studies on the current restructuring of the music industry (Herschmann, 2007), I did not identify either sovereign consumers or completely standardized masses, despite the fact that the present context is quite worrying. Actually, it can be argued that publics have been formed differently in the predigital and digital eras, although it is possible to identify continuities.

In spite of the high degree of corporate concentration and the dominance of the so-called 'majors' in the market, certain changes can be seen in the present-day music industry with regard to the relationship between those who produce and those who consume. On the one side, we see artists who are trying to develop new strategies and find alternatives for managing their careers, which depend less and less on the majors and more and more on the socialization of their productions. On the other side, we see consumers and fans who produce much-in-demand video clips of their idols; users who mobilize crowds of people to go to concerts; who work dedicatedly and voluntarily with social networks on the Web carrying out all kinds of activities for artists; who act as managers or go-betweens doing an important job of audience renewal or repositioning the artist's production within the genre or field of music (a clear example is the creation of tags by fans on the Internet); and consumers who are more interested in consuming music, now that it is available on technologies that fundamentally explore consumers' sensory aspects (Herschmann, 2007).

Clearly, the debate about the formation of publics/consumers is still ongoing: authorities and researchers from a variety of disciplinary fields have been trying to assess the relative influence of the family, school, the media, and public and private cultural enterprises in shaping the public within the current context marked by change (García Canclini, 2007). At the same time, government institutions dedicated to cultural dissemination find it difficult to acknowledge that their task of forming publics is no longer what it used to be. With precarious funds, such institutions are unable to compete with the work carried out by cultural industries in conjunction with society: they should promote educational experiences that effectively prepare individuals for the critical enjoyment of both art and the new languages that are now circulating intensively.

However, the education and training of critical spectators also fail to materialize not only due to the persistence of socioeconomic inequalities but also because cultural policies still operate based on models from the predigital context. Such policies insist, for example, on forming readers of books and spectators of the so-called fine arts. Unfortunately they are hardly ever geared towards educating spectators of new forms of art and entertainment consecrated by the communication and cultural industries. In parallel fashion, it can be argued that the industry is in a process of convergence, uniting languages and combining spaces: 'books are being produced, but so are audiobooks, and films are being made for cinema halls, but also to be watched on the sofa, using a mobile phone, etc.' (García Canclini, 2007).

Consequently, in recent years we have witnessed many significant changes that require researchers to develop tools to enable them to evaluate these transformations in a way that is neither deterministic nor overly simplistic. For example, people are now buying less from music stores, but at the same time we are seeing growth in the consumption of music video games, in addition to a significant increase in sales of musical instruments. Another example that could be given is the fact that the number of bookstores has decreased but there has been an increase in the number of Internet cafés and portable media for sending written and audiovisual messages.

Before reaching any hasty conclusions, therefore, these changes should be analysed – as suggested by certain media historians, such as Briggs and Burke (2004) – systematically in a long-term time series.

Final considerations

As can be appreciated through this chapter, the concept of 'circuit' – therefore the need to take into account the 'production of culture and the culture of production' (Du Gay, 1997) – was an important inspiration (almost a kind of research protocol) to the research work by a segment of scholars of cultural studies, more committed to a Marxist interpretation of social reality. However, the adoption of a theoretical-methodological approach that demands a global and complex perspective based on the idea of integrating the spaces of production and reception is not unique to cultural studies, or to its UK matrix. Indeed, it is an obsession found in various theoretical fields in different places and at different times. Within the Latin American model, I will mention the important work of Jesús Martín Barbero and the protocol he developed based on the notion of 'mediations'. Martín Barbero's concern rests not only on communication processes – with the condensing of networks of power and cultural production – but also on the emphasis he places on the need to assess the social uses of the media (Martín Barbero, 2002, 2003).

It is also essential to highlight the example of numerous studies in the specific field of the political economy of communication: these are works that seek to develop a global perspective on the dynamics of production and consumption – they operate as though these were an integrated pair – produced by leading researchers, such as Garnham (1990), Richieri (2008), Schlesinger (Schlesinger et al., 2001), Mosco (2005), Tremblay (1995), Bustamante (2001, 2002, 2003), Miège (2000) and Mattelart (Mattelart and Mattelart, 1997; Mattelart and Neveu, 2004).

It is true that, after analysing different theoretical trends in the field of communication, it could be said that there are now a significant number of researchers increasingly committed to studies that seek to make broader interpretations, conducting their analysis from an interdisciplinary perspective. García Canclini (2005) notes the wide public interest – even from experts – in a number of books that build up a global view based on the combination of different fields of knowledge, such as philosophy and social sciences. These are works that explore the rules of production, circulation and consumption of capital, goods and multitudes, as well as the way in which each one relates to the others. In a sense, they can be said to be works that produce 'mappings'. These mappings certainly do not translate into traditional cartography as such, but they do – as Martín Barbero (2002) suggests – form a necessary 'archipelago' of sorts. Although the number of researchers engaged in conducting these types of study may still be far from the ideal, the impact of this scientific output on the sphere of communication and related fields has to be recognized.

In spite of the fact that these studies face significant methodological challenges (some of which have been pointed out in the course of this text), we can conclude by highlighting some of the structural difficulties encountered by researchers dedicated to actively working with a broad research agenda:

- First, the shortage of available and reliable public data that can be used for research, which often makes more complex analyses quite difficult to accomplish. The obvious debate about the absence of cultural indicators – or indicators related to communication and culture – in a significant number of countries is an illustrative example of the situation faced by researchers today.
- Second, the scarcity of financial resources for carrying out such studies. This type of research almost always necessitates being able to rely on abundant and well-qualified human resources. It also involves most particularly conducting numerous research activities, many of them quite laborious and some aimed at producing primary data on the field of communication and culture. It should be emphasized that

the situation encountered in different locations and regions – such as in Latin American countries – is rather variable. Some countries have a more structured institutional framework that offers greater support for research when compared with others.

- Finally, it is necessary to highlight the lack of greater support from organizations or, rather, of clearer positioning in relation to the studies on the part of the institutions to which the researchers belong. Researchers nearly always complain about their lack of time, which they waste on the 'sterile productivist system' – which is hegemonic in the academic world – or on secondary and/or bureaucratic activities. In addition, researchers are always committed to building collaborative networks, which are fundamental for conducting their work, but which are often weakened for want of solid institutional support. Therefore, when assessing the limitations of the research conducted on behaviours, social practices and consumptions – especially in the Latin American context – it is also necessary for us to consider the precarious conditions in which most of these studies are carried out.

We might conclude by coming back to the arguments set out at the beginning of this text: perhaps the development of an interdisciplinary perspective that combines the political economy of communication with cultural studies – that overcomes the false dichotomy between these currents (Kellner, 1998) – is a crucial step that may enable progress to be made in the field of study on cultural practices and consumption.

Note

1. Richard Johnson (1986/1987) also proposes a model similar to the one put forward by Hall, based on a diagram of the circuits of production, textuality and reception, parallel to the circuits of capital highlighted by Marx.

References

Briggs, Asa and Burke, Peter (2004) *Uma social da mídia*, Rio de Janeiro: Zahar.
Bustamante, Enrique (2001) *La televisión económica*, Barcelona: Gedisa.
—— (coord.) (2002) *Comunicación y cultura en la era digital. Industrias, mercados y diversidad en España* (2nd edition updated 2004), Barcelona: Gedisa.
—— (coord.) (2003) *Hacia un nuevo sistema mundial de comunicación Las industrias culturales en la era digital*, Barcelona: Gedisa.
Certeau, Michel de (1994) *A invenção do cotidiano*, Petrópolis: Vozes.
Du Gay, Paul (org.) (1997) *Production of Culture, Culture of Production*, London: Sage.

Du Gay, Paul; Hall, Stuart; Janes, Linda; Mackay, Hugh and Negus, Keith (1997) *Doing Cultural Studies: The Story of the Sony Walkman*, London: SAGE Publications.

Escosteguy, Ana Carolina (2009) 'Quando a recepção já não alcança: os sentidos circulam entre a produção e a recepção', *Revista E-Compós*, 12(1), 1–15.

Ferguson, Marjorie and Golding, Peter (1998) *Economía política y estudios culturales*, Barcelona: Bosch.

García Canclini, Néstor (2005) *Diferentes, desiguais e desconectados*, Rio de Janeiro: UFRJ.

—— (2007) *Lectores, espectadores e internautas*, Barcelona: Gedisa.

Garnham, Nicholas (1990) *Capitalism and Communication*, London: SAGE Publications.

Hall, Stuart (2005) *Da diáspora. Identidade e Mediações Culturais*, Belo Horizonte: UFMG.

Herschmann, Micael (2007) *Lapa, cidade da música*, Rio de Janeiro: Mauad X.

Johnson, Richard (1986/87) 'What Is Cultural Studies Anyway?' *Social Text*, 16, 38–80.

Kellner, Douglas (1998) 'Vencer la línea divisoria: estudios culturales y economía política', in Ferguson, M. and Golding, P. (orgs) *Economía política y estudios culturales*, Barcelona: Bosch, 185–212.

Martín Barbero, Jesús (2002) *Oficio de cartógrafo: travesías latinoamericanas de la comunicación en la cultura*, México: Fondo de Cultura Económica.

—— (2003) *Dos meios às mediações: comunicação, cultura e hegemonia*, Rio de Janeiro: UFRJ.

Mattellart, Armand and Mattelart, Michèle (1997) *História das teorias da comunicação*, Porto: Campo das Letras.

Mattelart, Armand and Neveu, Erik (2004) *Introdução aos estudos culturais*, São Paulo: Parábola.

Miège, Bernard (2000) *Les industries du contenu face à l'ordre informationnel*, Grenoble: PUG.

Mosco, Vicent (2005) *The Digital Sublime: Myth, Power, and Cyberspace*, Cambridge, MA: MIT Press.

Richieri, Giuseppe (2008) 'As plataformas digitais e a evolução da indústria audiovisual', *Observatório*, 2, 85–95.

Schlesinger, Philip; Miller, David and Dinan, William (2001) *Open Scotland? Journalists, Spin Doctors and Lobbyists*, Edinburg: Polygon.

Tremblay, Gaëtan (1995) 'The Information Society: From Fordism to Gatesism: The 1995 Southam Lecture', *Canadian Journal of Communication*, 20(4), 461–482.

Williams, Raymond (1992) *Television, Audiences & Cultural Studies*, London: Routledge.

8
Cultural Consumption and Media Power

Francisco Sierra

All symbolic production is the inevitable result of a process of exchange and translation that is culturally mediated by the entire social system. In other words, the media are an institution that is historically and socially determined by the cultural system. And, for the same reason, their signifying practice cannot be understood without taking into consideration the political economy that conditions and governs the forms of informational representation. Consequently, analysing the media presupposes an attempt to understand the social change, and the technological, cultural and economic-political transformations that

> affect ways of representing, of the building of one's own truth and memory, desire and its *pregnancies*, the projections and expectations that human beings place within the spectrum of symbolic and cultural practices in relation to the self-understanding they come to about their own existence as individuals, but also in terms of their belonging and inclusion in the communities with which they identify themselves and in which they are recognized.
>
> (Brea, 2007)

Along the same lines, in contrast with conventional empiricist psychosociological perspectives, the study of cultural consumption has, in recent decades, sought to address the dynamics of interaction with the media from a more heuristically potent and reflective theoretical approach based on a historicocultural interpretation of the audience.

> Research in many different fields [has] thus been perforating the old unidirectional scheme of communication, diffusive, authoritarian, persuasive, educational, manipulator of empty minds or mass-man,

> to take a step forward towards a vindication of the receiver, which is also that of the capacity of the common man to structure the meaning of existence.
>
> (Ford, 1987)

Thus the text – and the productive mediation – has been displaced in favour of the pre-eminence of the public and its social interactions: from a reading of the signifieds to the signifiers, or, in other words, from informed reception to historically and socially significant interaction. The importance given to popular culture has thus opened up new directions for the social theory of communication in the study of problems of class, ideology and power, beyond the orthodox structural Marxism and liberal empiricism prevalent in positive sociology, thereby favouring an analysis of communicative uses focused on audiences as points of departure and arrival. This greater concreteness in communicological research has, however, ultimately resulted in a kind of apology of mass culture, which tends in general to distance itself almost entirely from the structural constraints determining all cultural production, particularly when we are talking about media industries.

Freed from the yoke imposed by reductionist concepts in the interpretation of fundamental terms, such as that of ideology – whose orientation was at first dominated by the Althusserian approach, since the fledgling school of cultural studies burst onto the social science scene in the 1970s – media culture studies have undergone a significant theoretical change in the most pragmatic and conservative sense of the word.

According to Barker and Beezer (1992), 'Cultural studies research is now less a matter of decoding the operations of power and resistance' than of 'giving voice to the meanings that are made in the here and now'. How far these meanings reach, where they may lead and what possibilities they may encompass are questions ignored by culturalist idealism when it comes to thinking about the scope and determination of social mediation. Cultural studies thus ends up representing a disjointed analysis of the practices of information consumption, outside the structures of production and circulation of social discourse. In fact,

- There has been a movement away from the notion of textual power to a restricted and limiting valuation of the strategies employed by readers and audiences:

> Cultural studies has shifted ground so that the concept of class has ceased to be the central critical concept. At best, it has become one 'variable' among many – but now frequently understood as

> just a mode of oppression, of poverty; at worst, it has dissolved away altogether. At the same time the primary focus has shifted to issues of subjectivity and identity, and to those cultural and media texts which inhabit and address the private and domestic domains. Simultaneously there has been a shift to a methodology which restricts interpretation to those offered by participants, sees them as empowered, and draws attention away from structures.
>
> (Barker and Beezer, 1992)

- Ethnography is, in this line of thinking, considered the only safe method to capture the full density of meanings of audience activity. This now makes it very difficult to maintain any notion of textual power as being complementary to the interpretations of publics when attempting to validate our understanding of ideologies. If the expression is allowed, in the terms of a certain postmodern discourse, we could argue that the original intention of understanding the main narratives of political rejection has been replaced by a willingness to explore those less evident – and superficially less heroic – stories of the everyday production of meanings, to such an extent that research sometimes even goes so far as to replace the preoccupation with power relations between texts and audiences with issues relating to forms of objectification and dominance embodied in the research process itself.
- All cultural activity is perceived, moreover, as a form of resistance to the inequalities of power and possession. In contrast to any theoretical claim that sees the subject as a product of public discourse, cultural studies identifies resistance with indiscriminate activity as a form of generalized and not specific opposition to mechanisms of dominance.
- The utopian celebration of cultural differences has, as a result, lost sight of the analysis of social determination. The obsession with recording and describing the familiar dynamic of reception, in its natural or domestic habitat, is preventing a thoroughgoing commitment to issues of textual power, of how families understand their place in the broader context of the social framework, and how this same framework conditions their access to cultural capital in the unbalanced field of our late-capitalist postmodernity.
- This leads to a logical theoretical domestication marked predominantly by the loss of context in which ultimately it is difficult to understand how and, above all, why TV – or other media such as the Internet – is used as a private communication resource in daily life.

- In summary, cultural studies has replaced macrosociological variables by issues of subjectivity and identity, at the microlevel, abstracted, in the concretion of the immediate, from the cultural and media texts that dominate domestic consumption and that ultimately mediate the general process of sociocultural reproduction.

In other words, the theoretical and political integrity that inspired this new line of study in the analysis and interpretation of active reception by audiences has been lost in the rhetorical game of discourse, when, paradoxically, and due to the development conditions of cognitive capitalism, the economic-cultural perspective that encouraged this knowledge policy on communicational phenomena now more than ever requires a clear and definite alternative for interpreting media consumption and the cultural relationship between the media and the social system as a whole as an ideological process and a space of representation of differences and class struggle. Issues such as

> institutional definitions of audiences (for example, in the broadcasters' departments of audience research); the emergence of new genres (which specify their own epistemological and communicative frames); the need to transcend binary ways of conceiving texts and viewer involvement (for example, as open versus closed); the effort to integrate new work on cognition; and the reformulation of the old question of the power and influence of the mass media (questioning, for example, the assumption that casual viewing is more resistant to effects than is concentration) require more reliable answers than the clichés that are now widespread in this current of mediological studies.
>
> (Barker and Beezer, 1992)

Nowadays, however, what seems to dominate is the eclecticism and positivity of the results of empirical research. The only thing that lends consistency to the different theoretical accumulations of this approach as a paradigm is its opposition to any determinism, to the extent that as a rule it tends to involve a tacit acceptance of extreme relativism as the only norm common to particular experiences of symbolic consumption by different audience segments.

However, in the postmodern culture of translation (the ductile), the simulated (the reality of reality) and the aleatory, if there is one thing that communicological research needs then it is comprehensive criticism of its legitimizing link that, from praxis, can transform such a logic according to the community requirements of social dialogue. It would be as well, then, to take into account the need for an epistemological reflection that overcomes the theoretical-practical excision, historicizing communication to link the moment of communicational analysis with the need for social change – all the more so when in the current development framework for the so-called 'information society', culture and knowledge are factors that directly determine the expanded reproduction of capitalist relations – and to seriously ask ourselves how effective *arrangements* of identification and citizenship take place, what mechanisms operate in the subjectivization and socialization that are now hegemonic in the age of transforming the world into a work of art. Furthermore, we need to begin by seriously asking ourselves how to activate new mediations and other research programmes in order that the contemporary struggles of the citizenry might enable other possible cultural mappings to be drawn, prefiguring new biopolitical machines and another type of individual and collective *arrangement* for social emancipation.

In the following pages I will attempt to outline some of the considerations in this regard by picking up a number of the main debates that have taken place over the past two decades between political economy and cultural studies, based on the work of Armand and Michèle Mattelart and the contributions of Italian neo-Marxism in its current interpretation of the creative and innovative ways of appropriating information and knowledge media and resources characteristic of cognitive capitalism.

Critical theory and cultural criticism of mediation

To paraphrase Marx, a topical problem shares the fate of any problem that is justified by its content – in other words, that is reasonable – in that it is not the solution but the problem in itself that constitutes the main difficulty. For this reason, true criticism does not analyse answers but rather questions. In the age of celebrating cultural populism, it is now time therefore to begin to ask what we scholars think about the media and cultural mediations, and on what basis. And on this point the Adornian questioning of the possibility or not of critical theory is more pertinent than ever now that we are hearing claims about the end of utopias due to the usurpation of any future imaginary by technoinformational devices, with the escape velocity of a future that is present, and is effectively tending towards the abolition of temporality. And even more so when all the social actors participate in the games of speaking and communicating, share contexts of communicative action, and develop scattered and rhizomatic resources of socialization. One of the characteristics of so-called cognitive capitalism consists, in this regard, in subsuming the general social intelligence on the basis of a new revolutionary process that, in a similar way to how Gramsci described the transformation of the social universe of Fordism and Taylorism, is tending to anthropologically alter the world of work, society and culture.

In this context, the debate taking place between political economy and cultural studies, which takes us back to the problem of studying consumption in the digital age, should no doubt be radically reformulated since, to some extent, the discussion has focused excessively on the problem of the subject, ethnomethodologies and the linguistic turn in the treatment of reception and everyday life on the other side of the screen, based on a limited historical reading, when it was more important to salvage the idea that any mediation is productive, and that there can be no mediation without production. The emphasis on surreptitious and ambiguous concepts such as the 'creative industries', or the commitment to development processes through stressing and concentrating public policies on the cultural dimension of capitalizing social networks, are merely contemporary forms of a new theoretical revisionism about which Armand Mattelart and Michèle Mattelart (1987) already cautioned two decades ago in *Pensar sobre los medios*.

In the era of immaterial labour, far from activating the emancipatory power of the singular, the new culturalist idealism serves to mask and reproduce the asymmetries and inequalities in the communication-world, which is why, now more than ever, it is essential to place the emphasis on the material conditions of existence in order to recover the reconstructive and critical potential of cultural studies and the critical theory of mediation. Because linking communication analysis to historicosocial praxis, to the real and concrete world of social actors, constitutes the basic axial framework that enables critical thinking to reveal the constituent logics of mediation, by linking information processes, general production and the symbolic universe from the point of view of social change and reproduction, which determines any media experience. This must be based on two new premises:

- The critical analysis of reception does not necessarily mean giving priority to production over consumption. Irrespective of the law which states that any supply creates its own demand, the important aspect in the critical and interpretative recovery of the complex dynamic of mediation is not necessarily the insistence on the relationship between capital and labour but rather addressing in detail the determinations of the contradictory relationship between subject and object in the global context of capitalist reproduction. In this sense, cultural studies in communication emerged precisely as an interdisciplinary field of analysis and historical criticism centred on the processes of social production and circulation of symbolic forms via collective dissemination media, based on the study of the institutional relations and practices that affect every cultural experience mediated in the social context and the life worlds (Featherstone, 1990; Grandi, 1995). And this institutional dimension, a constituent of mediation as a productive system, must be the ideal general sphere for understanding the everyday domestic and intrafamily ways of life of the subjects of reception.

- That is to say, the problem of the relationship between material goods and the symbolic entails analysing the general social logics of communication development. Unlike reductionist approaches to ideology, social structure and cultural functions in information theory, the socioanthropological study of the media must call attention to the importance acquired by information consumption as a process for producing meaning in the formation of cultural identities, highlighting the activity of publics in their interaction with mass culture channels and messages, as part of a broad, complex, contradictory and open process of social mediation, not one that is articulated around communication and cultural industries alone.

In other words, research on cultural consumption has to shift from culture to politics, and from contents and acts of everyday consumption to cultural codes, and consider, beyond the immediate, the relationship between public and private, between work and non-productive activity, as well as the role of the state in relation to cultural consumption.

Indeed, if we were to ask ourselves what contribution cultural studies has made to media analysis by interpreting the stage of reception, the answer would be precisely this: its capacity for openness and multidisciplinary integration. The usual fragmentation between disciplines that traditionally governed the study of communication and culture as separate and autonomous fields of mediation was later able to be replaced by an interdisciplinary vision in which the mediations of cultural industries began to be regarded as contiguous and integrated realities. For the first time in history, this was to involve a critical review of disciplinary compartmentalization, of barbaric thinking – Edgar Morin's dixit – the heir to sociological positivism, explaining social forms of producing knowledge and popular culture, by researching the disciplinary conditions that establish the issues, topics, methods and objects of communication research itself. We can therefore state that

> Both political economy and cultural studies are part of the same tradition in the social sciences. It could be said, following Foucault, that they owe their origin, in the first case, to the discovery of work, which explains wealth, and in the second, to the discovery of the grammar imposed quite literally by forms of representation.
>
> (Narváez, 2009)

The problem, basically, is that, in a context of the disarticulation of critical theory,

> the word 'culture' has also become an ideological and teleological resource for avoiding questions that are extremely uncomfortable for the system: for example, for contrasting it with politics and economics, using the argument, in the first case, that nowadays, at a supposedly more advanced stage of modernity, the new citizenries must not be regarded as being interested in power, the state and the public sphere but rather in daily life... and in the second case, that citizens' demands are now related to cultural recognition rather than economic redistribution. In other words, the same culture that created capitalism as an ethical stance has been responsible for eliminating the debate on capitalism by steering the discussion towards resulting problems such as overmodernity (Augé) or demodernization (Touraine), the society of risk (Beck), the information age (Castells) and, in the most daring example, towards globalization or the neutral version of imperialism, as Mattelart calls it.
>
> (Narváez, 2009)

The dominance of rhetoric and propaganda over the criticism of technocratism, irrespective of civic ethics, is a tangible sign of this social, theoretical and practical decomposition, in which it is possible to identify an ethnomethodological drift that loses sight of the structure and historical evolution of communication. For this reason, as Martin Serrano (2006) points out, it is necessary 'to invert the analysis in order to understand the construction of the rebuilding of the social sciences, and rebuild the sociohistoric meaning behind this intention'.

Considering the state of the art and the *drift* suffered by cultural studies with regard to reception, what is needed is a radically materialist overhaul of critical theory, and the production of emancipatory intelligence on culture based on at least three principles:

- No heuristic inquiry and particular methodology is immune to general paradigms. The multiple fabrics woven by the field of society, communication and culture do not give account of a finished object – that of collective communication – rather, this is a field that is always in a continuous process of production, caught between the norm of consensus and mobilizing contestation, between ideological imposition and domination, and counterhegemonic flights or disputes, between the orderly economy of signs and the generous outpouring of information, between continuity and rupture or, to use the apt expression coined by Lourau, between the instituted and the instituting. In contrast with what is stated by James Lull (1997), the cultural variation of the consumption process is not so diverse and unique as to invalidate theoretical power and the possibility of generalizing definitive explanations on specific audiences.
- Any discourse is integrated into a system of resources. A culturological reading along these lines entails, in other words, the integration of the transforming dialectic of the cultural system with knowledge of the forms of ideological control, through the analysis of the structures of social determination and the study of the live and unpredictable dynamic of marginal forms of cultural expression and representation in the interstices of the structure of society, from a critical and emancipatory vision. In other words, the dematerialization of information products due to the influence of digital technologies does not involve a process of disintermediation or disinstitutionalization of social mediation.
- There is no culture without politics. According to the writings of Williams, the active notion of culture presupposes a communicational actor in continuous dialogue with the symbolic universe, others and their time, and is the means of interweaving the *tensional* and contradictory aspects of society. The dilemma in this hypothesis is not recognition versus redistribution. As Narváez points out,

> Human beings are born both ethnicized and classed. Ethnicized through language; classed through their socioeconomic position. But since there are no classes without a language, or languages that are not socially rooted, under capitalism, ethnization becomes a form of enclassment due to unequal participation in the distribution of legitimate and empowering cultural resources at the same time that under capitalism enclassment becomes a form of

> ethnization which translates into a lack of recognition (discrimination) of a condition of cultural deficiency resulting from the non-possession of economic resources.
>
> (Narváez, 2009)

This unequal distribution poses a political problem that demands of theory the politicization of culture, in contrast with the culturalist apoliticism prevalent in studies on cultural reception and consumption.

If we accept that the media fulfil the role traditionally played by cosmologies – visions of the world that are at the same time particular perceptions of the people that give meaning to reality – compartmentalizing space and time, symbolizing it via the consumption of images and mediatized social discourses, it is necessary to ask ourselves what people do with the cultural products of the information media, such as the concrete mechanisms of production, use, and material and symbolic conservation of forms and devices of collective memory and imaginary, broadening the scope and vision of the readings made of this reality at the present time. What is the social significance of media cultures in the contemporary social universe? What is the relationship and the link formed between the mass media and other social communication practices? How are the dominant relations of social production and reproduction reproduced and modified by the mediating action of media discourses? What processes of subjectivation and identity occur in the social information mediation process? What type of culture is formed and transformed with the development of mediated communication? What are the characteristics of the new regime of cultural transmission and socialization imparted by the mass media?

Ultimately, establishing the principle of the centrality of communicative social mediation points to a map or field of multiple interdisciplinary dilemmas and problems from which to explain the processes of modernization and transformation of cultural traditions and their collective representation, and even the integration of the local and the global in the public sphere, with the confusion and the codetermination of popular cultures and media cultures or the change and affirmation of identities and senses of belonging, which would certainly require an open and sociocritical approach, as advocated from the very beginning by cultural studies – on the condition, of course, of beginning by insisting on the need for a theoretical reconstruction of meaning that goes against the dominant line of research, which extends from antagonistic politics to the condescending assertion of the equality of the modern individual due to the fraternity of social networks in the Web 2.0 era.

Cultural diversity, reception and cognitive capitalism

The variety and complex application of digital technologies in contemporary forms of collective action evince a new and productive social universe that stretches from counterhegemonic activism to the linking of thematic networks in blogs, or the mobilization of proliferating crowds via mobile communications:

> The interconnected and ahistorical space of the flows tends to impose itself on places, which are increasingly segmented and incapable of sharing cultural codes. Martín Barbero... considers that in the contemporary world, the idea and experience of identity surpass the interpretative frameworks of both an anthropology of the traditional-native (i.e., the logic of place), as well as a sociology of the modern-universal (i.e., the logic of the flows). Because nowadays identities, which are increasingly multilingual and transterritorial, are constituted not only from the differences between cultures that have developed separately but through the unequal appropriations and combinations that diverse groups make of elements from different societies and from their own.
>
> (Abril, 2003)

The problem of diversity in the cultural industries now emerges, therefore, as a nuclear concept indicative of a far-reaching change in the media and sociocultural mediations. Insofar as digital technology extends the possibilities of detecting and recording consumption habits thanks to new online measurement techniques and methods, and, as Postman observed, any technology is the bearer of a philosophy that sparks social processes of innovation, the contradictory and open dynamic of building the new system of digital mediation points, in this line at least, to the need to rethink numerous substantive issues concerning the stage of reception. That's because, among other reasons, as Gonzalo Abril (2003) cautions, 'multimedia languages help to develop not only a new sensomotoric intelligence but an entire epistemic *modus operandi*, which Maragliano describes as a worldly, horizontal and "participatory critique".'

In this scenario, thinking about audiences beyond the audiometer, entails contextualizing the fact of reception and digital technological innovations within the broader framework of the sociocultural changes characteristic of the early twenty-first century. It is only in this context that we can imagine the structural limits to the new demands of consumption from publics and the future role of the audience prefigured by battles such as that of News International Corp. for control of home multimedia services for digital TV, Internet and telephone communications. That's because, ironically, the dialectic that encourages changes in consumption habits is always accompanied by this type of strategy, which instead of democratizing the media seeks to restructure and redefine marketing activity according to the new technological and social environment that meets the specificities and the segmented diversity of audiences based on the demands of globalization and the dominant development model, which govern the traditional mediation structure. An obvious example of this logic is the international introduction of digital terrestrial television (DTT), where industrial concerns about the use and usefulness of decoders and interactive systems, which will affect the demand and industrial development of the sector, have dominated the process, leaving citizens in the dark as to the debate about both the audiovisual model for TV and the supply, uses and technological applications. In her doctoral thesis on the introduction of DTT into the EU, García Leiva (2008) in fact shows how this has led to the formation of citizen-users, while in general there is a degree of silence that accompanies a clientelistic relationship based on the ignorance of the audience and a complex social planning centralized by the large media conglomerates and the electronics industry.

In short, the insistent apology of semiotic democracy and postmodern pluralism as a premise for some of the approaches in vogue within cultural studies, as the common sense of communication theory, seems, in the light of these situations, like the re-edited version of a sort of solipsism equivalent to the reductionist norm of the text-centric perspective that it seeks to criticize, with its defence of the autonomy of the sovereign consumer proving to be a veritable array of arguments in favour of the free market and information and communications technology (ICT) companies. In other words, the postmodern dominance of the language and social thought of difference in the culturalist analysis of authors such as Clifford Geertz or Georges Marcus has been translated, in its application to communication, into a sort of idealist optimism on symbolic diversity and cultural pluralism, which in the field of the media limits all possibility of regulatory policy.

In such conditions we may well ask questions about the future of critical thinking, and it may even be debatable whether there are real alternatives and forces willing to restore the encouragement and incentive that inspired the original scientific bases that gave rise to this new culture of research, by attempting to define a way of thinking about communication that is committed to the various forms of subculture and popular communication for an emancipatory praxis, beyond the new liberal rhetoric that participates in the principle of market pluralism and the supposed sovereignty of the consumer. Thus, for example, in response to cultural relativism and the extreme valorization of the principle of audience pleasure as a form of cultural resistance, Morley proposed years ago, along this same line, coming back to the work of Stuart Hall to rediscover the operativity of ideology in contexts of media consumption, starting from the domestic arena, initially taking on himself the challenge signalled by Murdock, to develop a correct form of cultural studies conceptualizing the relationship between the two poles of the communication process – the material and discursive aspect and the economic-cultural aspect (Morley and Chen, 1996). But this and other proposals suggested from within the field of cultural studies ultimately ended up agreeing with the idea that cultural practices and interpretive acts on the part of the public are independent from economic and political structures, by dint of the fact that each subgroup or specific culture constitutes and autonomous interpretative community, which not only consumes the messages produced by the media in a different way but also filters and symbolically repositions the process of constructing the features of identity each receiver uses to decode and interpret media texts, according to their specific cultural circumstances.

For this reason, now more than ever, it should be recognized, in agreement with John B. Thompson (1993), that a critical theory of communication requires at least:

- conceptually, the examination of symbolic forms and their relationship with the social contexts within which they are produced, transmitted and received;
- historically, the reconstruction and development of the technical means of transmission and the institutional forms within which these technical means have been deployed and are deployed at the current time;
- theoretically, the reflection on the nature of the overall process of mediation and the impact it has on political and social life in the modern world and its implications for political and social theory in general and for the theory of ideology in particular.

We must at the very least, then, put forward a critique of certain visions of interactivity and the digital audiovisual sector as the scenario for a resurgent cultural democracy. The conception of the spectator emancipated on the basis of the potential of new technologies has, according to Schiller (1993), a blind spot: the impossibility of locating where the power lies in these new media. Since the mid-twentieth century,

> The West's efforts to stop and divert the almost global movement in favour of a change in the international informational and cultural order has received support from the explanations of cultural power based on active audiences. This theory has served to downplay, if not to place in doubt, the influence of the cultural power concentrated in the media.
>
> (Schiller, 1993)

As a consequence, the new theory of reception has ended up separating the political and economic arguments about cultural production from the analysis concerning elemental forms of private consumption.

This is to say that the problem with the privatization of cultural consumptions and of qualitative research on audiences is that it has idealized the forms of observation and analysis of the social, the criteria for interpreting reception through a fascination for capturing and discovering the particular moments of symbolic apprehension of concrete reality without questioning who produces meaning and what it signifies in ideological terms, the modes and content of cultural consumption. In short, the fact that the familiarity of the tone in which the language of the media is used masks the coercion and constraints of the code set up by the apparatus of domination is often overlooked in a very simplistic manner. The methodology thus becomes doubly diffuse since communicological research only yields to the rhetoric of liberal pluralism, and is lacking in an ideological point of inflection regarding the initial approach to the object or stage of reception. Thus, as a result, the basic inequality in the social order and in the possession of symbolic capital is assumed to be inherent to this order by the cultural studies of audiences themselves, when it is precisely the budgetary restrictions imposed by the regime of free competition that now in fact limit the desire for knowledge of consumption and demands not induced by publics.

Although since the beginning of the digital revolution demand has not ceased to grow, more is known about the quantitative than qualitative aspects of audiences, which enables us to state that their tastes, interests and needs are given very little consideration and that this contributes to the concealment of their political-cultural dimension. If we observe, for example, the case of the introduction of DTT, we can see that, during this process, not only has citizen participation in the production of messages or decision-making not been promoted,

> But also choice for viewers has not improved and their interaction in and with the programmes has not increased, demonstrating that although... the logics of social and cultural profitability have gained more discursive weight, their concrete expression in policy options has not prevailed in the various performances, loaded, in fact, in the short term with strong political, and at times also economic, content. (García Leiva, 2008)

To summarize our reasoning, we could say about this point that in the digital era not only have receivers been absent from the centre of the structural transformations of the new communication, but also they have been condemned to emulate the traditional social logics of mediation. Moreover, the study of audiences has not sought to vary its imaginary, and has thus fallen into multiple contradictions. The fact is, as Watzlawick (1979) points out, the problem of the knowledge context leads to the inappropriate apprehension of the object of study. Since they are unable to grasp the complexity of the relations between a reality and the context in which it occurs, between the organism and its environment, researchers tend to attribute to the object of study properties that it does not possess, except by extension of the same or other contexts or, as is often the case, in keeping with the industrial or technological vision of communication. When, in contrast with the common sense of reception studies, it would seem more than reasonable in the new information ecosystem to propose strategic aspects such as the forms of socialization of the new media culture, the degree of connectivity or the types of public participation in cultural contents and consumptions, by defining new use and consumption indicators to evaluate, based on the perceptions shared by audiences, the concrete practices of interaction, as well as the evolution of consumptions through longitudinal studies and non-induced or hidden demands on new communication services and devices. In this regard, there is a notable lack of research on community, collective and group forms of social appropriation of new technologies, as well as analysis of the impact on the social structure of the electronic modernization process in policies such as the accelerated introduction of DTT or the analogue switch-off.

We might, then, suggest that the problem of diversity in the cultural industries and the digital era is not only a matter of the plurality of supply, or even of the representative diversity of contents, formats and programmes distributed, but of the diversity of access available to the audience, the plurality of voices, groups and interests represented in the contents and in the participation of the media system.

> The problems of access for socially marginalized voices require investigations of a similar nature. This point is closely related to another one: the degree of homogeneity (or homogeneous trend) of media content. There is ample evidence that the news (in particular) not only tends to focus on a narrow set of problems, especially as defined by governments or other elite or official sources.
>
> (McQuail, 1998)

However, the same author states that

> What was once a radical criticism of the media seems to have been silenced or deflected to a great extent. Several of the prominent representatives of cultural theory now do not set any examples for the regulatory policies of the media. On the contrary, they are undermining them. The result seems to be, on the one hand, a project for a regulatory policy of the media that is increasingly more trite and inefficient and, on the other, a study project and criticism of the (mainly popular) culture of self-compassion, both remote and uncommitted.
>
> (McQuail, 1998)

Radical constructivism, the populist view and extreme contextualism are at the root of such an approach, which has permanently separated the traditional programme of regulatory policy from the cultural strategy of the media. Social equality, ethics, taste and aesthetics, the economic bases, art and cultural identity are dealt with by cultural studies in relation to the universe of communication without questioning the possibility, however minimal it may be, of a serious critical reflection that might stimulate contemporary public debate about the social and cultural role of the media. An intellectual project that – as Ferguson and Golding (1998) criticize – extols the virtues of eclecticism, relativism and a changing objective as a research agenda can hardly commit itself to a long-term media policy. With very few exceptions, such as that of Tony Bennett (1997), who calls for a more general regulatory policy that situates the most relevant issues relating to communication and culture in the context of the power relations that traverse any social practice, problems such as democracy and communication policy are absent from the culturalist agenda or, in the best-case scenario, are treated in a frivolous and superficial manner. The social action of the media has thus been gradually deanchored from its material basis of understanding, in a form of theoretical idealism and methodological pragmatism. Overlooking the historical realities of the inequality of access to cultural capital, informational concentration or the political rationales of info-entertainment and the market, media populism has thus introduced liberal economic assumptions into cultural analysis, thereby defining the processes of communicative interaction in distributive terms, without making any assessment of the material dimension of ideology, to say nothing of the historical detachment of the social movements and class formations to which the new left was linked from its advent, particularly the culturological approach to communication.

Thus, by moving away from the crudeness of economic reductionism and the base-superstructure model in a sort of pendulum motion, cultural studies has completely distanced itself from the material base and, to a large extent, also from politics. To paraphrase Eulalio Ferrer (1996), the critical theory of communication and culture has gone 'from being a struggle of classes to a struggle of phrases'. It is well worth remembering, in this regard, that the introduction of cultural studies occurred in a historical period marked by a swing to the right and extreme conservatism in both Europe and the USA, and by transformations in the structure of information as a result of three interrelated processes:

> The restructuring of cultural production and exchange on a global scale, in part associated with radical developments in the means of production with new technologies of information and communication; the restructuring of the relations of cultural production, involving in particular a social and economic repositioning of intellectuals; the specialists of symbolic representation; the restructuring of the relationship between political and cultural power, involving a potential redefinition of the role, and potential powers, of both state and citizen.
>
> (Garnham, 1998)

In this setting, the complex articulation of the economic, political and cultural spheres with which subordinate groups try to define their cultural self-determination was addressed on the basis of a vague, abstract idea of power, which favoured a lax and liberal interpretation of consumption and media cultures that would end up repeating the habitual errors characteristic of methodological individualism, irrespective of social structures and cultural history.

However, any critical theory requires both a historical and a structural perspective. No analysis of reality is of any value unless it takes a parallax view by revealing the past and projecting the architectures of the present onto the structural forms of the future. In other words, the sociocritical approach to cultural consumption depends on the capacity to relate or transfer the cognitive value, from the territory of reproduction and the archive to the field of production. It is thus necessary to place greater emphasis on those case studies dealing with both structure as well as content and audience, to obtain a comparative analysis of cultures, territories and channels. It is a matter of

> situating the productivity of meaning and significance (of reception practices) in a specific context of stabilized concepts and fortified social institutions and showing and laying bare the dependencies and interests of all kinds which from each of these contexts affect the production of narratives and imaginaries – whether these and they themselves are declared to be hegemonic or counterhegemonic, institutional or antagonistic.
>
> (Brea, 2007)

This was, at the outset, the priority task of cultural studies: to aim to explore the potential of receivers to resist and rebel against the real forces of the dominant ideological power.

Through the establishment of broad oppositions between the concepts of power/ideology and culture/participation, among others, the original aim of cultural studies was initially to try to provide viable solutions to the need to transform and reform radical projects. 'What can be done about the oppressive relations we are revealing? What forces are there, even if only potentially, that could lead to liberation? What strategies suggest themselves for supporting emancipator forces? And in consequence, what will count as liberation and emancipation?' (Barker and Beezer, 1992). These are the starting points from which research in communication and culture was to work in following this line. The answers to such questions, as is to be expected, require recourse to interdisciplinary theoretical approaches and a non-positivist and sympathetically imaginative methodological perspective on the common sense of publics in their appropriation of products of mass culture, which, as Williams points out, regards the search for connections between mass products and cultural relations and the understanding of the role of ideology in relation to popular culture as a process of symbolic hegemony-building (Williams, 1997; Stevenson, 1998). Or, in

Gramscian terms, it is a matter of seeking to better understand the true relation between hegemonic culture and civil society, by founding a critique to actively intervene in the field of mediation that is capable of reconstructing the complex networks of power and dependency – since, in accordance with Francis Pisani (2008), social networks lead to a diffuse form of exposure in the dual sense of enabling us to see and placing us in a situation of potential vulnerability.

In this logical framework, network analysis must be applied as a powerful heuristic tool of structural research. It is essential to remember, however, that we have two paradigms of social network analysis: the structural model or that of social (nomothetic) systems, and historical (ideographic) analysis. Based on the choice of this methodology, we can opt for different alternatives for researching reception, such as small-world networks, scale-free link distribution or studies on social capital and appropriation, along the line taken by Putnam. Each one of these proposals puts the emphasis more on either structure or agency, which is why, as Martín Serrano (2006) rightly states, these methodologies bring us back to general paradigms and principles of communicological research, from the epistemological point of view. And, in this regard, it should be stressed that a critical theory without emancipatory potential, without a communication policy, is, quite simply, a useless box of tools.

As we learned from Bourdieu, the activity of researching is not simply a question of methodology or a set of rules guaranteeing the logic of veridiction that fences off the object of knowledge, but rather a task that consists in illuminating, with the right intention of epistemological vigilance, the discovery of the truth, constructing a logic of enlightenment. The objectivity and overall progress of knowledge are compatible here with the democratization of information for the reproducibility of the results and conclusions found. In this endeavour we must be clear as to from where we are observing, how we construct our research object, what hypothesis we formulate, and why and how we plan the fieldwork. Only in this way will we be able to consistently conceive the creative act of contemporary cultural consumption in which the whole continuous flow of ricochets and circulations that characterizes the mode of being of cognitive capitalist production is a valorization of the network that constitutes it, provides it with feedback and continually updates it in an endless stream of echoes and refluxes. Hence the problem of consumption, which is the drama of a cultural output that is 'increasingly collegiate and distributed, the result of a participative process of echoes and resends that is increasingly broad and expansive, culminating in a general effect of intellection, of collective intelligence' (Brea, 2007).

This would require that a scientific policy of critical analysis of reception prioritizes at least three strategic lines of approach:

- The politics of representation: brands have colonized and commoditized the public space, narratively appropriating the imaginaries of rebellion and resistance. Thus, for example, advertising discourse has managed to codify the desire for freedom by converting audiences' libidinal passions, feelings and aspirations and transferring them from sex to consumption, at the cost, of course, of negating and trivializing the public sphere.

> Faced with the process of undifferentiated absorption at the heart of the broader entertainment industries, and their assumption of the tasks of engineering the individual and the social, it is the responsibility of cultural practices to develop and interpose mechanisms of criticism capable of revealing the interests and dependencies associated with each production of imaginaries of identification.
>
> (Brea, 2007)

As we argued earlier, in line with McQuail (1998), the need for regulatory guidance in the global media age is a demand that is increasingly evident in an environment of intensive development and growth of the collective media as strategic agents of contemporary economy and society. Problems such as globalization, cultural identity, traditional forms of national and popular culture, the economic domination and commercialization of symbolic contents, and even personal privacy more than justify the development of political reflection in this regard.

- The politics of the event: critical theory must produce experience and community. It is no longer so much a question of producing alternative imaginaries – other figures of representation, other narratives, other referents of identification – as of developing spaces and mechanisms that foster encounters, exchange and the commons.

> It is not a matter of providing the subject of experience of new stories or imaginaries of recognition; it is a matter of situating him in intensified contexts of relational encounter with other subjects of experience, in order that the processes of subjectivation and socialization that emerge there are achieved not in adhesion

> to any specific structure of founding narrative; but rather in the shared awareness of withdrawal and contingency.
>
> (Brea, 2007)

Critical theory, in one sense, is by definition innovative; it seeks to multiply dissent and diversify interpretations by creating bridges and original forms of observation in contrast or, as Bourdieu (2003) would say, as a 'firewall'. It is precisely here, where the greatest imbalance can be seen in the change processes between instituted forms of discourse and radical needs, that critical theory must question the social function of science.

- Economy of communication and culture policies: and, obviously, it is also necessary to describe and criticize the structures of power and inequality that the capitalist mode of production prefigures in the asymmetrical forms of cultural access and consumption, by pressing for the socialized implantation of new economies of distribution in the dialectic between communal forms of appropriation and the enclosures imposed in the struggle to privatize cultural codes and shared means of expression with digital technological innovation.

In conclusion

By way of notes in the margin on the problem under discussion, and taking into consideration the arguments presented throughout this chapter, we can therefore conclude, in accordance with the observations of Mattelart (2006), that cultural diversity in the digital age is not exclusively or largely determined by the plurality of supply or even by the representative diversity of contents, formats and programmes distributed, but rather, on the contrary, by the diversity of access available to the audience, the plurality of voices, groups and interests represented in the contents and, of course, by the participation and capacity to determine the model and structure of the system of means of representation.

If demanding studies on reception is to serve any purpose, then it is precisely along these lines, as an expository, sociocritical function, conceived as the will to power, as the shift from a cultural policy centred on consumption to a communication policy concerned with the dimension of production or of social projection, in terms of access and democratic control of the media. The need, then, to think about citizenship requires that we seriously reconsider the new concepts of the public and the common. A conceptual and epistemological debate that, although relevant in itself, is really about not repeating the traditional separation between theory and practice as has usually been the case in the Anglo-American line of cultural studies. In this endeavour, various lines of development must be prioritized – namely,

- The problematization of social demand or the problem of defining the 'radical needs' of communication. From Agnes Heller (1998) we know that in order to revolutionize daily life, an alternative cultural policy needs to consider the forms of reproduction and the moral economy of the crowd, as Michel de Certeau (2000) described in his day. This challenge, in our view, lies in tackling the problem of the social function of empirical knowledge that historically the more or less orthodox Marxist version of critical thinking has consigned to the analysis of forms of cultural identification, interaction and consumption. If we can transcend questionable formulations such as that of analytical Marxism or any form of methodological individualism that is not in accord with, or we might say is contrary to, the sociocritical approach, then thinking about audiences, structurally analysing logics of reception both quantitatively and qualitatively, using a more productive and integrative historicocritical approach, could no doubt help to advance the scientific programme of political economy – and more importantly still, to give greater consistency to the political proposals to democratize the media, from the point of view of social needs, thus avoiding any a priori formulation in public debates on the social function of the media.
- The integration of levels of analysis and approaches in the age of liquid modernity. The complexity of cognitive capitalism, the intricate and rhizomatic structure of network society, irrespective of the conceptual framework of interpretation that we adopt, presents a new context of social mediation that at the very least requires of us as scholars an integrated and complex approach to the different levels of analysis of reality that as far as possible can give account of the fluid forms of exchange and circulation of cultural capital, messages and repertoires. This entails not reproducing commonly used dichotomies, as is usual, for example, in the debate between the local and the global; in order to try to build bridges and conceptual systems of relation between the micro and the macro, between the ethnographic view and the historical and cultural perspective, along the lines of some outstanding analyses, such as that of Richard Hoggart (1995).

- The reformulation of the problem of ideology. Based on the original concept of cultural materialism identified by Raymond Williams (1980), studying the forms of consumption and reception in the political economy of communication involves recovering the critique of the myth of transparency, by reviving the notion of the opacity of cultural representations and of the praxis of the individuals themselves. In this regard the study of ideology cannot remain aloof from the analysis of the complex abstract forms of mediation at the service of the complete subsumption of society as a whole by capital. In keeping with David Harvey (2004) and Fredric Jameson (1991), an ideological critique of the speculative rationality of financial capital and the determination of symbolic contents requires, in addition, that any empirical analysis be based on a critical theory of postmodernity that is capable of providing a response to Foucault's paradox on archive and representation, as well as the problem of the political economy of the sign.
- The politicization of cultural consumption as a problem of *koiné* and citizenship. Lastly, the Sisyphusian challenge for emancipatory thinking continues, as it was in classical industrial society, to reverse the dominant discourses that regard citizens as consumers, now in vogue with the new forms of possessive individualism. Fighting a guerrilla war of communication in the new biopolitical struggles as a counterhegemonic struggle against the populist logic of proclaiming cultural democracy which, in practice, ends up closing down spaces of freedom and autonomy, the problematization of the relationship between citizens and the media requires, in our opinion, the necessary redefinition of commonly used notions such as the idea of public interest and, in general, the forms and strategies for defending democratic communication politics and the strategies of opposition and struggle for social change, from the recognition of the emergence of a new subject and a new political subjectivity, and, of course, based on the recognition of the formation of a new social context. Conservative sociologists such as Daniel Bell have since the 1980s been undermining the desire for the welfare state to progress by demanding the defence of the idea of the public household as a justification for reducing the social rights of the subordinate sectors of society. In addition, critical development theory now questions the role of the state as a guarantor of the conditions of self-determination for the population, while the process of cultural globalization advances, repeating the mythified forms of power and domination characteristic of capitalist barbarism, dismantling government structures and

> public control at the national level. Under these circumstances, it then seems logical to think that, in the age of cognitive capitalism, we must face the theoretical and critical challenge of thinking, no longer exactly without a state but at least from a postnational view that would enable us to see the contradictions and imbalances of the system for organizing information and knowledge, which is experienced and endured by the masses in the age of networks of cooperation and intelligent social production. This, consistently speaking, entails refining and redefining the concept of public service, politicizing the ways of producing knowledge, and recovering, for example, the emancipatory potential that Latin American critical theory once had precisely on account of its tradition of social praxis.

This and this alone is the strategic task involved in politicizing the analysis of cultural consumption – to not forget that the abstraction of daily life or, in our case, of the practices of cultural reception and consumption may ultimately escape the logic of intellectual workers' conditions of knowledge production. However, to recall the words of Benjamin, there is no document of culture that is not at the same time a document of barbarism and creative destruction of capitalist production. Ultimately, then, one has always to walk the streets to find again the rocky roads to freedom.

References

Abril, Gonzalo (2003) 'El séptimo día. Notas sobre la comunicación en la era digital', *Revista Científica de Información y Comunicación IC*, 1, 11–20.

Barker, Martin and Beezer, Anne (eds) (1992) *Reading into Cultural Studies*, London: Routledge.

Bennett, Tony (1997) *Popular Culture: Past and Present*, London: Routledge.

Bourdieu, Pierre (2003) *Contrafuegos. Reflexiones para servir a la resistencia contra la invasión neoliberal*, Barcelona: Anagrama.

Brea, José Luis (2007) *Cultura RAM. Mutaciones de la cultura en la era de su distribución electrónica*, Barcelona: Gedisa.

Certeau, Michel de (2000) *La invención de lo cotidiano*, México: Universidad Iberoamericana.

Featherstone, Mike (1990) *Global Culture: Nationalism, Globalisation and Modernity*, London: SAGE Publications.

Ferguson, Marjorie and Golding, Peter (eds) (1998) *Economía política y estudios culturales*, Barcelona: Bosch.

Ferrer, Eulalio (1996) *De la lucha de clases a la lucha de frases*, Madrid: Taurus.

Ford, Aníbal (1987) 'Aproximaciones al tema de federalismo y comunicación', in Landi, O. (comp.) *Medios, transformación cultural y política*, Buenos Aires: Legasa, 59–87.

García Leiva, Mª Trinidad (2008) *Políticas europeas para la transición digital en televisión. Análisis comparado de las políticas de TDT en el Reino Unido y España*, Madrid: CSIC.

Garnham, Nicholas (1998) 'Economía política y la práctica de los estudios culturales', in Ferguson, M. and Golding, P. (eds) *Economía política y estudios culturales*, Barcelona: Bosch, 121–144.

Grandi, Roberto (1995) *Texto y contexto en los medios de comunicación*, Barcelona: Bosch.

Harvey, David (2004) *El nuevo imperialismo*, Madrid: Akal.

Heller, Agnes (1998) *Teoría de las necesidades en Marx*, Barcelona: Península.

Hoggart, Richard (1995) *The Tyranny of Relativism: Culture and Politics in Contemporary English Society*, London: Chatto & Windus.

Jameson, Fredric (1991) *El postmodernismo o la lógica cultural del capitalismo tardío*, Barcelona: Paidós.

Lull, James (1997) *Medios, comunicación, cultura*, Buenos Aires: Amorrortu Editores.

Martín Serrano, Manuel (2006) 'Para reconstruir el sentido que tiene el intento de deconstruir las ciencias sociales', *REIS: Revista Española de Investigaciones Sociológicas*, 114, 137–154.

Mattelart, Armand (2006) *Diversidad cultural y mundialización*, Barcelona: Paidós.

Mattelart, Armand and Mattelart, Michèle (1987) *Pensar sobre los medios. Comunicación y crítica social*, Madrid: Fundesco.

McQuail, Denis (1998) *La acción de los medios*, Buenos Aires: Amorrortu Editores.

Morley, David and Chen, Kuan-Hsing (comps.) (1996) *Stuart Hall. Critical Dialogues in Cultural Studies*, London: Routledge.

Narváez, Ancízar (2009) 'La globalización como expansión alfabética anglosajona' (mimeographed document), Bogotá: Pedagógica Nacional University.

Pisani, Francis (2008) 'Redes sociales y vigilancia participativa', *El País*, Madrid, 8 May.

Schiller, Herbert I. (1993) *Cultura S.A. La apropiación corporativa de la expresión pública*, México: Universidad de Guadalajara.

Stevenson, Nick (1998) *Culturas mediáticas. Teoría social y comunicación masiva*, Buenos Aires: Amorrortu Editores.

Thompson, John B. (1993) *Ideología y cultura moderna. Teoría crítica social en la era de la comunicación de masas*, México: UAM-X.

Watzlawick, Paul (1979) *¿Es real la realidad?*, Barcelona: Herder.

Williams, Raymond (1980) *Marxismo y literatura*, Barcelona: Península.

—— (1997) *La política del modernismo*, Buenos Aires: Manantial.

Part IV

Challenges in Thinking about Communication and Culture

9

Digital Networks and Services: A New Political and Technological Agenda

Luis A. Albornoz

When analysing the technology–society binomial in his famous work on the medium of TV, Raymond Williams (1974) advocated an interpretation that regards technology as an object looked for and developed on the basis of certain purposes and practices (known social needs) that precede it. This involves stepping back from both so-called technological determinism and from the viewpoint of symptomatic technology, two perspectives deeply rooted in modern social thought that depend for their formulation on the isolation of technology. While technological determinism understands that 'new technologies are discovered, by an essentially internal process of research and development, which then sets the conditions for social change and progress, the view of symptomatic technology 'assumes that research and development are self-generating, but in a more marginal way. What is discovered in the margin is then taken up and used'. Distancing himself from both perspectives, Williams was to state that broadcasting, like any other technology, is the result of 'a set of emphases and responses within the determining limits and pressures of industrial capitalist society'.

Following Williams' line of thought, the comprehensive digitization of a significant part of all cultural contents – a process that covers both the manufacturing of devices for producing, playing and receiving, and

This chapter is an updated version of the chapter 'Redes y servicios digitales. Una nueva agenda político-tecnológica', published in the Spanish edition of this book, *Poder, medios, cultura. Una mirada crítica desde la economía política de la comunicación* (Buenos Aires: Paidós). I am grateful for the support provided by the São Paulo Research Foundation (FAPESP), Brazil, through the 2014/03219-6 grant process.

the installation of physical and wireless networks – is the intrinsic result of earlier industrial transformation and its new social forms.

As indicated by the results of a collective research study conducted at the beginning of the last decade (Bustamante, 2003), we are witnessing a new digital cultural landscape still under construction from a technological perspective but, above all, from the social and economic point of view. This landscape is being carved out by the highly dynamic and complex relationships established between public authorities at various levels (international, national and local), corporations belonging to the different branches of industry (from large national and multinational business conglomerates to small, medium and microenterprises) and the citizenry (organized into interest groups or not). In this complex social game, each player acts based on their own interests and needs.

Digital communication technologies and their attendant changes in the production, circulation and consumption of cultural contents must therefore be analysed, while taking into consideration a series of interrelated processes that precede and accompany them. These notably include:

- Normative 'deregulation' or 'reregulation': understood as a change of position by the state regarding a set of economic activities (audiovisual industry, telecommunications) that encourages the private sector to play a part. This, like other processes that have affected the sphere of culture and information in recent decades, has been driven by policies of a neoliberal bent. With its own characteristics in each region and country, the result of this process is a significant increase in the weight of the corporate sector within the field of communication and culture.
- Large-scale business concentration: a process that has been witnessed for decades at both the national and international level in the absorption and mergers of commercial firms. The most visible result is the formation of large conglomerates with a presence in different branches of the cultural industries.
- The growth in the production, dissemination and consumption of multiple flows of cultural content (Miège, 2000): particularly evident in the audiovisual sector and encouraged by the expansion of new forms of dissemination (broadcasting of content via cable and satellite).
- The internationalization of capital, agents and content: a process that is not new and that for the last century has accompanied the development of certain cultural industries, such as the cinema and recording

industries, but which in recent decades has spread to other sectors – TV, publishing.

- The 'financialization' of the informational and cultural sphere: this is a more recent change. It first involves the entry of financial institutions into the different branches of the production of information and culture, thereby displacing traditional actors. Second, it is evident from the fact the main media conglomerates are listed on the stock exchange. This process (flotation, distribution of dividends among shareholders, capital increase) deepens short-term commercial logic in the field of information, communication and culture.

The new political and technological agenda

In this social, political and economic context, the comprehensive digitization of the cultural industries brings with it new social problems that arouse controversy and conflict between independent creators, business agents, copyright management bodies, citizen-users, public administrations and consumer organizations. These are new thematic areas in need of producing knowledge regarding the positioning and actions of public powers, the corporate sector and the citizenry.

In this sense the development of the various digital networks, led by the Internet, presents itself as a new field of battle in which some of the disputes typical of the cultural industries in their analogue phase are revisited: public service versus commercial interest, political control versus freedom of information, regulation versus *laissez-faire*, standardization and homogeneity versus cultural diversity, commercial control versus privacy.

Given the evident social, cultural and economic importance acquired by the content and services accessed through digital networks, the international expansion of these networks poses a range of problems that give rise to a new political and technological agenda. This agenda serves as a focus for social debate and renews questions about the relationship between technological innovation and social change. In response to the celebratory discourse that accompanies technology implementation in the various facets of social life, which equates technological innovation with development, it is necessary to evaluate technological progress and question its ends, means and consequences.

The following section presents several areas of the current debate, which covers aspects related to public policies, business strategies and social uses.

Internet access: A fundamental right?

The Internet has been (and is) considered to be the main entrance point to the so-called 'information society', understood as a political-economic project in which information and communication technologies play a central role (Lacroix and Tremblay, 1997; Garnham, 2000; Mattelart, 2002; Becerra, 2003; Crovi, 2004). So important is it that states and international organizations have come to postulate the need to establish public policies to guarantee access to the network of networks for the various social sectors and to form 'digital citizens'. The aim is to thereby eliminate the major disparities ('digital divide') observed at both the international level and within nations, which was a problem addressed without concrete results at the two-part WSIS (Geneva, 2003; Tunis, 2005) organized by the International Telecommunication Union in the middle of the last decade.

Some general data may give us a rough idea about the prevailing inequality of access to the Internet. According to the Internet World Stats portal, only 39 per cent of the world's population are Internet users. At the regional level, while 84.9 per cent of the inhabitants of North America access the 'network of networks', the figure for Africa barely exceeds 21 per cent.[1] For their part, data from December 2013 on the group of 34 countries that make up the OECD indicate that the average penetration of fixed broadband (DSL variants, cable, fibre/LAN) is 27 connections per 100 inhabitants, based on a broad spread of average values ranging from those of Switzerland (44.9), the Netherlands (40.4), Denmark (40) and France (37.6) to those of Chile (12.9), Mexico (11.4) and Turkey (11.2) (OECD, 2014).

When considering infrastructure development alone, it can first of all be observed that in most countries not all geographical areas have Internet access. As has happened in the past with the development of other networks, remote regions with a scarce population do not prove profitable for network operators and are therefore not provided with coverage. Second, within the context of limited interbusiness competition – oligopolistic structures containing operators that hold dominant positions – Internet access providers impose different sales modalities with varying connection speeds.

As part of its supranational policy with regard to the information society, the European Commission has begun to explore the possibility of including broadband access in the universal service obligations for telecommunications to ensure that no citizens are excluded from digital society. Having achieved basic broadband coverage for all citizens in 2013, the Digital Agenda for Europe sets as a target the universalization of ultrafast broadband by 2020 (minimum speeds of 30 megabits per second).

At the national level, countries such as Finland have established that Internet access should be regarded as a fundamental right of all citizens. By virtue of the decree issued by the Ministry of Transport and Communications, since 31 July 2010 every Finnish home has been provided with a minimum connection of 1 megabit per second, which must reach a 100 megabits by 2015 (Government of Finland, 2009). In the case of Spain, since 2011, Internet access at a speed of 1 megabit per second has been classified as universal service.[2] This means that any citizen, regardless of their place of residence, has the right to digital equality, which is understood as a universal right to Internet access with broadband connections that comply with the rules on quality, accessibility and affordability. However, it is disputed whether the basic broadband speed for data transmission of 1 megabit is sufficient to ensure functional Internet access as universal service provision (Síndic de Greuges, 2013).

This series of government announcements could be marking a trend towards the democratization of access to Internet infrastructures. However, for the time being, these are just isolated cases; and, in the context of the vast majority of Latin American countries, such measures for democratizing access are highly unlikely. Moreover, the unquestionable importance of these provisions has aroused reactions of different kinds: while Internet access providers maintain that 'it makes no sense' to increase costs for companies in the sector by including Internet in universal service, Internet users' associations consider the minimum connection speeds involved to be very low and demand reasonable prices, in view of the high tariffs charged in certain markets.

Net neutrality

Another controversial aspect related to the development of digital networks and their generic transport capabilities is that known as 'net neutrality', a principle whereby a network access provider may in no way discriminate against any kind of content or service offered online and transmitted through that network, whether it is fixed or mobile. Examples of a violation of this principle, tacitly established since the early years of digital network development, are the blocking of peer-to-peer (p2p) file-exchange systems by the cable operator Comcast in the USA in 2008, and the ban on the use of the Skype service on mobile telephony networks enforced by telephone operators such as T-Mobile (Germany) and Movistar (Spain) in 2009.

On the opposite side of the fence from the advocates of the principle of net neutrality – producers of online content, applications and services, and users' associations – we find the telecommunications and cable operators. Arguing that they are responsible for the establishment, maintenance and future development of networks, these operators claim the right to discriminate by applying different speeds and/or tariffs according to the service offered by third parties. Among other initiatives, access providers have put forward the idea of creating a 'Google tax': a sort of toll paid to online search engines that generate a large number of visits for the use of their infrastructure.

It should be remembered that there is no agreed definition regarding what is meant by net neutrality, a principle that brings together multiple aspects and that is currently being debated on numerous forums. According to the document *Contribución de España a la consulta pública sobre Internet abierta y neutralidad de red en Europa* (Government of Spain, 2010), net neutrality

> emerged as a principle of 'non-discrimination' derived from the... guarantees of end-to-end connectivity and respect for the integrity of the information transmitted, the specific aim of which is for all communications to be treated equally regardless of their origin or destination and the type of information transmitted.

Formulating the principle in these terms and applying it to the area of digital networks would lead to the prohibition of commercial practices currently in force – pricing based on consumption or, in the case of flat-rate plans, pricing based on connection speed. In this regard, the document itself immediately establishes that net neutrality should not be understood in the strictest sense to mean that all users should receive an identical type of service, since both traditional and modern networks 'offer multiple access products that differ in regard to capacity or guarantees of quality (and therefore price) in order to respond to the wide variety of users' needs'.

By way of conclusion, the Spanish authorities consider it 'more appropriate' to regard net neutrality as a principle that

> seeks to prevent *undue discrimination* on the part of providers of electronic communications networks and services, which should be considered to include any practices of blocking, restricting or managing traffic that have anti-competitive results, or those that contravene the requirements of end-to-end connectivity and respect

> for the content of communications generally applied to electronic communication services.

At the international level, following almost three years of debate and a highly active campaign by cyberactivists grouped around the online platform Neutralidad SI, in July 2010, Chile became the first country to enshrine the principle of net neutrality. In its single article, the law establishes that access providers

> may not arbitrarily block, interfere with, discriminate against, hinder, or restrict the right of any Internet user to use, send, receive or offer any legal content, application or service via the Internet, or any other type of legal activity or use carried out via the Web.

In May 2012, the Netherlands became the second country in the world to integrate the principle of net neutrality into its legislation. The regulations include several points aimed at providing users with greater protection against possible disconnections and the control of traffic content of by Internet service providers. The Dutch law also stipulates that users can only be disconnected from the network in the event of fraud or non-payment of bills.

The debate about net neutrality has become particularly heated in the USA, a country where the firms grouped together in the Open Internet Coalition (Google, eBay, Amazon, Flickr, YouTube, Facebook and PayPal, among others) are pitted against the network communication and technology companies (Cisco, Motorola, Nokia or Alcatel). Both lobbies are exerting considerable pressure on the body responsible for defining communication policy, the Federal Communications Commission (FCC), whose authorities established the criterion of net neutrality in December 2010 through the Open Internet Order.

However, in early 2014, the judgment of a federal court of appeal in Washington in the case of *Verizon Communications Inc. vs. FCC* seems to have brought about a break in the political direction hitherto pursued by the electronic communications regulator. The court found in favour of Verizon, one of the major telephone operators, in the suit it had filed against the FCC for having prevented it from being able to establish different download speeds. The judicial organ accused the FCC of overstepping its function, since in 2002 the FCC itself had classified Internet service providers as information services and not as telecommunications services, meaning that it has no power to regulate them. The ruling also considered that Verizon has the right to create the rules of access to its services, while maintaining the principle of net neutrality, but on the condition that it does not overstep its powers. This decision forced the FCC to review the regulations to make it easier for Internet connection providers to offer services with different speeds in exchange for extra payment. In April 2014, the FCC announced its proposed new rules, which grant broadband Internet service providers (e.g. Comcast and Verizon) the 'right to build special lanes' with faster connection speeds for companies (e.g. Netflix, Disney and Google) willing to pay a higher price. Those voices most critical of the FCC's proposal argue that the regulator is giving in to the interests of the large telecommunications companies, which raises two problems: that only large companies would be able to afford such a tariff (which could have an impact on the subscribers to the service) and that the current ecosystem which has enabled the consolidation of dozens of start-ups would disappear.

For its part, the EU undertook an extensive public consultation, between 30 June and 30 September 2010, in which it invited all the sectors concerned – public authorities, service and content providers, consumers, businesses and researchers – to address the following questions: Should access providers be allowed to adopt traffic-management practices that give priority to one type of traffic over another? Can traffic-management practices create problems and have undesired effects for users? Can the level of competition between different access providers and the transparency requirements of the new telecommunications framework be sufficient to prevent potential problems while allowing consumers to choose? Is there a need for further actions to ensure fairness in the Internet market, or should industry take the lead in this area?

As a result of this consultation, the European Commission issued a communication entitled 'The Open Internet and Net Neutrality in Europe' (European Commission, 2011), which seeks to promote the neutral and open nature of the Internet. The document focuses on the obstacles facing Internet neutrality: the blocking or regulation of traffic by certain network operators, which restrict access to services (online TV, videoconferencing, etc.) or to Internet pages; traffic congestion, which needs reasonable management; and the lack of transparency, which prevents users from making informed choices about services. In this regard the communication states that

> the fact that some operators, for reasons unrelated to traffic management, may block or degrade legal services (in particular voice over IP [Internet protocol] services) that compete with their own services can be considered to run against the open character of

the Internet. Transparency is also an essential part of the net neutrality debate. Obtaining adequate information on possible limitations or traffic management enables consumers to make informed choices.

Given this precedent, in April 2014 the European Parliament voted in rules that prevent Internet access providers from blocking or restricting services or content to manage their network traffic.[3] This decision was taken following months of campaigning by the digital rights advocates and technological service companies that support this legislation (Body of European Regulators of Electronic Communications; Save the Internet campaign; Avaaz.org platform) in the face of opposition from telecommunications operators, which argue that rates for different speeds and services help them to invest in upgrading networks.

Brazil, for its part, adopted the Civil Framework Law in April 2014, dubbed the 'Internet Constitution', which introduces respect for civil rights in the use of the Web. The Civil Framework, the result of a broad discussion involving numerous institutions and prominent figures, enshrines the principle of neutrality, limits the responsibility for intermediaries (Internet service providers), and guarantees the freedom of expression and privacy of users. With respect to net neutrality, Article 9 of the regulations (Government of Brazil, 2014) stipulates that:

> The entity responsible for the transmission, switching or routing is obliged to treat any data packet in an isonomic manner, regardless of content, origin and destination, service, terminal or application.

Any agreements established in the future by the small number of Internet operators and main providers of goods and services will be vitally important in shaping the online landscape, since they have the ability to negatively affect the diversity of the different content and initiatives that populate networks (Albornoz, 2011). The problem is compounded when we take into consideration the fact that some access providers offer their own online services, such as e-mail or news-aggregation portals.

From a business perspective, Alcántara and de Ugarte (2010) note that 'on the pretext of allowing bilateral negotiation between Internet service operators and providers, the aim is to limit competition for those players with the greatest financial clout'. Thus, argue these consultants, 'eliminating net neutrality would not mean greater market freedom, on the contrary, it would destroy the competitive and meritocratic market that is the Web today'.

E-commerce versus piracy

One of the most controversial and complex problems on the current political and technological agenda, which is intrinsically linked to the possibilities of commodifying cultural production in digital networks, is that posed by the right to commercialize cultural goods and services contemplated both by the system of authors' rights in the Latin sphere and the system of copyright in the English-speaking sphere. Addressing this issue involves swimming in troubled waters: caught between the necessary remuneration of cultural workers for their creative labour and the right of every citizen to benefit from culture; between property rights and the public domain.

The main actors in the cultural industries attribute the causes of the current, and future, crisis suffered by various sectors (particularly the music industry) to both the sale of illegal physical copies as well as free downloads and exchanges carried out by millions of users via networks and digital devices. Large firms and copyright-management companies represent the main opponents of some of the changes in the area of cultural consumption, which have been promoted by the emergence of digital networks, and seek an automatic transposition of the relations and conditions that underpinned the development of the cultural industries in the past. Combating the sale and purchase of copies outside legal marketing channels, and free downloads and exchanges of content – songs, films, TV series and so on – is therefore seen as a priority.

Supported by the governments of the major countries, the main actors in the cultural industries have thus been investing valuable resources and articulating efforts at the international level on four identifiable fronts of action: education, legislation, the justice system, and law enforcement and technology.

In terms of education, the aim is to encourage 'responsible Internet use' among users and to obtain the 'collaboration' of digital network access providers. To this end, social awareness campaigns have been organized, some of them international in scope, about the pernicious effects of 'digital piracy'. Many of these campaigns criminalize widespread social uses, such as free downloads via p2p networks.

With regard to legislation, the objective of the majors and rights-management companies is to influence the enactment of measures 'adapted to new technologies'. Thus, in some countries, the main representatives of the cultural industries have managed to ensure that the tax on digital media and devices is gradually extended from blank compact discs to mp3 players and pen drives, although not without opposition from hardware manufacturers and computer users. For their part, countries such as France, the UK and Sweden have already taken steps towards introducing systems of warning messages with subsequent disconnection or monetary fines for those individual Internet users who perform free downloads of copyrighted content. Outside the Western European context, in 2009 South Korea and Taiwan reformulated their respective legislation to pursue 'pirates'.

With respect to the justice system and law enforcement, the aim is for the repressive apparatus of the state to play a more leading role, through faster legal proceedings as well as an increase in the number of police personnel engaged in the fight against 'piracy'. Public demonstrations of unauthorized copies of CDs and DVDs being destroyed by steamrollers have become an everyday sight.

Lastly, at the technological level, a defence is made of the need to use technologies to establish a 'clean market free from competition'. This has resulted in the development of technological devices, known as digital rights management systems, the purpose of which is to prevent contents from being copied and/or the same content from being used in various electronic devices. In practice, however, content encryption systems have not been successful in counteracting the skills of users, so we are now witnessing their virtual disappearance.

In summary, these are a set of actions implemented on the four different but interrelated levels. As can be observed, the main business associations maintain their stance of making no attempt to differentiate between those practices that are profit-oriented (sale of physical copies of content) and those that do not seek direct economic benefits (exchanges and free downloads between consumers). Efforts are thus being made to criminalize social practices of distribution and consumption that have spread on an international scale as the level of Internet penetration has increased. To get an idea of the scope of the abovementioned practices, it should be noted that only 5 per cent of the 20 billion music files circulating annually are actually sold (Attali and Olivennes, 2008).

Software: Closed or open systems?

The penetration of digital networks is accompanied by the growing importance of free or open source software (OSS). These are IT programs that are collaborative, shared and low-cost, in contrast with so-called proprietary software, patented by large multinational corporations, the use of which involves expensive licensing, implementation and maintenance contracts.

Broadly speaking, software is considered 'free' if it guarantees the freedoms to (a) use it for any purpose; (b) study how it works and modify it – for which purpose it is necessary to know the source code, a fundamental tool for finding out whether the software has functions that control or invade the user's privacy; (c) distribute copies of it; and (d) improve it and make the improvements public.

In addition to the pioneering work carried out by many non-profit organizations (e.g. Free Software Foundation or Mozilla Foundation) and users associations in developing free software, in the last few years, efforts have been made by the public authorities of various countries, which see the use of free software as a commitment to democracy.

The 'Informe sobre el panorama internacional del *software* de fuentes abiertas' (CENATIC, 2010) confirms that the level of adoption and development of OSS varies considerably between different geographical regions of the world. This variability tends to correlate with the degree of information society development exhibited by a region or country. Countries with stronger economies, such as the USA, Australia and the countries of Western Europe, thus display high levels of both information society development and the use of OSS. For their part, the regions of Africa, Latin America and Eastern Europe record low values in relation to both the rates of development of their information society projects and the use of free software.

In the Latin American context, in spite of showing a level of information society development similar to that of Argentina, Mexico or Chile, the South American giant, Brazil, stands out from the rest of the countries in the region due to its higher level of free software adoption and development – comparable to that of countries such as India and China. According to the CENATIC (Centro Nacional de Referencia de Aplicación de las Tecnologías de Información y la Comunicación basadas en Fuentes Abiertas) report, the reason for this notable situation lies in the impetus that the Brazilian Government 'has been able to give to all areas of the OSS ecosystem: the publication of regulations, mass migration in public sector agencies and companies, development of OSS products (goods and services) by public universities and the creation of a collaborative portal for the actors in the Community'.

In the middle of the last decade, the Brazilian Government presented the *Guia livre. Referência de Migração para Software Livre do Governo Federal* (Government of Brazil, 2005). The reasons highlighted for the adoption of free software by the state included the need to adopt open standards for e-government; the level of security provided; the elimination of compulsory changes that proprietary models periodically impose on their users; technological independence; the development of local knowledge; the possibility of auditing systems; and independence from a single bidder. The *Guia livre* also emphasizes respect for the principles of impersonality, efficiency and reasonableness, and explains that:

> The state benefits directly from the adoption of Free Software, in regard to both its structuring to meet social demands as well as its role as a development promoter. We thereby enable the integration of policies of administrative modernization and social inclusion based on information technology and industrial development.
>
> (Government of Brazil, 2005)

As can be seen, there are a variety of weighty arguments for adopting free software for Internet use. The advantages for the citizenry as a whole in this regard are clear. The current challenge involves incorporating OSS and applications into state-of-the-art digital devices (laptops, mobile phones, tablets, multimedia players, etc.). Examples of such initiatives include those of the Open Handset Alliance, an organization set up by hardware, software and telecommunications companies dedicated to developing open standards for mobile devices at the same time as the launch of the Android (Google) system for smartphones; or that of the Mozilla Foundation, the driving force behind the free and open source Web browser Firefox, which is working on launching a multiplatform browser for use in telephones and other mobile equipment.

Commercialization of personal data

Investments in advertising via digital channels are steadily increasing and in some countries now rank third behind those made in TV and the written press. At the same time this growth has led to the development of a series of new advertising modalities[4] and practices of various kinds which exploit users' personal information available on networks, to the point of intruding into the sphere of personal privacy. This is made possible by the use of IT devices that request personal data in order to obtain access to certain content and services (online registration) and scrutinize the behaviour of each user in digital networks.

On the Internet, for example, cookies – tracking systems that store information about the browsing activity of each Web surfer – are an essential tool for advertising agencies and advertisers. The data provided by cookies (repeat visits, keywords, Internet output) make it possible to produce consumer profiles and, subsequently, to put together customized advertising messages, what in advertising jargon is known as behavioural advertising. In this regard, the Spanish Data Protection Agency (AEPD) points out that despite the fact that online behavioural advertising may 'bring benefits to the Internet industry and users themselves, the impact it has on the protection of personal data and privacy is considerable'.

In the EU the growing implementation of IT devices that record data and generate profiles from information on digital network use, thereby violating the privacy of millions of users, has set alarm bells ringing. Between 2006 and 2007 the number of companies in Western Europe using advertising techniques based on individual behaviours increased by 150 per cent (Jupiter Research Corporation, 2008). In this context the community data-protection authorities[5] have questioned the current opt-out systems, and in an opinion issued in June 2010, recalled that the new directive on privacy in telecommunications, number 136/2009, introduces the obligation of obtaining the informed consent of Internet users before installing information-collection mechanisms in personal computers.[6]

As the director of the AEPD, Artemi Rallo (2010) declared before the Constitutional Commission of the Spanish Congress: 'understanding the soul of users is the top priority of Internet services and their main economic asset'. In this quest the major service providers of this network repeatedly overstep the limits of respect for privacy. The following cases illustrate the actions undertaken by the agencies responsible for ensuring the protection of personal data in digital networks (Rallo, 2010):

- Ten data protection authorities – several of them European, along with those of Canada, New Zealand and Israel – representing over 300 million people, addressed a letter to Google in April expressing their concern about the threat to privacy posed by the launch of the social network Google Buzz, given that Google included Gmail users as members of the social network without their consent and automatically listed as 'followers' those people with whom they communicated most frequently via Gmail; all of this without properly informing them.
- The EU data-protection authorities sent a letter to Facebook in May, rejecting the unilateral change in the privacy setting for users of the social network, since the company had introduced a default privacy policy that enabled all users of the network to access the data of each user and even allowed the data to be published in search engines. This was a unilateral modification of the privacy options for users

who at the time might have adopted an option that better protected their privacy.

- The European authorities wrote to Google, Microsoft and Yahoo! in May, reiterating the need to limit the period of time for which records of Internet searches are kept to six months.
- The AEPD began a sanction procedure against Google in October after finding evidence of infringement of the regulations in force when inspecting the acquisition and storage of data from wireless networks by the vehicles used to photograph the streets of Spanish cities for its Street View service. The data collected include e-mail addresses with names and surnames, access to social networking accounts and websites, or user codes and passwords with personal data that identify the account holders and, in some cases, allow access to sensitive data.
- In October the AEPD initiated an inspection procedure against Facebook with regard to the transmission of the data of users – and, in some cases, their friends in the social network – to advertisers and other companies. The transmission of these data was alleged to have taken place via several of the most popular applications programmed on the Facebook platform. One month later the organization initiated similar actions against the social network Myspace.

As these cases demonstrate, the situation is a complex and delicate one. The vast majority of users are not aware of the data trafficking and commercial practices brought about by the use of networks. In the opinion of many experts from the field of law, the right to data protection and privacy on the networks is a fiction, and as new services are launched – such as behavioural advertising – it becomes apparent that it is necessary to establish new operating rules capable of guaranteeing the privacy of citizens.

Government control of networks, services and contents

Through the press we are constantly exposed to news of episodic tensions involving national governments, companies at the forefront of technological innovation – such as Yahoo!, Skype, Microsoft, Google and Research In Motion (RIM) – and digital network users. These tensions are related to the tendency on the part of governments of different political bents, from one-party authoritarian regimes to Western capitalist democracies, to seek to regulate the functioning of digital networks and services. As explained by Armand Mattelart (2009), control of the content circulating via the networks, the focus of attention for regulation, is an extremely delicate matter which calls into question the very privacy of the networks as a space for addressing issues of social relevance and sharing content of various types.

Nation states justify their interventions – electronic surveillance programmes, the blocking of services and content, legal closures of websites, demands for access to content-storage servers, national intranets and so on – by claiming to safeguard 'national security' in turbulent contexts (terrorist attacks, popular uprisings, one-party systems, etc.). Moreover, commercial firms eager to increase their presence in attractive markets have been observed to enter into secret agreements with various governments without alerting their users to the danger posed to their privacy.

Some of the most high-profile cases have involved the governments of the USA or China. The US authorities expanded their electronic surveillance programmes following the terrorist attacks of 11 September 2001, without paying much heed to civil liberties. In the event of detecting that national security may be at risk, the US Homeland Security Agency has been able to request the encryption codes of any communication from fixed and mobile telephone companies since 1994, and from providers of Internet connections and IP telephony – technology that allows calls to be made via the Web – since 2004: a practice implemented during the George Bush administration (2001–2009) without prior legal authorization. The USA also issued a government order in May 2009 for Microsoft to block its instant messaging service, MSN Messenger, in Cuba, Syria, Iran and North Korea, countries on which the USA had imposed a trade embargo.

In the land of the Asian giant, a growing market of 300 million Internet users, Google came to a controversial secret agreement with the Chinese Government, in force between 2005 and 2010, which included censorship of its search engine results. During that period, government regulators had the right to monitor and censor the content provided by the firm based in Mountain View (California). This censorship was allegedly aimed at defending the local culture and values, including the political regime. To this end, Chinese telecommunications law prohibits any organization or individual from using the Internet to disseminate content that seeks to 'subvert state power, undermine national security or that incites ethnic hatred and secession, or transmits pornography or violence'.

Since the Google-China agreement came to an end in early 2010, after the US company reported having suffered a cyberattack launched from

Chinese territory, the situation has not changed to any great extent. The chief analyst of new technologies at *El País* newspaper, Tomás Delclós (2010), summarizes the current state of affairs as follows:

> Google, which had threatened to pull out if it was unable to work without censorship, finally opted to leave the Chinese version of its search engine out in the cold, subject to cuts by the authorities in Beijing. And it directed its Internet users to a free version of its search engine in Hong Kong. China, in turn, which was to renew the company's business permit this year [2010], did so without complaint while accepting a cosmetic modification of the Google search engine. Unhappy about the direct diversion to Hong Kong, the Chinese accepted that instead of automatically sending local Internet users to google.com.hk when they wished to consult its search engine, they should go through google.ch and from there click on the other Google.

The *Enemies of the Internet/Countries under Surveillance* report (RWB, 2010), produced by Reporters Without Borders (RWB), denounces that during 2009, 60 countries exercised some type of censorship of the Internet, a figure double that recorded in 2008. The report also highlights the fact that the Web is increasingly being swallowed up by national intranets whose contents are 'approved' by the respective political authorities. From the international non-profit organization's perspective, the Internet network is gaining importance as a space in the context of the dispute over the dissemination and reception of information:

> The fight for free access to information is being playing out to an ever greater extent on the Internet. The general emerging trend is that a growing number of countries are attempting to tighten their control of the Net, but at the same time, increasingly inventive netizens demonstrate mutual solidarity by mobilizing when necessary.
>
> (RWB, 2010)

Another area of conflict has centred on the mobile phone network for BlackBerry devices, manufactured by the company RIM. BlackBerry offers different services – e-mail, instant messaging, Internet browsing – with one of the most secure message-encryption services on the market. RIM uses complex codes to encrypt messages as they travel between phones and what is known as a BlackBerry Enterprise Server. There are only two ways to decrypt the messages: using codes located in the telephonic devices themselves or in each company's BlackBerry server. To complicate matters further, RIM assures that it does not have a master key that enables it to access all these codes and decrypt all the messages pouring through the vast BlackBerry network.

India, Saudi Arabia and the United Arab Emirates have all sought access to RIM servers for reasons of national security. The Indian authorities, which also extended their request for indiscriminate access to the servers of other companies such as Google or Skype, allege that the 2008 terrorists attacks on Mumbai were coordinated from Pakistan by terrorists who used this type of telephone. In the wake of those attacks, the government pushed through new legislation that gives it the power to intercept any technological communication if any risk to national security is suspected.

In June 2013, news broke of the 'Snowden case', which reveals the crude reality of the surveillance of global telecommunications carried out by the US Government via the National Security Agency (NSA). The secret documents disclosed by the former CIA employee Edward Snowden, through a select group of major newspapers (*The Guardian, The Washington Post, The New York Times, Der Spiegel, Le Monde* and *El País*), recount that, in the name of national security and the fight against Islamic fundamentalist terrorism, the intelligence agency conducts global espionage that includes the communications of both millions of citizens and political leaders from different countries. The consequences of the revelations made by Snowden have yet to be seen, and they may come to affect the future operation of the Internet (Lefébure, 2014).

When questioned about the risk of the loss of freedom experienced by citizens due to the control exercised through digital technology, the sociologist Ulrich Beck (Doncel, 2014) made the following reflections:

> The more global the control of information, the more awareness of the problem will disappear. This is the paradox of digital risk: that the closer we are to disaster, the less we perceive it. This is an intangible threat that does not affect lives (like terrorism), the survival of humanity (climate change) or property (the financial crisis). The violation of our freedom does us no physical harm. However, it puts at risk achievements of civilization such as personal freedom and privacy and institutions such as democracy and justice. At the same time, we are seeing something that is unheard of. We know of this risk thanks only to the courage of one person: Edward Snowden. This has not happened in any empire.

Lastly, it should be mentioned that the recent *Enemies of the Internet* reports published annually by the international non-governmental organization RWB focus on those companies that put their knowledge at the service of authoritarian regimes (RWB, 2013), and governmental bodies and agencies that implement censorship and online surveillance (RWB, 2014). The 2014 report singles out the Pakistan Telecommunication Authority, North Korea's Central Scientific and Technological Information Agency, Vietnam's Ministry of Information and Communications, and China's State Internet Information Office as entities that have used the defence of national security as a pretext to far exceed their original mission for the purpose of censoring journalists, bloggers and other information providers. The report also points to the actions of three agencies operating in countries that have traditionally boasted of defending freedom of expression and the free flow of information: the NSA in the USA, the Government Communications Headquarters in the UK and the Centre for Development of Telematics in India.

Closing thoughts

The renewed political and technological agenda regarding digital networks and their generic transport capabilities, briefly summarized in this chapter, is extremely complex in nature. It also reveals the clash of interests concerning issues of crucial importance for the functioning of democratic societies, such as public interest, personal privacy, free circulation of information or respect for citizens' rights.

There is no doubt that the sought-after development of digital infrastructures, which open up new spaces for the circulation of information and cultural content of all kinds on a transnational scale, is being driven by economic interests. The primacy of financial interests over those of a sociocultural nature in the initial phases of rolling out networks and their services has resulted in uneven development: inequalities in the level of penetration and access – exclusion of territories and social sectors – marketing policies based on the relation between price and connection speed, profoundly unequal access to fixed broadband, the designing of networks and digital services exclusively as commercial segments, the powerful influence of the advertising industry, self-censorship and covert agreements on the provision of services in certain markets, and the list goes on.

This state of affairs has encouraged countries and their institutions to act in different directions. On the one hand, we find those states that, in keeping with their commitment to a social democratic model, understand that one of their obligations given the new digital landscape is to ensure equal access to networks for all citizens. Initiatives designed to include the Internet in the catalogue of universal services or to enshrine the principle of net neutrality are certainly steps towards democratizing information, communication and culture. However, guaranteeing access or preventing discrimination in certain services would appear to be necessary, but insufficient, conditions for achieving equal opportunities in the digital arena.

In this regard, through public policies that integrate the fields of education, communication and culture, and industry and technology (Albornoz, 2005; Sierra Caballero, 2006), it is necessary to form citizens so that they can participate in producing and take advantage of the range of cultural expressions, to establish a strong presence of a public domain that is democratizing in nature at the level of both infrastructure and services, and to encourage the presence of other – collaborative, not lucrative – logics in the digital arena, as demonstrated by the examples of free software or creative commons licences. Moreover, in relation to so-called digital 'piracy', it is the duty of the public authorities to seek to achieve a balance between the protection of cultural creators and artists, and the rights of citizens. It is essential to think that technological innovation cannot just be placed at the service of pre-existing structures of control and cultural commercialization, but rather that it is possible to encourage the organization of new productive structures, by exploring different property and contract regimes.

A second notable aspect of the actions undertaken by states has to do with the defensive attitude that prevails in many of the initiatives to regulate, if not censor, digital networks. Threatened by the loss of political control over informational and cultural flows, and by the capacity of the new digital environment to introduce new actors and content into the process of social organization, states adopt initiatives that may harm civil and political liberties, in the name of safeguarding national security. In this sense, any regulation that might affect the rate of flows moving through digital networks has to have limits, in compliance with the content of Article 19 of the Universal Declaration of Human Rights (1948): 'Everyone has the right to freedom of opinion and expression; this right includes freedom to hold opinions without interference and to seek, receive and impart information and ideas through any media and regardless of frontiers.'

Furthermore, when reviewing the new political and technological agenda, there emerges another aspect for consideration: the secrecy that guides the conduct of governments and corporations. In general, technological multinationals have been employing a strategy of 'country-by-country solutions'; in other words, they make agreements with the authorities of each foreign country in which they set up operations according to its political and regulatory security demands. The nature of these agreements is kept secret – that is to say, they take place behind the backs of citizens and users of digital services and content.

This secrecy was made evident in the covert negotiations carried out in the framework of developing ACTA[7] or in the concerted campaign of pressure by the USA to force the Spanish authorities to adopt legislation penalizing free downloads via the Internet.[8] For its part, the mass spying carried out by the US intelligence services disclosed in the Snowden case reveal a very grave problem of invasion of privacy. This is quite clearly an attack against the democratic functioning of societies. Such a lack of transparency also has a direct impact on the possibilities for researchers to come to fully know and analyse the social reality.

However, this panorama, marked by the primacy of economic interests, the lack of transparency and the undermining of civil liberties, has not prevented political-cultural alternatives to the dominant model and uses undesirable to the legitimate powers that be from emerging in the new spaces of interaction opened up by digital networks and services. The use of digital networks to debate important social issues, mobilize collectivities or share content are an eloquent example of this fact. But the consolidation of networks as part of the political and cultural public space – that is to say, as a 'space of significant social interaction where ideas and values are formed, transmitted, supported and opposed; a space that ultimately becomes the training ground for action and reaction' (Castells, 2009) – is a matter that entails the necessary will, hard work and articulation of numerous social groups. In this sense, the in-depth study and rigorous analysis that academics can contribute in their capacity as knowledge workers is of paramount importance.

Notes

1. Figures updated to 31 December 2013 by Internet World Stats: www.Internetworldstats.com.
2. Article 22 of the Spanish General Telecommunications Act (Law 32/2003) describes universal service as 'the defined set of services guaranteed to be provided to all end-users regardless of geographical location, with a given level of quality and at an affordable price'. In addition to 1 megabyte per second Internet access, this service includes telephony, telephone directories, booths, functional narrowband Internet access or a social subsidy for users with special social needs.
3. The law has to be ratified by parliament after the May 2014 elections. In addition the EU states must each separately approve the regulations.

4. The new advertising modalities most notably include online social advertising and online behavioural advertising in different types of segmentation (keyword, contextual, geographical search) and retargeting (Pérez Bes, 2010).
5. Set up under Article 29 of Directive 95/46/EC, the Article 29 working party is the EU's independent advisory body on data protection and personal secrecy. Opinion 2/2010 on online behavioural advertising is available at http://ec.europa.eu.
6. The European Commission issued a communication entitled 'A comprehensive approach on personal data protection in the European Union' (November 2010), setting priorities and establishing the broad outline of Europe's future legal framework.
7. The Anti-Counterfeiting Trade Agreement, promoted from late 2007 by the USA and by business groups, seeks agreement between governments and companies to deal with 'the proliferation of counterfeit goods and pirated works protected by copyright in the global market', by implementing a battery of measures to prevent 'piracy', and establishing control and surveillance systems for Internet traffic to prevent it from being used to disseminate copyrighted works (see Santini, 2010).
8. Revealed by the WikiLeaks portal, the campaign, conducted between 2004 and 2010, included 'meetings with ministers, secretaries of State and middle-ranking officials from the departments of culture and industry... with companies that provide network access such as Telefónica, collaborations with the interested parties – SGAE [Sociedad General de Autores y Editores], Federation for the protection of intellectual property (FAP), Association of Music Producers Promusicae – and visits of senior officials from US government and industry:... Christopher Wilson, the *number two* in foreign trade, and Dan Glickman, the all-powerful president of the Motion Pictures Association' (see Elola, 2010).

References

Albornoz, Luis A. (2005) 'Políticas públicas e industrias culturales: el desafío de la diversidad', *Anuario ININCO*, 17(2), 114–138.

—— (2011) 'Questionamentos em torno da diversidade cultural na Ibero-América', in Barros, J.M. and Kauark, G. (orgs) *Diversidade cultural e desigualdade de trocas*, Belo Horizonte: PUC Minas/Itaú Cultural, 101–112.

Alcántara, José F. and De Ugarte, David (2010) 'Una pésima idea', *El País*, Madrid, 9 August.

Attali, Jacques and Olivennes, Denis (2008) 'La gratuité va-t-elle tuer la culture?', *Problèmes économiques*, 2.939, 3–6.

Becerra, Martín (2003) *Sociedad de la información: proyecto, convergencia, divergencia*, Buenos Aires: Norma.

Bustamante, Enrique (coord.) (2003) *Hacia un nuevo sistema mundial de comunicación. Las industrias culturales en la era digital*, Barcelona: Gedisa.

Castells, Manuel (2009) *Comunicación y poder*, Madrid: Alianza.

CENATIC (Centro Nacional de Referencia de Aplicación de las Tecnologías de la Información y la Comunicación basadas en Fuentes Abiertas) (2010) 'Informe sobre el panorama internacional del *software* de fuentes abiertas,

2010', Almendralejo (Badajoz): Centro Nacional de Referencia de Aplicación de las Tecnologías de la Información y la Comunicación basadas en Fuentes Abiertas.

Crovi, Delia (coord.) (2004) *Sociedad de la información y el conocimiento. Entre lo falaz y lo posible*, Buenos Aires: UNAM/La Crujía.

Delclós, Tomás (2010) 'Google y China. La 'guerra fría' y digital de dos gigantes', *El País*, Madrid, 5 December.

Doncel, Luis (2014) 'Conversaciones con futuro – Ulrich Beck: "Esta crisis no se superará sin la iniciativa ciudadana" ', *El País*, Madrid, 17 August.

Elola, Joseba (2010) 'EE.UU. ejecutó un plan para conseguir una ley antidescargas', *El País*, Madrid, 3 December.

European Commission (2011) 'Communication from the Commission to the European Parliament, the Council, the European Economic and Social Committee and the Committee of the Regions of 19 April 2011 – The open internet and net neutrality in Europe (COM(2011) 222 final), Brussels: European Commission.

Garnham, Nicholas (2000) 'La théorie de la société de l'information en tant qu'idéologie', *Réseaux*, 18(101), 53–91.

Government of Brazil (2005) *Guia livre. Referência de Migração para Software Livre do Governo Federal*, Brasília: Grupo de Trabalho Migração para Software Livre.

Government of Brazil (2014) Lei no. 12.965, de 23 de abril de 2014 (Marco Civil da Internet), Brasília: Presidência da República.

Government of Finland (2009) Decree no. 732/2009 of the Ministry of Transport and Communications on the minimum rate of a functional Internet access as a universal service, Helsinki: Ministerio de Transportes y Comunicaciones, Finland.

Government of Spain (2010) 'Contribución de España para a la consulta pública sobre internet abierta y neutralidad de red en Europa', Madrid: Secretaría de Estado de Telecomunicaciones y para la Sociedad de la Información, Ministerio de Industria, Turismo y Comercio, Spain.

Jupiter Research Inc. (2008) *European Search Marketing Executive Survey 2007*, New York: Jupiter Research Inc.

Lacroix, Jean-Guy and Tremblay, Gäetan (1997) 'The "information society" and cultural industries theory', *Current Sociology*, 45(4), 1–153.

Lefébure, Antoine (2014) *L'affaire Snowden. Comment les États-Unis espionnent le monde*, Paris: Éditions La Découverte.

Mattelart, Armand (2002) *Historia de la sociedad de la información*, Barcelona/Buenos Aires: Paidós.

—— (2009) *Un mundo vigilado*, Barcelona: Paidós.

Miège, Bernard (2000) *Les industries du contenu face à l'ordre informationnel*, Grenoble: Presses Universitaires de Grenoble.

OECD (Organisation for Economic Co-operation and Development) (2014) 'Fixed broadband penetration and population density (December 2013)', *OECD Broadband Statistics (December 2013)*, Paris: OECD.

Pérez Bes, Francisco (2010) 'Nuevos retos legales: la publicidad en las redes sociales', *Telos – Cuadernos de comunicación e innovación*, 85, 58–68.

Rallo, Artemi (2010) 'Comparecencia del Director de la AEPD ante la Comisión Constitucional del Congreso. 1 de diciembre de 2010', Madrid: Spanish Data Protection Agency.

RWB (Reporters Without Borders) (2010) *Enemies of the Internet 2010. Countries under Surveillance*, Paris: RWB.
RWB (Reporters Without Borders) (2013) *Enemies of the Internet 2013 Report. Special Edition: Surveillance*, Paris: RWB.
RWB (Reporters Without Borders) (2014) *Enemies of the Internet 2014 Report: Entities at the Heart of Censorship and Surveillance*, Paris: RWB.
Santini, Simone (2010) 'Ya sabemos por qué ACTA era secreto', *Periódico Diagonal*, 131, Madrid, 23 July.
Sierra Caballero, Francisco (2006) *Políticas de comunicación y educación. Crítica y desarrollo de la sociedad del conocimiento*, Barcelona: Gedisa.
Síndic de Greuges (2013) *Internet de banda ancha como servicio universal: el derecho a la igualdad digital*. Barcelona: Síndic de Greuges de Catalunya.
Williams, Raymond (1974) *Television. Technology and Cultural Form*, London: Fontana.

10
Communication and Epistemological Struggle

César Bolaño

This chapter takes up an earlier reflection (Bolaño, 2009) on the epistemological struggle incumbent upon the political economy of communication, which is regarded as an alternative critical reference framework for the field of communication in general, at a time when the Third Industrial Revolution is making the capitalist mode of production increasingly computer-based and communicational thanks to an extensive shift towards the subsumption of intellectual work and the general intellectualization of labour processes and consumption (Bolaño, 1995, 2002). Under these conditions the so-called communication (and information) sciences end up taking on an uncommon centrality in the epistemological struggle affecting the entire field of the social sciences since the foundational moment of the critique of political economy.

Epistemology and politics

As Pérez de Soto (1998) argues, 'Epistemology is not a theoretical problem. It is a problem that proves to be practical when the association between epistemology and politics is noted.' This can be expressed in highly didactic fashion by turning to Mayo (2005), another Latin American author.

> The problem of objectivity is not, therefore, that of the discussion about the absolute or relative (limited) nature of knowledge. The difficulty lies in the fact that, in the social sciences, there coexist different theories with equal claims to scientific validity. In addition, this coexistence does not occur on equal terms. On the contrary, certain theories...contain the hegemony of their discipline, even though they are shown to be incapable of eliminating rival theories.

Mayo quotes the famous paragraph by Marx and Engels from *The German Ideology* (1845–1846), in which these thinkers state that the dominant ideas in a given time are always the ideas of the dominant class – that is to say, that the social class that holds material power also possesses spiritual power, and he concludes that this does not mean that the subordinate classes are incapable of producing opposing theories to the dominant ones but that, on the contrary, 'the differences in the way these classes are inserted in the production process... create the conditions for the emergence of social theories that challenge the hegemonic theories' (Mayo, 2005).[1]

This was precisely how Marxism set itself up as a critique of political economy and has continued over time to serve as an alternative theoretical paradigm. In reaction to 'the unimaginative fantasies of eighteenth-century romances à la Robinson Crusoe' and the naturalization of the bourgeois individual ideal, 'a product of the dissolution of feudal society on the one hand and of the new productive forces evolved since the sixteenth century on the other' (Marx, [1857] 1978). Marx would undertake his critical endeavour, aimed at revealing the reality of the capitalist system behind the mask of appearances that the old political economy tended to reproduce in its thinking.

It is the immanent critique of what was the first of the social sciences, which emerged in close relation to the development of capitalism, and particularly of industrial capitalism – and of the industrial bourgeoisie – in the case of the classical school of political economy. Therefore, if political economy represents the scientific ideology in the service of capital, then the critique of political economy establishes itself as a scientific paradigm in the service of the antagonistic class – the industrial proletariat – claiming its place in the struggle to radically transform reality in accordance with workers' interests.

In economics, the reaction to Marx's criticism – which takes the labour theory of value of classical economists to its logical extreme, clarifying its inconsistencies and drawing from it the most radical conclusions – was to mark a complete break from that founding paradigm and the redefinition of the discipline in a positivist sense. Value ceased to have an objective foundation and came to be based on purely subjective criteria. 'Value ceased to be a social issue and became a psychological problem. It was not by chance that neoclassical economists adopted the methodological individualism method' (Mayo, 2005).

Weber's sociology also adopted methodological individualism, abandoning the essentialist version employed by economists in favour of a methodological solution – analysis of the actions of different social actors and their individual motives, without recourse to the concept of class – that does away with the idea of totality. 'The elimination of the concept of totality from the area of social theory reinforces the effect of the "suppression" of social classes, since it hinders the perception of the problem of social change' (Mayo, 2005).

Durkheim's organic functionalist model, for its part, did break with methodological individualism, restoring a model of objectivity that is close to the sciences of nature, and reinstating the idea of totality, but replacing the idea of conflict with that of social pathologies and normality. In every case (Weber, Durkheim), these are solutions offered by bourgeois thinking to the challenge laid down by Marx, meaning that 'the achievements of classical sociology... were only possible because the theoretical challenge of Marxism and the unfulfilled promises of economics had shaken the main ideologies of the bourgeoisie' (Mayo, 2005), which is to say, in Mayo's opinion, classical economics, political liberalism and methodological individualism.[2]

When Marx was producing his works, the industrial bourgeoisie had already abandoned its revolutionary programme and was concerned with maintaining the order of capital against the revolutionary struggle of the working class. In these conditions, vulgar economics and neoclassical thinking could do nothing else but seek to mask the reality of the system, its essence, by taking refuge in methodological individualism.

Indeed, sociology emerged as a reaction but went much further, at a time when other bourgeois sciences – such as anthropology and the *soi-disant* 'scientific management' of Taylor and Fayol – were being founded. At any rate, the Marxist paradigm eventually surfaced in most of them, and so, for example, Freud would make way for Reich, while academic sociology would adopt Karl Marx as one of its founding fathers. Even in the neoclassical field, Marx's influence on such a significant author as Schumpeter was undeniable. This was the peak of bourgeois thinking and an extremely creative time for academic output in the social sciences, with the clear definition of the two main opposing paradigms that nevertheless retained a significant capacity for dialogue and even articulation as evidenced by certain hybridizations, such as 'Weberian Marxism' or 'Freudian Marxism'.

Communication and capitalism

The emergence of the so-called information and communication sciences as specialized academic fields would take place under very different circumstances. Although their precursors can be traced back to the start of the twentieth century, it was in the context of the Cold War that their development was to unfold, influenced mainly by neoclassical economics and US functionalist sociology. The great critical school that would dedicate itself to studying the field of communication was the Frankfurt School, responsible for defining some of the main categories, such as the technical reproducibility of works of art (Benjamin, [1936] 1989) or cultural industries (Adorno and Horkheimer, [1944] 2001).

But the big issue that would mobilize the new field was that of development. And here there emerged a second critical current influenced by the Frankfurt School and French structuralism, in Althusser's version of Marxism, but mainly encouraged by such authors as Paulo Freire, the so-called Latin American structuralism of Raúl Prebisch, Celso Furtado and the Economic Commission for Latin America and the Caribbean (ECLAC), and by dependency theories or the theatre of Augusto Boal. This type of critical thinking, which emerged in Latin America and had a significant international impact, would also find an important correspondence in the field of communication. In every case, the central problem was that of development, bearing in mind the failure – or, in the best-case scenario, the impasses – to which the import substitution industrialization processes had led.

It is worth underlining that capitalism and international relations at that time had changed dramatically, beginning with Spain's defeat in the Spanish-American War (1898) and concluded at the end of the Second World War. From the point of view of productive forces, the twentieth century inaugurated so-called monopolistic capitalism, a situation in which the level reached by the process of concentration and centralization of capital inherent to the capitalist mode of production would end up promoting a qualitative change of order that demanded a profound reconfiguration of the state – which would only take place in the 1930s – and of the structure of systems of domination, with the emergence of the cultural industries and the structural change in the public sphere (Habermas, [1962] 1984; Bolaño, 2000).

This change – which took as a given what Marx defined as the Second Industrial Revolution, with the 'production of machines by machines' (Marx, [1867] 1980) – would be accompanied by a violent imperialist dispute over the redivision of global space among the new capitalist powers in addition to Russia (Lenin, [1916] 1979). US hegemony within capitalism cannot be separated from the formation of a new capitalist culture at the global level, whether from the point of view of 'material culture', to use Furtado's concept,[3] or from the point of view of the 'superior culture' represented by the US model for organizing industrialized cultural production, which was to make such a bad impression on Adorno.

This was the great victory of capital, which ended up constituting its own form of symbolic production marked by the dual contradiction – capital-labour, economy-culture – which had characterized the system from the outset, getting rid of the need for other institutions, such as the Church or the family,[4] in order to establish ideological domination, by constituting a global culture, in the anthropological sense (Bolaño, 2000). This 'popular international culture', to use Renato Ortiz's (1996) felicitous expression, is modelled on US popular culture, which spread worldwide throughout the last century thanks to the actions of the oligopolistic companies of Hollywood and the phonographic industry.

In this framework, broadcasting, much like telecommunications, established itself as a typically national industry, whether state-owned or private, monopolistic or oligopolistic. It linked up with the global oligopolies mentioned above to form a powerful and highly capillarized mechanism of social control and manipulation. Given this make-up, the field of communication became the central pillar for building hegemony at the national and international levels. The case of Brazil following the military coup of 1964, in which both local and national oligarchic, political and economic interests were articulated through a system of affiliations between broadcasting licensees, is a radical example of the efficiency of this system of social control (Brittos and Bolaño, 2005).

Such a strongly established capitalist culture was perfectly suited to the needs of the social communication (advertising) of the great monopolistic capital and of the social reproduction (propaganda) of the capitalist state of the period (Bolaño, 2000). From the viewpoint of international relations, it was the work of US capitalism that superimposed itself on the former British imperial system, based on a written press organized in the mould of the old bourgeois public sphere of competitive capitalism and articulated by the major news agencies (see Kaul, 2006).

With regard to Third World countries, the key issue of the post-war period with the division of the world into two antagonistic blocs was to be that of development. In the case of Latin America – unlike African and Asian countries, which had been colonized more recently and would soon undergo a wave of decolonization – the experience of over a century of independence with patterns of social organization resulting, as in the case of Brazil, from a cultural mixture with a broad hegemony of the European element, called into question the imitative model. In the framework of the Cold War, the Soviet-type socialist option – adopted by Cuba – put on the agenda, for most of the local elites and for the hegemonic power, the need for new dependent development strategies.

The theoretical matrix of the communication projects for development, with their diffusionist base, was that of US academic sociology, the founder of the communication sciences, which emerged within a new hegemonic structure that no longer placed that European tradition of economic or sociological thinking at the forefront, but instead the new material and spiritual culture of US monopolistic capitalism. They thus formed part of a much bigger whole that could only be understood in the holistic moulds of the likes of Furtado (1984), for example, or of a critical political economy whose historically determined objective was none other than culture in the broadest sense.

In these terms, US hegemony encompasses both elements of a technological nature linked to the dynamism of the military-industrial complex, as well as that material culture that determines patterns of production and consumption, and models of behaviour that guarantee social reproduction as a whole. The cultural industry and the big mass-communication systems form part of this whole; and their function is to mediate between the systemic interests of capital and of the state, and the world inhabited by the broadest strata of the population, by fulfilling the advertising and propaganda function in the service of capitalist accumulation and legitimization of the system respectively (Bolaño, 2000).

This particular mode of regulation, to use the expression coined by the French or neo-Marxist Regulation School, is not inherent to capitalism but is instead a historical construction typical of monopolistic capitalism as structured under US hegemony, which eventually spread across the world, with significant local particularities, but while always guaranteeing the global hegemony of the 'American way of life' and the articulation of the national broadcasting oligopolies and monopolies with the global oligopoly of Hollywood, the music industry and US 'showbiz'.

In this scenario, the new sciences of communication took on the task of supporting projects for integrating the periphery, following the diffusionist logic that saw in the development of the mass media the possibility of overcoming what was regarded as backwardness. Critique of this functionalist paradigm was to come from both Europe, with the Frankfurt School, and Latin America. The young intellectuals who were to introduce communication studies in Latin America, undoubtedly influenced by the hegemonic paradigm, would soon take up the critical stance proposed to them by the abovementioned Latin American tradition, which was to be developed in their specific field, achieving great international notoriety by debating the possibility of establishing a New World Information and Communication Order (NWICO), derived from the idea of setting up a New International Economic Order.

The theoretical paradigm, of both ECLAC as well as what Marques de Melo (2000) quite rightly insists on defining as the Latin American School of Communication, was critical but not necessarily Marxist. However, Latin American structuralism as a whole was to be strongly and increasingly influenced by Marxist critique. Thus, both dependency theories and the output of the economists from Campinas State University (UNICAMP) and the Marxist critique of dependency theories or of cultural imperialism formed part of a broader debate that was treated in Latin America as a legitimate piece of the history of Marxist thinking, which recovered local or universal authors and traditions.

In the 1980s and 1990s, this debate was interrupted, mainly by the advance of postmodern and liberal perspectives, which benefited from the crisis in socialist thinking that followed the collapse of the Soviet Union. Thus, for example, a line of Latin American critical thinking as important as that of cultural studies, which incorporated hitherto underrated contributions, such as those of anthropology, to formulate a Marxist-style critique of the determinism of dependency theories, would eventually abandon Marx's frame of reference in favour of the paradigm of postmodernity, whose main representative, Fukuyama (1992), after 200 years again took up the old liberal ideology of the end of history, ingeniously but vacuously dressed up in Hegelian clothing, in the service of the US political establishment.[5]

Other major theoretical shifts were, first of all, the spreading of dependency theories to other regions of the world – with the prominent work of Samir Amin – and, second, the advance of postcolonial studies, which emerged, as in the case of the founding work of Edward Said, in the field of Marxism, but which would eventually make a similar *démarche* to that of cultural studies towards the postmodern paradigm. This was certainly a regrettable development from the point of view of critical thinking, but in the long term opened up a perspective of progression insofar as it enabled a South–South academic dialogue to be established on a common basis historically constructed within the Marxist thinking that in both cases continues to be a paradigmatic alternative present in the work of various authors who seek to maintain the spirit of its founding fathers. The role of the political economy of communication is fundamental in this respect.

The political economy of communication: The challenges ahead

What is now known as the political economy of communication emerged independently in different places and under different influences as a Marxist critique of communicational thinking, in other words as an alternative critical paradigm for the whole academic field of communication. Such was the case in North America, with Dallas Smythe in the 1950s; in the UK with Nicholas Garnham and other academics, from the late 1970s and mainly in the 1980s and 1990s; and it was also largely the case in France, a contemporary of the British School, influenced by the heterodox economic thinking of William Baumol, but which with Bernard Miège and his colleagues adopted concerns inherited from German Marxism and from Raymond Williams himself, who also strongly influenced the British School (Bolaño, 2009).

This has also been the case in Latin America since the 1980s. The first works in the Latin American field (Muraro, 1974, 1987; Arriaga, 1980; Portales, 1981; Bolaño, 1988, 2000;[6] Portales, 1981; among others) emerged in autonomous fashion, directly influenced by the aforementioned Latin American debate, as a Marxist critique – or Marxian as it was referred to at the time – of dependency theories and cultural imperialism, either in dialogue with authors such as those of the Latin American School of Communication, which included figures like Armand Mattelart, Herbert Schiller and Elizabeth Fox, or by taking up the left's critiques of ECLAC and dependency theories. Contact with European contributions, and even with those from Canada, would take place later, beginning in the 1990s, when the conceptual bases of the Latin American group had already been defined.

If the first task of the political economy of communication in all its variants must be, as suggested in the final point above, to support the rebuilding of the critical field of communication as a whole, by offering a holistic and interdisciplinary paradigmatic alternative linked to the most general critical paradigm of historical materialism, this must be carried out according to three lines of action:

- Establishing, first and foremost, an effective dialogue between the various schools of the political economy of communication in the epistemological field, supported by the definition of categories of analysis and conceptual hierarchies; seeking to maximize the explanatory power of the whole and establish fronts of dialogue with other currents and fields of critical thinking. This does not at all mean creating any kind of consensus or orthodoxy but, rather, on the contrary, setting up a field of permanent production and debate by stimulating creativity and multiple theoretical fertilization.

- Recognizing the particular importance of the Latin American contribution, taking into account the widespread ignorance of this contribution that still prevails in other areas. In order for the political economy of communication as a whole to begin to play a significant role in the international critical field, it is essential to break with any eurocentrism within the discipline itself, which will only be possible with an effective commitment on the part of European and American colleagues to translate, read and disseminate works produced in Latin America.
- Attempting to preserve the critical nature, the realism and the commitment to the truth that characterizes Marx's original thinking, and his *engagée* participation in the workers' struggle against domination and exploitation. The tasks proposed in the theoretical and epistemological field – the rebuilding of critical thinking and, within it, the development of the paradigm of critique of political economy – are not abstract notions but rather the demands of a historic moment marked by productive restructuring and the consequent transformations in the subjective factor, and the crisis of global hegemony.

The first two guidelines are among the principles that inspired the creation of Latin Union of Political Economy of Information, Communication and Culture (ULEPICC), with a view to ensuring a greater impact of critical thinking on the field of communication. The third is more complex, and the more effective the actions to promote the previous two, the better it will be accomplished, since it demands the mobilization of our collective 'sociological imagination', which requires of everyone academic rigour and political will. The essential thing in this regard is to know how to use the instruments of critique and reason that we have inherited and sought to develop to understand the particularities of the present moment, discover its contradictions and trends, and formulate diagnoses, proposals for change and realistic utopias.

Notes

1. So it is also impossible to talk about an essential scientific method. For Pérez de Soto (1998), 'the scientific method is the ideology of the scientific community'. He refers to Lakatos and his theory of research programmes, recalling that in it 'there are research techniques, and each programme sets itself research techniques consistent with its stable core, with the set of problems it

has defined, but there is nothing akin to a scientific method that can be taught in the abstract and applied to any object. This explains why, in Lakatos's view, physicists and chemists do not take courses in scientific method. Teaching the abstract subject of "Scientific Method" is a vice more common to Social Science Faculties.'

2. Mayo (2005) insists that, if Durkheim's sociology breaks with the tradition of the old political economy, it does not do so in relation to the French theoretical tradition ('in fact, Comte had already argued that society should be considered as a whole'). In addition, this break was heavily influenced by the low levels of development of economics in France. In contrast, in the 'Anglo-Saxon' countries, with their strong tradition of economic studies, the other break represented by the neoclassical school was to predominate. In every case the shift took place mainly as a response to Marx, whose critique of political economy in the latter half of the nineteenth century posed a threat to the conquests of the bourgeoisie's social thinking from Smith and his precursors until that time.
3. On the concepts of material and spiritual culture in Celso Furtado, see Rodríguez (2009).
4. As Williams (2000) makes clear, the establishment of broadcasting systems represents a false autonomy of the nuclear family, which, on being freed from the old institutions inherited from precapitalism, submits to the new central core of the great cultural industry; a shift that follows the trend towards fragmentation identified by Marx, which is now reaching a peak with the expansion of telematics networks, particularly the Internet.
5. Important and renowned Latin American authors would end up being influenced by this ideology, not via Fukuyama but through the US reception of French poststructuralism, which extensively sterilized the critical contribution of an author as important as Foucault. But this regression has not only affected Latin America, where cultural studies was able to remain fairly critical, when compared with the academic regression undergone by its 'Anglo-Saxon' counterparts, in opposition to the committed and militant Marxism of their founding fathers.
6. In the References this refers to the 2000 edition of a PhD thesis submitted in 1993 to the Institute of Economics at UNICAMP. Meanwhile, the book dating from 1988 resulted from the master's thesis presented in 1986. The second revised and updated edition is listed in the References.

References

Adorno, Theodor W. and Horkheimer, Max ([1944] 2001) *Dialéctica de la ilustración*, Madrid: Trotta.

Arriaga, Patricia (1980) *Publicidad, economía y comunicación masiva (México-Estados Unidos)*, Mexico City: CEESTEN/Nueva Imagen.

Benjamin, Walter ([1936] 1989) 'La obra de arte en la época de su reproductibilidad técnica', in *Discursos interrumpidos I. Filosofía del arte y de la historia*, Buenos Aires: Taurus, 14–60.

Bolaño, César R. S. (1988) *Mercado brasileiro de televisão* (2nd edition revised and expanded, 2004), São Paulo: EDUC.

—— (1995) 'Economía política, comunicación y globalización', *Nueva Sociedad*, 140, 138–153.
—— (2000) *Indústria Cultural, informação e capitalismo*, São Paulo: Hucitec.
—— (2002) 'Trabalho intelectual, comunicação e capitalismo. A re-configuração do fator subjetivo na atual reestruturação produtiva', *Revista da Sociedade Brasileira de Economia Política*, 11, 53–78.
—— (2009) 'A centralidade da chamada Economia Política da Comunicação na construção do campo acadêmico da Comunicação: uma contribuição crítica', in Bolaño, C. R. S. (org.) *Comunicação e crítica da economia política: perspectivas teóricas e epistemológicas*, Aracaju: UFS, 97–112.
Brittos, Valério Cruz and Bolaño, César R. S. (org.) (2005) *Rede Globo: 40 anos de poder e hegemonia*, São Paulo: Paulus.
Fukuyama, Francis (1992) *The End of History and the Last Man*, London: Penguin Books.
Furtado, Celso (1984) *Cultura e desenvolvimento em época de crise*, São Paulo: Paz e Terra.
Habermas, Jürgen ([1962] 1984) *Mudança estrutural da esfera pública*, Rio de Janeiro: Tempo Brasileiro.
Kaul, Cahndrika (org.) (2006) *Media and the Empire*, London: Palgrave Macmillan.
Lenin, Wladimir Illich ([1916] 1979) *Imperialismo. Fase superior do capitalismo*, São Paulo: Global.
Marx, Karl ([1857] 1978) *Contribuição para a Crítica da Economia Política*, São Paulo: Abril Cultural.
—— ([1867] 1980) *O Capital. Crítica da economia política* (first volume), São Paulo: Civilização Brasileira.
Mayo, Ariel E. E. (2005) *La ideología del conocimiento. Introducción a los modelos epistemológicos de las ciencias sociales*, Buenos Aires: Jorge Baudino Ediciones.
Melo, José Marques de (2000) 'Escola latino-americana de comunicação: gênese, crescimento, perspectivas', in Melo, J. M. and Gobbi, M. C. (orgs) *Gênese do pensamento comunicacional latino-americano*, São Bernardo do Campo: Methodist University of São Paulo, 19–32.
Muraro, Heriberto (1974) *Neocapitalismo y comunicación de masas*, Buenos Aires: Eudeba.
—— (1987) 'Economía y comunicación: convergencia histórica e inventario de ideas. Con especial referencia a América Latina', in *Invasión cultural, economía y comunicación*, Buenos Aires: Legasa, 67–131.
Ortiz, Renato (1996) *Mundialicação e cultura*, São Paulo: Brasiliense.
Pérez de Soto, Carlos (1998) *Sobre un concepto histórico de ciencia. De la epistemología actual a la dialéctica*, Santiago de Chile: LOM.
Portales, Diego (1981) *Poder económico y libertad de expresión*, Mexico City: ILET.
Rodríguez, Octavio (2009) *O estruturalismo latino-americano*, Rio de Janeiro: Civilização Brasileira.
Williams, Raymond ([1974] 2000) *Tecnologia e forma culturale*, Rome: Editori Riuniti.

11
Culture and Communication: A Political Economy View

Delia Crovi Druetta

Despite the resistances stirred up by the political economy of communication and culture among certain scholars in the knowledge field of communication, its effectiveness in highlighting the situation faced by communication systems has been undeniable, particularly in those societies characterized by the concentration of the media in private hands. Unfortunately, with the exception of the analysis of the sector's legislation and a number of direct interventions by experts in the processes of the legal framework, the remaining approaches to understanding communication problems have not been easy for society as a whole to comprehend. This lack of comprehension tends to lead to a lack of interest in understanding both the media's production processes and their economic structure, which is something that Wolton (1992) already cautioned against with reference to TV. And this position reaffirms a certain immutability of the media with regard to their modes of being, and producing and distributing content, as though it were something given and not subject to change.[1] For example, the elucidation of certain technological mechanisms may not be accessible to receivers, which is why ordinary citizens behave like users of services they neither question nor are able to explain, regarding it as a form of knowledge reserved for experts.

From a Latin American perspective, it is worth remembering that since the 1960s the data provided on the economic structure of the media have bared their business status and the collusion of the media corporations with those in power, leading them to be seen as allies of anti-democratic processes and natural predators on national and regional cultures. However, while these types of study have from the outset served as a denunciation, helping to lend transparency to the integration of national – and especially private – communication systems, it does not seem possible to extend these benefits to all cultural spheres,[2] whether mediatized or not, without questioning the limits not only of the political economy of communication but also of the knowledge field of communication.

The ample discussion on the topic indicates that perhaps the only consensus is that the frontiers of the political economy of communication and culture are permeable and its objects of study can be analysed from different points of view: cultural studies, politics, economics and/or communication, among others. This multiplicity of approaches, alongside the fact that the starting point is taken to be the porosity of its limits, raises questions that deserve to be explored. Regarding the reflections in this chapter, I would like to point out that in my opinion the main challenges now facing the political economy of communication and culture are (a) the articulations between economics and communication; (b) the complexity of defining the scope of culture as the framework in which the political economy of communication and culture operates; (c) the environment of the economic crisis and its correlates in political economy of communication and culture research; and (d) inescapable emerging issues.

Articulations between economics and communication

Let us remember that as early as the late 1990s, when referring to the infocommunicationalization processes that constitute the information society, Bernard Miège argued that the articulations between communication and economics resulted in two scenarios for analysis. The first relates to the increasing industrialization of information, culture, and social and professional exchanges, in which he believed a shift towards content was taking place. The second concerns the role played by communication technologies as accompaniments to social, socio-organizational and cultural changes (Becerra, 1998). Miège pointed out that while the actors in the former scenario are companies of all sizes, involved in network industries, their materials and content, those in the latter are more diverse and also more numerous. Among them he identified all the institutions of society and even users, bearing in mind the inequities existing with regard to access to communicational goods.

So far the political economy of communication and culture has focused its reflections primarily on the first articulation of economics-communication: the growing industrialization of information. However, while the second scenario covers particular circumstances in which communication is present, it also offers a dimension that is too wide-ranging, even for the research possibilities available in the political economy of communication and culture. But it is not a question of giving up on what we are unable to fully comprehend, but rather of considering a necessary self-reflection of an epistemological – as well as methodological – nature, which would enable us to make the frontiers less porous and, at least, to highlight any unresolved issues.

In my view, therefore, the increasing social mediatization represents the first major challenge for the political economy of communication and culture: rethinking its limits, avoiding building rigid boundaries that prevent this type of study from being extended to areas of culture that require a critical stance. An important part of this challenge relates to the questioning levelled at the political economy of communication and culture on account of its distancing from cultural aspects and of an ideologically committed perspective. Without ignoring the very clear interests present in some of these demands, it is necessary to open up the richness of political economy in order to combine it with another kind of analysis, as certain colleagues are already doing. Building bridges towards other perspectives on communication processes would enable us to increasingly grasp their complexity and that of the actors involved.

The search for an answer to this first question on the articulations between economics and communication in the political economy of communication and culture leads us directly to two new approaches: one theoretical and the other related to the conditions in which social science research is conducted.

The complexity of defining the scope of culture

Is it possible to incorporate all cultural processes into the analysis carried out by the political economy of communication and culture, which primarily involves dealing with the complexity of defining this term, and then tackling the problem of encompassing its countless manifestations?

After reviewing the topic from the perspective of the literary-philosophical, anthropological, Marxist and symbolic traditions, Gilberto Giménez Montiel (2005) performs an analysis of what he calls the internalization and objectifying of culture, at the end of which he focuses on a specific case – the Atlixco Valley in Mexico – through which he tackles a series of social phenomena linked to territoriality. During this process, and following the line taken by Pierre Bourdieu, he concludes that culture regarded as a whole comprises two moments of existence: one as symbols objectified according to certain ritual practices or everyday objects, and another as internalized symbolic forms and mental structures. Objectified forms and internalized forms are dialectically related. And he adds that

> This strategic distinction, often forgotten in sociological and anthropological studies, assumes that there can be no culture without a subject or subject without a culture. It follows, therefore, that there is no sense in talking about 'material culture', that is to say about its objectified forms if we do not transfer them to concrete social actors, to their ways of life and to a 'space of identity'.
>
> (Giménez Montiel, 2005)

These points, with which I concur, help to propose certain limits for the political economy of communication and culture, but also suggest that research focusing on objects alone should rescue the subject from oblivion. According to Giménez Montiel, given the difficulty of studying subjectivized forms of culture, sociologists and anthropologists[3] have focused on studying objectified forms: festivals, rituals, dances, food, clothes and so forth. These difficulties can be extrapolated to a number of studies by the political economy of communication and culture that, faced with the difficulty of studying subjectivized forms of culture, have concentrated on objectified ones, which are more accessible in terms of description and observation, such as the technological generations of a particular communication apparatus. This limitation can even be extended to research on a company, treated as an objectified form, which strips it of its subjective dimension; or, in other words, in the absence of the subjects-actors involved in the process of production, distribution and consumption of communicational content.

However, in his summing up on the internalization and subjectivization of culture, Giménez Montiel also recovers the notion of social representation,[4] and does so in recognition of a resurgence of the importance of collective phenomena and the rules of social thought.

> The study of 'naïve' thinking or 'common sense' now becomes essential. It is recognized that identifying the 'worldview' that individuals or groups hold and use to act or take a stance proves indispensable for understanding the dynamics of social interactions and clarifying the determinants of social practices.
>
> (Giménez Montiel, 2005)

To recognize the rules of social thought and the emergence of collective phenomena as inherent features of cultural representations becomes indispensable for the political economy of communication and culture in societies where the application of certain technological developments involves an uncommonly heavy load of individualism, which by contrast has brought with it an unexpected collective use – including social mobilizations orchestrated via mobile telephony or the Internet, the organization of artistic events using digital media and political campaigns on the Internet or mobile devices. These alternative strategies for appropriating media originally designed to be consumed individually and in isolation constitute responses to neoliberal concentration, which deserve detailed examination by the political economy of communication and culture in order to begin to provide answers to the cultural (and economic?) value of these and other collective social practices.

Comparing political economy findings with a cultural perspective in the terms that I propose, following the line taken by Giménez Montiel, proves to be an essential dialectic for outlining proposals that allow for explicit public policies on culture and communication. This explicit nature, which is so elusive in many countries that call themselves democratic, would avoid us being faced with surprises resulting from negotiations between groups in power and the *de facto* powers of the media and telecommunications,[5] which remain hidden from civil society.

Along with the subjective dimension and the emergence of collective social phenomena, Giménez Montiel (2005) also adds the spatial and territorial aspect: 'Territory – with its characteristic and typifying landscapes – continues to be the object of strong emotional attachment and is presented as a screen on which communities project their imaginary, values and identity'.

The picture that describes each territory, whether rural or urban, establishes particular imaginaries, values and identity, which when reflected from the perspective of the political economy of communication and culture would make it possible to produce a – hitherto incomplete – mapping of the structure of national and regional communication systems, which would reflect sociohistoric conditions, legislation and also public policies in this regard. It is not a question of eliminating the inescapable process of cultural globalization but rather of rescuing from oblivion the concept of territory whose map of inequities and deficiencies is increasingly linked to economic vicissitudes as well as political plaudits.

In Latin America, the communicational inequalities and digital divides that persist within countries are poorly reported in political economy of communication and culture studies, perhaps with the partial exception of Brazil. This, which is not due to a lack of interest but of opportunities for research – an activity that also involves conditions of inequality – prevents a thorough understanding of regional situations with regard to both the composition of the media structures and the representations and imaginaries of their inhabitants.

In short, the recovery of the subject, the emergence of collective phenomena that make it possible to understand the dynamic of interactions and social practices, the territory and the way identity is reflected within it are the features that must be present in any studies undertaken by a political economy of communication and culture.

In reviewing the classics of economics, and not as far as might be assumed from the cultural approaches of Giménez Montiel, Núria Almiron Roig reminds us of the need to concentrate on the four main concerns of those classics: history, ethics, totality and praxis.

> In short, addressing the historical context, taking moral philosophy as a guide, understanding the social as a whole and encouraging the researcher's commitment to reality. Four tasks that can unite all political economists of communication, whatever their academic tradition.
>
> (Almiron Roig, 2009)

In the context that I have proposed, answering the question of whether policies on communication and culture are necessary in the information society entails, first of all, having available political economy of communication and culture studies that effectively incorporate the cultural dimension such as I have described. It also implies insisting on the importance of effectively including communication in public communication policies.

The unequal division that territories bring to the social imaginary tends to produce unexpected results on this topic: in Mexico, on 2 October 2008, the Chamber of Deputies unanimously approved reforms of articles 4 and 73 of the Political Constitution, amendments that were made official on 30 April 2009 (Government of Mexico, 2009). The aim of the changes was to incorporate the right of access to culture and its free exercise, as well as to add to Article 73 the power of Congress to legislate in the area of copyright and other concepts of intellectual property.

The reforms emphasize the need to achieve a linkage between the public, private and social sectors, and the three levels of government with regard to cultural policies, as well as the right of access to culture in the services provided by the state. They also specify that the country constitutionally recognizes the respect for cultural rights as individual guarantees and establishes the state's responsibility in promoting and protecting their dissemination and development.

However, expression – as important as it was belated – does not make explicit reference to communication in any of its dimensions. Some specialists are of the opinion that, while necessary, the reforms are still anchored in the access phase, leaving cultural production in a kind of limbo, along with the training and protection of creators, which are issues of particular relevance at the present time. From my point of view, this oversight does no more than reaffirm the dominant perspective: in spite of the fact that some media we call public manage to survive, media communication belongs to the private sector, and as such it is a business that should not be contemplated in the Mexican constitution, much less in terms of culture. This is why the challenge of ensuring that communication forms part of cultural policies has not yet been accomplished, at least in certain national and territorial contexts.

The typifying landscapes confront us with situations that are unequal in terms of communication and culture. The political economy of communication and culture can and must give account of them from a global perspective that enables it to report, denounce where necessary, compare and, of course, propose the best ways to overcome the difficulties of the slippery policies on communication and culture.

A few paragraphs earlier I pointed out that seeking an answer to the first question led us to two new approaches: the first of a theoretical nature, which I dealt with very briefly from the point of view of culture,[6] and the other concerning the conditions of research work in the area of the political economy of communication and culture, which makes it possible to formulate new questions.

The environment of the economic crisis and its correlates in political economy of communication and culture research

Researching culture from the perspective of political economy offers a panorama that is so vast that it poses challenges of a methodological nature and leads us to ask questions about the conditions in which political economy of communication and culture research is conducted.

If we ask about the 'how', the answer may be short but vital: carrying out work of theoretical elaboration with the corresponding empirical validation. The abundance of essay-style works must be increasingly offset by specific empirical studies capable of constantly and comprehensively recording cultural changes and the structures of the infocommunications sector.

But a response that seems so clear and direct nevertheless suffers the impact of the current economic conditions faced by higher education institutions, which is where most of the political economy of communication and culture research is conducted. As a result of the crisis, private institutions are seeing their incomes decrease due to students' inability to pay high tuition fees, while public institutions are being subjected to budget cuts.

It is well known that many private institutions have neither an interest in nor a vocation for carrying out research, which is why the situation of public universities is of particular concern, since they bear the responsibility for conducting the bulk of the studies on all areas of knowledge, including those on communication. As has occurred in other social sectors, the privatization of the education system as a result of neoliberal changes has had a profound effect on teaching and research structures:

> This, of course, is not a blatant privatization aiming to result in the buyout of public universities by private capital, as though they were a profitable investment; it is more of a subtle privatization, which gradually puts in place all the mechanisms possible to ensure that the three products of public universities (graduates, knowledge and values) are channelled according to the differentiated competitive needs of private capital.
>
> (Villaseñor García, 2002)

This privatizing perspective on education, which links it closely with productive sectors, has gradually achieved a hegemonic position, thereby imposing limitations on social science research.

In 1945, Friedrich Hayek published a well-known article entitled 'The Use of Knowledge in Society', in which he argued that the most efficient economic system was one that made full use of existing knowledge, and also noted that knowledge should be the criterion considered in the allocation of economic resources. Almost 60 years on, his original proposals guide development-related research, but with particular readings: knowledge is not always the criterion for allocating resources, but, on the other hand, knowledge generation and application are being linked to development, which is understood as the economic growth of productive sectors. And as we know, this is the basis for the paradigm of a society characterized by knowledge, which demands results that can be immediately incorporated into those productive systems.

This situation has led, among other things, to quality being substituted for quantity, basic science for applied science, and to the putting forward of research agendas that are forced to overlook those topics that cannot be rapidly integrated into the labyrinth of productivity. What is now required is finalistic and complete knowledge integrated into specific products, which are awkward conditions for political economy of communication and culture studies. Amid this panorama, some groups of researchers, either through necessity or by choice, seek resources and funding in consultancy or other work whose results cannot always be shared with the scientific community, thereby creating a parallel circuit of products that are finalistic and opaque to the process of social construction of scientific knowledge.

For the social sciences, and in particular for the political economy of communication and culture, which is characterized by a critical perspective that contrasts cultural interest with those of the market, creating applied or finalistic knowledge entails reducing the range of possible sources of funding. In view of the crisis we are currently facing, and its consequent impact on university research budgets, the future outlook may be even more restrictive. There is nothing new about this statement, but it does pose the challenge of promoting a cultural change in the way we work and produce scientific knowledge, through the integration of networks that enable us to optimize efforts and also compare results.

Some inescapable emerging issues

I round off the reflections in this chapter by noting a number of topics that need to be addressed by the political economy of communication and culture in the short term. This is a personal selection and, of course, does not exclude others of great importance. I will mention just three: the so-called 'creative industries', the increasing industrialization of education and the role of the state in the digital society *vis-à-vis* the contribution of private agents.

Owing to its increasing importance, the topic of the creative industries is one that further complicates the dimension of the political economy of communication and culture's object of study.[7] Obligatory references in this regard include the works of Philip Schlesinger (2008), as well as the analyses carried out by Gaëtan Tremblay (1998) and, recently, Enrique Bustamante (2009), who notes that

> Most of the texts devoted to defending these 'creative industries' mix highly heterogeneous elements in varying amounts: they stress individual (and not collective) effort, combining them with the

> new digital technologies (not on social interaction), immediately exploiting them via patents (without questioning copyright but rather strengthening it), large organizations (and not SMEs), the need to enrich them using management techniques, their export projection (and not horizontal cooperation between culture and peoples). In short, unlike the cultural industries, the creative industries have lost all cultural and democratic complexes and are oriented exclusively towards the market and short-term profitability.
>
> (Bustamante, 2009)

This new type of 'industry' is being sold – particularly to the younger generations – as spaces of freedom and informality within the sphere of cultural corporations. There, creators must develop an active role, which leads them to become empowered and take responsibility for their own situation, turning the proposal into a sort of freedom on condition of parole or probation. In a more or less digitalized society, which mobilizes a new space-time dimension without limits, the creative industries are offered as an alternative to fixed hours and regulated spaces for working and studying, thus promoting a false emancipating vision.

We have heard a lot about the advantages to be gained from being an entrepreneur, but little is said about its correlates: subcontracting, lack of job security, individualism and the permanent requirement to reconvert through the constant generation of new and creative projects capable of producing profits in the short term.

> Creative individuals are abandoned to a specific area of freedom, independence and self-government. Here freedom becomes the despotic norm, job insecurity the rule, the borders between working time and free time become blurred just like those between employment and unemployment, and this precariousness spreads from work to the whole of life.
>
> (Raunig, 2007)

Another of the challenges I would like to consider is the relevance of the political economy of communication and culture systematically conducting studies on education systems. Some years ago now, Tremblay (1998) argued that this was an 'industrializable' sector, but that it had still not reached the status of industry. Once again, the territorial perspective might reverse these claims, since it is in those countries where budget restrictions for public education have been most acute that private education is becoming increasingly industrial in nature, in terms of both the behaviour of its academic staff and the serial production of educational content, thanks to the combination of digital resources and the structure of the companies offering education. In view of the crisis, many of these educational companies are accelerating their industrialization processes, in which they see a solution to the drop in income.

Education is first and foremost a cultural process involving the active participation of subjects. It is nourished by collective phenomena that encourage interaction and form part of daily social practices anchored in specific territories that house a dialogic identity construction, that essential look into the eyes of others, which is described so well by Jean-Paul Sartre (1944) in referring to a mirror: 'How empty it is. A glass in which I am absent.' Or in his famous phrase 'Hell is other people'.

Lastly, I would like to point up the challenge of the unfinished discussion about the role of the state in the digital society *vis-à-vis* the contribution of private agents. Starting from the heralded economic crisis, which was only acknowledged at the end of 2008, the complaints about the modest role of the neoliberal state and its scant interference in public affairs led the same old voices to be heard and new voices to speak out about the need to rethink its responsibilities. The studies on communication and culture conducted from the perspective of political economy have dealt extensively with this topic, which nevertheless has not yet been resolved due to the strong economic interests that would be affected by a more active position on the part of the state. The body of law that is emerging is clear proof of this clash of interests, which fuels the need to continue with the ongoing reflection on the active role of the state in favour of more democratic cultural and communicative processes.

Notes

1. When the so-called 'Televisa law' was debated in Mexico and resisted by a diverse group from civil society, quite a few of us who belonged to the group were approached by people interested in understanding mechanisms they found hard to grasp (e.g. technological convergence) but many simply admitted to not understanding – nor wishing to know – the ins and outs of the topic because they considered it to be complex. However, while the bulk of the population have difficulty in understanding technical mechanisms, they are able to grasp the business concentration represented by Televisa, TV Azteca, Telmex and Telcel, whose economic interests are evident in scheduling or the telephone service – that is to say, in tangible aspects of their daily lives.
2. From the perspective of these reflections, the political economy of communication and culture's objects of study reach beyond processes with an industrial component, typical of the analysis of the cultural industries. They also include

significant cultural and communicational manifestations (e.g. the Internet or cellular telephony), which are of interest to communication and culture.

3. He does not mention communicologists or communication because he sees this area of knowledge as an activity of symbolic exchange that cuts across culture as a whole, which is always anchored and defined from the social position of the subjects that communicate. This point of view downplays the importance of communication in its own right while at the same time viewing it as a substantive component of the cultural.
4. Developed by Moscovici, in 1961 and ignored for a long time by social scientists (see Moscovici, [1961] 1979).
5. In recent Mexican history such surprises have been a common occurrence. For example, in the so-called 'decretazo' (summary decree) and 'Televisa Law', coups administrated under the Fox government (National Action Party) to the detriment of the necessary democratization of the media. The first (10 October 2002) modified the Regulations of the Federal Law on Radio and Television, reducing from 12.5 per cent to 1.25 per cent the tax that private operators paid 'in kind' – time to broadcast various public messages. This change reduced the transmission of public messages from 180 to 18 minutes per day. The 'Televisa Law' was so called because the amendments to the Federal Laws on Telecommunications, Radio and Television (30 March 2006) were a response to the lobby of the main TV operator in the country. This then gave rise to a movement of intellectuals and politicians, who succeeded in only partly reversing the changes to those laws.
6. Communication's perspective on this topic is expressed in a fresh way in numerous studies and academic discussions. For an economic viewpoint, see Almiron Roig (2009), Bustamante (2009), Segovia and Almiron (2008) or Zallo (2008).
7. See Part II of this volume, 'Cultural or Creative Industries?'.

References

Almiron Roig, Núria (2009) 'Economía política y comunicación: una aproximación epistemológica a los orígenes', *Revista Latina de Comunicación Social*, 64, 563–571.

Becerra, Martín (1998) 'Las industrias audiovisuales ante la "revolución informacional" ' (interview with Bernard Miège), *Voces y Culturas*, 14, 143–160.

Bustamante, Enrique (2009) 'De las industrias culturales al entretenimiento. La creatividad, la innovación... Viejos y nuevos señuelos para la investigación de la cultura', *Diálogos*, 78, 1–25.

Giménez Montiel, Gilberto (2005) *Teoría y análisis de la cultura* (vols I and II), Mexico City: ICOCULT/CONACULTA.

Government of Mexico (2009) *Diario Oficial de la Federación*, 30 April.

Hayek, Friedrich (1945) 'The use of knowledge in society', *The American Economic Review*, 35(4), 519–530.

Moscovici, Serge ([1961] 1979) *El psicoanálisis, su imagen y su público*, Buenos Aires: Huemul.

Raunig, Gerald (2007) 'Creative Industries as Mass Deception', *Transform.eipcp.net* – European Institute for Progressive Cultural Policies. Available at http://eipcp.net/transversal/0207/raunig/en (consulted in September 2010).

Sartre, Jean-Paul (1944) *A puerta cerrada*, Buenos Aires: Losada.

Schlesinger, Philip (2008) 'Discurso de la creatividad: políticas e intelectuales' (keynote lecture), IV Pan-American Conference on Communication 'Industria de la creatividad: creatividad, industrias culturales y desafío para los comunicadores', Santiago de Chile: Mayor University.

Segovia, Ana I. and Almiron, Núria (2008) 'La cuestión fundamental no es tanto la concentración, sino el poder de clase sobre el discurso ideológico' (interview with Dan Schiller), *EPTIC Online, Revista de Economía Política de las Tecnologías de la Información y Comunicación*, 10(2).

Tremblay, Gäetan (1998) 'Une approche pertinente?' in Moeglin, P. (dir.) *L'industrialisation de la formation: état de la question*, Paris: Centre national de documentation pédagogique, 39–60.

Villaseñor García, Guillermo (2002) 'Políticas de educación superior en México y en el mundo', in Comboni Salinas, S., Juárez Núñez, J.M. and París Pombo, M.D. (coords) *¿Hacia dónde va la universidad pública? La educación superior en el siglo XXI,* Mexico City: UAM-Xochimilco, 57–68.

Wolton, Dominique (1992) *Elogio del gran público. Una teoría crítica de la televisión*, Barcelona: Gedisa.

Zallo, Ramón (2008) 'I+C: las políticas de comunicación y cultura', paper presented at the First International Conference of Asociación Española de Investigación en Comunicación (Spanish Research Association on Communication) 'I+C: Investigar a comunicación', Santiago de Compostela.

Index

9781137540072